MODERN HUMANITIES RESEARCH ASSOCIATION
EUROPEAN TRANSLATIONS
VOLUME 4

GERMANIC EDITOR
RITCHIE ROBERTSON

The Amber Witch

EDITED BY
BARBARA BURNS

The Amber Witch

Original by
Wilhelm Meinhold

Translated from the German by
Lady Duff Gordon

This Volume Edited by
Barbara Burns

Modern Humanities Research Association
2016

Published by

*The Modern Humanities Research Association,
Salisbury House
Station Road
Cambridge CB1 2LA*

© *The Modern Humanities Research Association, 2016*

Barbara Burns has asserted her right under the Copyright, Designs and Patents Act 1988 to be identified as the author of this work. Parts of this work may be reproduced as permitted under legal provisions for fair dealing (or fair use) for the purposes of research, private study, criticism, or review, or when a relevant collective licensing agreement is in place. All other reproduction requires the written permission of the copyright holder who may be contacted at rights@mhra.org.uk.

First published 2016

ISBN 978-1-78188-095-1

Copies may be ordered from www.translations.mhra.org.uk

CONTENTS

Introduction	1
Editorial Note	15
The Amber Witch	17
Notes to the Text	149
Bibliography	162

INTRODUCTION

For British readers, the nineteenth century was a time of widening horizons. The production of literary translations for the mass market was booming, and many German writers in particular became sought-after names among frequenters of lending libraries and bookshops. Opinion was divided in the face of the growing popularity of German fiction: while Charles Maturin famously lamented the 'plague ship of German letters',[1] another reviewer enthused about 'the solid and elaborate production of a more laborious and painstaking set of authors than any other country in Europe can boast of'.[2] However divergent the judgments of commentators may have been, this era heralded an important phenomenon of Anglo-German cultural relations, namely that of literary influence and exchange.

Compared with French literature, the dissemination of German works in Britain had a bumpy start. Germany's political weakness following the Thirty Years' War, and a general assumption that the country had little of aesthetic value to offer, impeded the potential for sharing cultivated ideas. Helped by the marriage of George III to Charlotte of Mecklenburg in 1760, however, as well as by the influx of seminal German texts through French, the situation began to change towards the end of the eighteenth century. By 1816 a writer in the *Edinburgh Review* was able to report on the 'astonishing rapidity of the development of German literature',[3] as the availability of good translations and the enthusiasm of the reading public expanded. While much that rose swiftly to popularity did not ultimately achieve canonical status, it catered to a demand in what Thomas Carlyle called the 'bowl-and-dagger department'.[4] Commenting on the German terror-dramas of Kotzebue, Grillparzer and Klingemann, Carlyle wrote: 'If any man wish to amuse himself irrationally, here is the ware for his money.'[5] German literary works, in the genres of both drama and prose, were embraced by a British market eager for thrilling tales of the supernatural, the bizarre and the savage. The Gothic romance offered an alternative to the

---

1. Charles Maturin, 'Preface', *Fatal Revenge; Or, The Family of Montorio* (London: Longman, Hurst, Rees, and Orme, 1807), p. iii.
2. J[ohn] S[tuart] B[lackie], 'The Importance of the German Language, and Reasons for its More General Cultivation in this Country', *The Edinburgh Literary Journal; Or, Weekly Register of Criticism and Belles Lettres*, 2 vols (Edinburgh: Constable, 1829), II, 163–66 (p. 164).
3. Francis Palgrave, 'Goethe's *Life of Himself*', *Edinburgh Review*, 26 (1816), 304–37 (p. 305).
4. Thomas Carlyle, 'State of German Literature (1827)', in *Critical and Miscellaneous Essays*, 4 vols (Boston: Munroe, 1839), I, pp. 28–94 (p. 41).
5. Thomas Carlyle, 'German Playwrights (1829)', ibid., pp. 390–435 (p. 406).

predominant Utilitarianism and materialism of the day,[6] satisfying the desire of the individual living in a relatively secure, civilised society to experience the cathartic sensations of pity and fear through a realm of villains, ghosts, ethereal heroines and narrow escapes.

Such a literary landscape offered a natural home to the work of the German writer Wilhelm Meinhold (1797–1851). His novel *Maria Schweidler: Die Bernsteinhexe* (1844), translated into English in 1846 as *Mary Schweidler: The Amber Witch* by Lady Duff Gordon, saw numerous editions and enjoyed widespread popular success. This suspenseful story of a guileless young woman, unjustly accused of witchcraft, was hailed as the leading German novel of its day,[7] and has since been described as 'the most important witch novel in the nineteenth-century English-speaking world'.[8] The full title suggests the mystery and sensation of the tale: *Mary Schweidler: The Amber Witch. The Most Interesting Trial for Witchcraft Ever Known; Printed from an Imperfect Manuscript by her Father Abraham Schweidler, The Pastor of Coserow in the Island of Usedom. Edited by William Meinhold, Doctor of Theology*. Written in the style of a seventeenth-century chronicle, *The Amber Witch* appealed to a readership which identified in Meinhold's work echoes of Daniel Defoe, Oliver Goldsmith, and Walter Scott. The young Oscar Wilde was enthused by Meinhold,[9] the English essayist Walter Pater was able by 1889 to refer out of context to 'the sorceress of the Streckelberg' without the need for an explanatory note,[10] and in 1895 the *New York Times* reported on proposals to include *The Amber Witch* in a list of the hundred best books.[11]

This good literary fortune emerged from humble beginnings. Meinhold was a Lutheran cleric on the Baltic island of Usedom, conservative in doctrinal conviction and irritable in temperament. Educated at home by an eccentric father, he was deprived of childhood fun and emotional sustenance, and as an aspiring writer suffered greatly from his rural isolation. His sole literary mentor was the poet Ludwig Gotthard Kosegarten (1758–1818), a clergyman on the island of Rügen and professor at the University of Greifswald, who introduced him to the works of Goethe and Schiller and encouraged him in his early creative

---

6. See John R. Davis, *The Victorians and Germany* (Oxford: Lang, 2007), pp. 68–69.
7. Richard M. Meyer, *Die deutsche Literatur des neunzehnten Jahrhunderts*, 4th edn, 2 vols (Berlin: Bondi, 1910), I, p. 64.
8. E. F. Bleiler, 'Introduction to the Dover Edition', *Five Victorian Ghost Novels*, ed. by E. F. Bleiler (New York: Dover, 1971), p. x.
9. In his *Reviews* Wilde described *The Amber Witch* and *Sidonia von Bork* as having been 'my favourite romantic reading when a boy'. See Oscar Wilde, *Complete Shorter Fiction*, ed. by Isobel Murray (Oxford: Oxford University Press, 1980), p. 3.
10. Walter Pater, 'Aesthetic Poetry', *Appreciations* (London: Macmillan, 1889), pp. 213–27 (p. 226).
11. 'An Old and Famous Story', *New York Times*, 17 March 1895, p. 31.

endeavours. Kosegarten's comment that in Meinhold 'a rough shell hides a sweet kernel'[12] indicates that he countered his pupil's insecurity and social ineptitude with a generous spirit. Meinhold's early poetry won qualified approval from Goethe,[13] and Jean Paul Richter commented favourably on a draft of his first tragedy, on a topic from Pomeranian history, describing him as being 'capable of true tragic expression'.[14] Meinhold made his name as a writer, however, through the publication of a short novel which was also a literary hoax,[15] a controversial and mischievous, even reprehensible, act for a man of the cloth.

While the intention behind Meinhold's hoax was arguably a principled one, the genesis of *The Amber Witch* is rather absurd, and understanding it requires some knowledge of the contemporary theological frame of reference. One of the greatest challenges to the nineteenth-century European Christian establishment came in 1835, in the shape of a work by the liberal protestant theologian David Friedrich Strauss. In *The Life of Jesus, Critically Examined*, Strauss effectively denied the divinity of Christ, asserting that the Gospel accounts of miracles were based not on historical fact, but on myths created by Christ's followers. As a traditionalist, Meinhold perceived Strauss's findings as an outright attack on the Christian church, and responded with customary truculence and almost unbelievable convolution. His plan was to set a trap for Strauss and his fellow scholars who claimed to be able to distinguish historical fact from fiction. He contrived to fake a seventeenth-century manuscript, claiming to have stumbled on it by chance and to have edited it for publication, to test whether it was indeed so easy to judge the authenticity of a work from a previous era. Meinhold's reasoning was that if critics could be taken in by a forgery, believing it to be an authentic document, then conversely they could be wrong in judging authentic documents to be forgeries. Naïve and logically flawed though this undertaking may seem, many were taken in by the ruse, and even when Meinhold some six months later explained in a newspaper article that the work was a forgery,[16] some were reluctant to believe it, seeing this, rather than the novel itself, as the bluff.

Commentators who had welcomed the text as evidence of the inhumanity of Germany's witch-hunting heritage and the culpability of the Church in this persecution were particularly disappointed to learn that *The Amber Witch* was

---

12. Cited in *Wilhelm Meinholds Briefe*, ed. by Walther Bethke (Greifswald: Universitätsverlag, 1935), p. 15.
13. See Goethe's essay 'Individualpoesie', in Johann Wolfgang von Goethe, *Sämtliche Werke*, ed. by Hendrik Birus et al., 40 vols (Frankfurt a.M.: Deutscher Klassiker Verlag, 1986–2000), XXII: *Ästhetische Schriften 1824–1832*, ed. by Anne Bohnenkamp (1999), p. 658.
14. *Wahrheit aus Jean Paul's Leben*, ed. by Christian Otto and Ernst Förster, 8 vols (Breslau: Max und Komp., 1826–33), VIII (1833), 271.
15. See Barbara Burns, 'Truth, Fiction and Deception in Wilhelm Meinhold's *Maria Schweidler, die Bernsteinhexe*', *Neophilologus*, 95 (2011), 627–38.
16. *Augsburger Allgemeine Zeitung*, 23 January 1844.

not an authentic document, and insisted that Meinhold prove his authorship. He did so by producing a signed testimony from the Synod of Usedom that as early as 1826–27 he had discussed his progress in writing the story with clerical colleagues and had read them excerpts from it. This statement was published in the *Novellen-Zeitung*,[17] together with the original version of the story — written in modern rather than antiquated German — in order to clarify the truth of the matter. Even three years after his public declaration that *The Amber Witch* was a piece of fiction, however, Meinhold was still fielding assertions to the contrary, and made a repeated attempt to set the record straight in the preface to his next novel: '*The Amber Witch* is still considered to be true, just as the Bible is considered fiction. Only recently (and who would fail to respect this) Heine declared in Paris that *The Amber Witch* was historical, apart from the closing pages.'[18] The German poet Heinrich Heine did not have a direct connection with Meinhold, but was a friend of the novel's English translator Lady Duff Gordon, who clearly had swayed his opinion.[19] While attention from as celebrated a figure as Heine was gratifying to a degree, it also highlighted afresh Meinhold's ill-judged trickery.

Those who observed these German literary shenanigans from the benefit of some distance were mildly amused by developments. A writer for the *London Quarterly Review* commented:

> Among Dr. Meinhold's victims were the Tubingen reviewers, either the redoubted Strauss himself or his faithful and acknowledged followers. These gentlemen, whose training in the infallible Hegelian philosophy has endowed them with an unerring judgement as to the authenticity of every kind of writing; whose well-tried acuteness can detect the *myth* in every form, who throughout the Gospel can discriminate, from internal evidence, the precise degree of credibility of each chapter, each narrative, each word, with a certainty which disdains all doubt — the School of Strauss pronounced the 'Amber Witch' to be a *genuine chronicle*! But worse than this, if Dr. Meinhold (as we understand a very pious and good man) is to be credited, they fell into a trap designedly laid for *them*. [...] We wish him joy of his success, and condole with Strauss and Co.![20]

---

17. Wilhelm Meinhold, '*Die Bernsteinhexe* von Wilhelm Meinhold. In ihrer ursprünglichen, neuhochdeutschen Gestalt vom Jahre 1826', *Novellen-Zeitung*, 3 July 1844, pp. 2–8.
18. Wilhelm Meinhold, *Gesammelte Schriften*, 7 vols (Leipzig: Weber, 1846–48), VII (1848), *Sidonia von Bork die Klosterhexe, angebliche Vertilgerin des gesammten herzoglich-pommerschen Regentenhauses*, p. x.
19. Duff Gordon first met Heine at the age of 12 in Boulogne in August 1833, and maintained her friendship with him until the poet's death in 1856. He dedicated to her his poem 'Wenn ich an deinem Hause // Des Morgens vorübergeh'. See 'Heine and Lady Duff Gordon', *Otago Witness*, 5 July 1894, p. 41, and also the Introduction by Duff Gordon's daughter Janet Ross to Lady Duff Gordon, *Last Letters From Egypt*, (London: Macmillan, 1875), pp. xxii–xxxi.
20. *London Quarterly Review*, 73 (1844), 107–20 (p. 120).

The *New York Times*, another ally in debunking the purveyors of liberal theology, likewise took Meinhold's part in the episode:

> Meinhold did not spare them [the disciples of Strauss] when they fell into the snare, and made merry with the historical knowledge and critical acumen that could not detect the contemporary romancer under the mask of two centuries ago, while they decided so positively as to the authority of the most ancient writings in the world.[21]

Not everyone viewed Meinhold's literary hoax so benignly, however. The Prussian King, Friedrich Wilhelm IV, whose interest had been sparked by an earlier, shorter version of the story in the periodical *Christoterpe*[22] and who had himself sponsored the novel's publication by Duncker und Humblot in Berlin, felt that he had lost face through the affair and regretted his involvement with a 'devious hypocrite'[23] and 'rogue'.[24] Interest in this quirky country parson who had pitted himself against the intellectual acumen of the academic elite caused Meinhold's reputation to grow in Germany for a time, but his notoriety was relatively short-lived. After the publication of another historical novel on a witchcraft theme, *Sidonia von Bork, die Klosterhexe* (1847), translated into English as *Sidonia the Sorceress*,[25] he faded into obscurity, retiring early as a result of tensions both with his parishioners and his ecclesiastical superiors, and died in 1851 at the age of fifty-four.

Recognition of Meinhold's achievement was generated predominantly through his popularity in the English-speaking world, and this was due in no small part to the talent and influence of his translators. Lucie, Lady Duff Gordon (1821–1869) was the daughter of the literary translator Sarah Austin and the legal

---

21. 'The Author of *The Amber Witch*', *The Eclectic Magazine of Foreign Literature, Science and Art*, 21 (1850), ed. by John Holmes Agnew and Walter Hilliard Bidwell (New York: Leavitt, Trow and Co.), p. 419. The author cites a correspondent for the *New York Times* without giving the date of the article.
22. *Christoterpe. Ein Taschenbuch für christliche Leser*: vol. 1841 contained parts of chapters 7, 9, 13 and 15; vol. 1842 had chapters 26 and 27.
23. Karl August Varnhagen von Ense, *Tagebücher*, 14 vols (Leipzig: Brockhaus, 1861–70), II, p. 269 (diary entry for 4 March 1844). Von Ense was closely involved in this matter and in his diary describes the king's reaction in detail, though it is not possible to know whether he quotes the king's precise words here.
24. Ibid., p. 272 (diary entry for 10 March 1844). It should be noted that Meinhold had already explained the hoax to the king before the novel's publication, therefore the king's anger must be attributed to embarrassment not at having been misled, but rather at having supported a writer who was deemed disreputable.
25. The translator was Jane Elgee, who later became Lady Wilde, mother of Oscar Wilde. William Morris wrote of her translation (first published by the Parlour Library in 1849): 'Lady Wilde's translation, which was the one through which we made acquaintance with Meinhold's genius, is a good, simple, and sympathetic one.' (William S. Peterson, *A Bibliography of the Kelmscott Press* (Oxford: Clarendon Press, 1984), p. 51.)

philosopher John Austin.[26] Sarah Austin was an estimable scholar and a widely travelled woman with an extensive range of correspondents. A friend of the German Prince Hermann von Pückler-Muskau whose letters she translated, among many works she also published the successful *Characteristics of Goethe* and *Fragments from German Prose Writers*.[27] Austin was a passionate advocate of the education of girls, and ensured that her daughter developed the cerebral as well as the social skills needed to fulfil her potential. John Stuart Mill, a frequent visitor to the family home, was taught German by Sarah Austin whom he affectionately addressed as 'Mutter', and took an interest in the development of the young Lucie. In 1826 the Austin family moved for almost two years to Bonn, in order for Lucie's father to study Roman Law under Barthold Georg Niebuhr and August Wilhelm Schlegel. This enabled Lucie at an early age to become fluent in German and develop a taste for reading German literature. Following her return to England and her marriage in 1840 to Sir Alexander Cornewall Duff Gordon, Baronet of Halkin, Lucie's Westminster home became a regular meeting place for writers including Dickens, Thackeray, Tennyson and Warburton, as well as a magnet for foreign visitors of repute. Thus her translation of Meinhold's story was executed in an environment of keen literary interest and anticipation. Having published her first translation project, Niebuhr's children's book entitled *Stories of the Gods and Heroes of Greece*, in her mother's name in 1842, it was time to forge her own creative identity, an undertaking in which her circle of discriminating lettered friends offered a considerable advantage.[28]

Duff Gordon received the sum of £50 for her work from the London publisher John Murray, who had previously taken many of her mother's translations. This was a flat fee, and such a contractual arrangement which did not include provision for royalties on sales proved somewhat unfortunate in light of the immediate popularity of the book which saw three editions in the first year alone. Rather than feeling resentful, however, Duff Gordon was pleased with the results of her first foray into professional translation, and used her earnings to repair the leaking roof of her London home. Duff Gordon's achievement was all the more

---

26. Lucy Duff Gordon's daughter, Janet Ross, documented the lives of her mother, grandmother and great-grandmother in *Three Generations of English Women: Memoirs and Correspondence of Mrs John Taylor, Mrs Sarah Austin and Lady Duff Gordon* (London: Murray, 1888).
27. See Hermann Fürst von Pückler-Muskau, *Tour in England, Ireland, and France, in the years 1826, 1827, 1828, and 1829: With Remarks on the Manners and Customs of the Inhabitants, and Anecdotes of Distinguished Public Characters*, trans. by Sarah Austin (London: Wilson, 1832); *Characteristics of Goethe from the German of Falk, Von Müller, Etc.*, trans. by Sarah Austin (London: Wilson: 1833); *Fragments from German Prose Writers*, trans. by Sarah Austin (London: Murray, 1841).
28. Lady Duff Gordon was not the only person to translate *The Amber Witch*. 1844 saw the publication of two English versions of the novel, the other by E. A. Friedländer (London: H. G. Clarke), which proved less popular than Duff Gordon's work.

gratifying, given the prediction of the German novel's first English reviewer in June 1844 that the original was 'incommunicable, we fear, in any translation'. The anonymous commentator interestingly alludes to the track record of Duff Gordon's mother as the benchmark for literary translation at the time: 'Who could translate it? Scarcely even Mrs Austin. The somewhat antiquated and provincial language, with its odd pedantic scraps of Latin […] could hardly be preserved by a translator, unless by uncommon care and felicity, without harshness and affectation'.[29] Undaunted by such defeatism, Duff Gordon proceeded with quiet determination to prove the experts wrong. Some fifty years later the succinct accolade for her work printed in the *New York Times* encapsulated the view of the late nineteenth-century literary establishment: 'As to Lady Duff Gordon's translation, it is the very best that ever was done.'[30]

The cleverness of Duff Gordon's translation of *The Amber Witch* resided in her ability to imitate the archaic style of Meinhold's original, while at the same time eliminating a number of the linguistic idiosyncrasies which had been part of the author's strategy in constructing his literary forgery, but had also made his work difficult to read. For example, her version obviates the need for many of Meinhold's editorial footnotes explaining dialect or obsolete terms as she largely uses standard English, albeit retaining the peppering of Latin terminology and antiquated syntax which create the illusion of a much older document. Duff Gordon seems intuitively to have sensed the risk highlighted by Sir Walter Scott when he observed of another writer that 'by rendering his language too ancient, and displaying his antiquarian knowledge too liberally, the ingenious author had raised up an obstacle to his own success'.[31] If Meinhold too had erred down this path, Duff Gordon managed subtly to retrieve his text for the Victorian reader, making it accessible without compromising its integrity as a chronicle of a bygone era. Such was her accomplishment that readers credited her as the originator of the novel, refusing to believe that her work was a translation.

While Duff Gordon's version is very faithful to the original, her female sensibilities caused her to sidestep some rather indecorous details of the narrative, such as the reference to the man defecating in the street (see note 129) or the devil's semen (see note 161). Generally, however, for a woman of her station she negotiates the earthier and disquieting aspects of the tale remarkably well, and does not otherwise abbreviate the sections describing the indignities of the witchcraft trial. Having read a number of factual accounts of such trials in preparation for completing her translation, she had not only become familiar

---

29. *London Quarterly Review*, 73 (1844), 107–20 (p. 108).
30. 'An Old and Famous Story', *New York Times*, 17 March 1895, p. 31.
31. Walter Scott, 'General Preface' to *Waverley Novels*, 25 vols (London: Dryburgh, 1929), I, p. xv. The reference is to Joseph Strutt's unfinished manuscript of *Queenhoo Hall* which was completed by Scott.

with the subject matter and to an extent inured to the grimness of the theme,[32] but had also gained an insight into the sophistications of the older English style which she would need to imitate. Duff Gordon retains Meinhold's expanded chapter headings providing a summary of the forthcoming action, in the manner of seventeenth-century works, and leaves the majority of the Latin phrases and quotations untranslated, as he does. Given her own sound training in Latin, it is perhaps surprising that she does not discriminate between the relatively accessible Latin terms and others for which an average dictionary is of little help, such as 'custos' (see note 44), or 'locamentum' (see note 62), nor does she correct the narrator's erroneous claim that the Latin chronograms in chapter 10 are written in hexameter. She does clarify, for the benefit of a British readership, that the Biblical citations are from Luther's version, an important point in referring to the Ten Commandments, for example, as they appear in a different order in the King James Bible. Presumably she regarded further editorial intervention as exceeding her remit, however, and may indeed have feared that removing some minor obstacles to understanding could have diluted the desired linguistic effect.

The fluency of Duff Gordon's translation belies the complexity and abstruseness of the German original. Work of such quality is a rare accomplishment in any era for a woman in her early twenties, without formal qualifications. Moreover, she was one of the first modern European scholars to produce a literary translation which led to greater fame for a work than it achieved in its language of creation. Meinhold himself recognised the debt her owed to his skilful English colleague, and dedicated to her his next novel, *Sidonia the Sorceress*: 'To the illustrious Lady Lucy Duff Gordon, the young and gifted translator of *The Amber Witch*, this work is respectfully inscribed'. Duff Gordon's translation saw several editions in her lifetime, but sadly she did not live to see the most sumptuous version, the David Nutt edition of 1895, dedicated to Lady Burne-Jones, which included five illustrations by her son Philip Burne-Jones. Entitled 'The Apparition of the Streckelberg', 'The Gallows Ghost', 'The Torture Chamber', 'The Doom of the Wheel', and 'The Bridal Gifts', these images conveyed the Gothic mood of the novel to good effect.

The enthusiasm for Meinhold's work emanating from Duff Gordon's circle was shared by writers and artists alike, and the social connections and mutual tastes of a fashionable British cultural elite had a ripple effect which brought the work of this obscure Pomeranian cleric to a broad audience. One of the few portraits of Lady Duff Gordon was sketched by her friend George Frederic Watts, who in turn was a close associate of Edward Burne-Jones and William Morris.

---

32. A literary periodical many years later reported on Lady Duff Gordon's recollections of reading these witch trial accounts and of feeling deeply moved at the fate of a particular woman who was unjustly accused. See Caroline Norton, 'Lady Duff Gordon and Her Works', *Macmillan's Magazine*, September 1869, pp. 457–62.

The Pre-Raphaelites were irresistibly drawn to Meinhold, in particular his second novel *Sidonia the Sorceress*. His writing, as Patrick Bridgwater puts it, 'took them back to the boyhood reading they never outgrew, and to the fictionalised "middle ages" in which they lived'.[33] After the initial commercial success of the English translations, the Burne-Jones and Morris families were together responsible for keeping Meinhold's work in the public eye through important new editions. In 1893 William Morris re-published *Sidonia von Bork* in his own Kelmscott Press, writing in the press announcement that both this novel and *The Amber Witch* were 'almost faultless reproductions of the life of the past; not merely antiquarian studies, but presentations of events, often tragic, the actors in which are really alive'.[34] Burne-Jones's son-in-law, John William Mackail, who became Oxford Professor of Poetry and President of the British Academy, wrote the introduction to the 1928 Oxford University Press edition of *The Amber Witch* in the 'World's Classics' series, a publication which bore testament to the work's enduring prestige.

The fact that Meinhold's writing was widely respected in Victorian England and had set a standard against which works by other authors were measured is evidenced in numerous literary commentaries. For example, the biographer of George Eliot reported on Daniel Gabriel Rossetti's view of Eliot's historical novel *Romola*: 'He did not think that the tone and colour of Italian life in the fifteenth century were caught with that intuitive perception of a bygone age characteristic of a Walter Scott or a Meinhold'.[35] Another reviewer, evaluating Mrs Gaskell's short story 'Lois the Witch' (1859), remarked that the cruelty of the innocent young heroine's persecutors 'is represented with a force which reminds us of Meinhold himself and of his *Amber Witch*'.[36] Such observations confirm Meinhold's status in Britain as a writer of considerable reputation who was regarded as part of the literary establishment, a far cry from his position in his native Germany.

Comparisons between the work of Meinhold and that of other British writers abound in the literary reviews of the day. The English poet and critic Sir Edmund Gosse identified a link with the early Gothic novelist Ann Radcliffe, suggesting that Meinhold 'had a tincture in his veins of the Mrs. Radcliffe sensationalism'.[37] Parallels of characterization were readily drawn between Meinhold's Pastor Schweidler and Goldsmith's Dr Primrose, especially in light of the widespread

---

33. Patrick Bridgwater, 'Who's Afraid of Sidonia von Bork?', in *The Novel in Anglo-German Context: Cultural Cross-Currents and Affinities*, ed. by Susanne Stark (Amsterdam: Rodopi, 2000), pp. 213–28 (p. 216).
34. William S. Peterson, *A Bibliography of the Kelmscott Press*, p. 51.
35. Mathilde Blind, *George Eliot* (London: Allen, 1883), p. 150.
36. Oliver Elton, *A Survey of English Literature, 1830–1880*, 2 vols (London: Arnold, 1920), II, p. 301.
37. Edmund Gosse, *Leaves and Fruit* (London: Heinemann, 1927), p. 196.

popularity in Germany of *The Vicar of Wakefield*.[38] More recently E. F. Bleiler has speculated on the influence of James Hogg's *The Private Memoirs and Confessions of a Justified Sinner* (1824),[39] which shares with Meinhold's narrative the elements of the discovered manuscript introduced by a fictitious 'editor', as well as the theme of religious zealotry. While it remains a matter of hypothesis whether Meinhold had read any of these works, it is known that he was familiar with Walter Scott and Daniel Defoe. Scott's novels had begun to appear in German translation in the 1820s, and his technique of constructing his historical works from a template of preface, text and footnotes is echoed in Meinhold's approach. The early Meinhold critic Rupprecht Leppla outlined a series of parallels in plot development between *The Amber Witch* and Scott's *Ivanhoe* which make a strong case for Scott's impact on his German counterpart.[40]

The most influential contemporary review, however, drew attention to Meinhold's debt to Defoe, and provided a sentence which was later seized upon for marketing purposes: 'If this little work [...] be a fiction, it is worthy, we can give no higher praise, of De Foe.'[41] Applauding Meinhold's descriptive talents, the commentator drew attention to the believability of the work in terms of bringing not only individuals but also localities to life:

> If there be a part of the world of which we were utterly ignorant, it is the coast of Pomerania, yet just as we know more about old London from De Foe's 'History of the Plague', and of low London life from his 'Colonel Jack', than from pages of antiquarian lore, so from this little book, in which there is not a line of *description*, we think we know the Streckelberg, the way to it, its juniper-bushes, its caverns, and its sea-shore, certainly far better than if we had studied the best geographical treatise or local guide.[42]

It was this resourceful combination of fact and fiction that impressed British readers and endeared them to an unknown German writer who seemed to be continuing in a narrative tradition which they recognized and appreciated. Mackail too accentuates the legacy of Defoe in his tribute to Meinhold:

---

38. Goethe refers to the novel in *The Sorrows of Young Werther* and also writes of it in his autobiography: 'Now Herder came, and together with his great knowledge brought many other aids, and the later publications besides. Among these he announced to us the *Vicar of Wakefield* as an excellent work, with a German translation of which he would make us acquainted by reading it aloud to us himself. [...] A Protestant country clergyman is, perhaps, the most beautiful subject for a modern idyl; he appears, like Melchizedek, as priest and king in one person', *The Autobiography of Goethe: Truth and Poetry, From My Own Life*, trans. by John Oxenford (London: Bohn, 1848), p. 368.
39. E. F. Bleiler, 'Introduction to the Dover Edition', p. ix.
40. Rupprecht Leppla, *Wilhelm Meinhold und die chronikalische Erzählung* (Berlin: Ebering, 1928), p. 141.
41. *The London Quarterly Review*, 73 (1844), 107–20, p. 107.
42. Ibid., p. 108.

Both writers produce the illusion of reality in their stories by an infinity of minute detail; and in both the illusion is so great that in *The Amber Witch*, as in *Moll Flanders* and the *Journal of the Plague Year*, the fictitious narrative may be, and was, taken as a transcript of actual occurrences. How far Meinhold may have been directly indebted for his method to German translations of Defoe there is no evidence. But in him the genius of Defoe was reincarnated.[43]

It is clear that the accumulation of meticulous historical and ethnographic detail in Meinhold's narrative was a major factor in persuading readers of its credibility as an authentic seventeenth-century chronicle of events. The author's outstanding achievement as a researcher was somewhat overlooked, however, by those who rushed to lambast him as a forger. In his subsequent attempt to resolve the confusion Meinhold in a sense does himself an injustice when he declares: 'Not a single word of the entire thing is true, except that during the Thirty Years' War there was a sheriff in Pudagla who is briefly described by an old pastor in Coserow as very tyrannical. Everything else is pure fiction.'[44] Apart from the fact that the main storyline is invented, the text is underpinned by years of study of regional history, folklore, law, theology, numismatics, and flora and fauna, and demonstrates a firm grasp of Latin as well as of local dialect. Meinhold refers authoritatively to the work of the influential early jurists and philosophers who opposed witch-hunting in Europe, such as Balthasar Bekker, Friedrich von Spee, and Christian Thomasius, and also draws heavily on the annals of Johann Micraelius and Carl Heller, as well as on the Pomeranian periodical *Pommersche Provinzial-Blätter für Stadt und Land* to which he was himself a contributor. His story features major historical characters and events, such as the landing of King Gustavus Adolphus of Sweden with his army on the island of Usedom in 1630, and minor figures of little significance, plucked from the obscurity of regional documents of the era (see, for example, note 64). Meinhold's assertion therefore that his story is 'pure fiction' is an oversimplification, intended for rhetorical effect, which belies an erudite author's complex interweaving of multiple sources.

While the theme of witchcraft has had timeless appeal for creative writers and social historians across Europe, the first half of the nineteenth century witnessed a particular surge of interest in the subject. An important source for Meinhold was Georg Conrad Horst's six-volume collection of magical texts entitled *Zauber-Bibliothek* (1821–26),[45] and he also read Walter Scott's commercially successful *Letters on Demonology and Witchcraft* (1830) which commented on Scottish

---

43. Wilhelm Meinhold, *The Amber Witch*, intro. by J. W. Mackail (London: Oxford University Press (World's Classics), 1928), p. vi.
44. Wilhelm Meinhold, preface to the second edition of the novel, *Gesammelte Schriften*, 7 vols (Leipzig: Weber, 1846–48), I (1846), p. xx.
45. Conrad Georg Horst, *Zauber-Bibliothek: Oder, von Zauberei, Theurgie und Mantik, Zauberern, Hexen, und Hexenprocessen, Dämonen, Gespenstern, und Geistererscheinungen*, 6 vols (Mainz: Kupferberg, 1821–26).

witchcraft trials.[46] Historical material was used too by Ludwig Tieck as a basis for his novella *Der Hexen-Sabbath* which appeared in 1832,[47] paving the way for numerous later engagements by German writers with the topic.[48] In England Meinhold's *Amber Witch* was followed by several witch-themed publications, the most famous of which was W. Harrison Ainsworth's *The Lancashire Witches* (1848). All of these works tapped into an enduring scholarly and popular fascination with women who were deemed to threaten the fabric of society by being agents of the Devil. With the advance of science and rational philosophy a nineteenth-century readership was equipped to question and to reassess the superstition and prejudice of a previous era, yet this stood in tension with residual Victorian uncertainties surrounding appropriate responses to women who did not fit conventional models of behaviour, making the witch motif a seductive one.

Unlike the older notion of witches as individuals (male or female) endowed with special wisdom and innate supernatural powers, those identified as witches in the early modern period were women believed to have a pact with the Devil, to practise harmful magic, and to meet secretly with others of their kind. The accusation of witchcraft was readily attached to 'the old, the widow, the deformed, deaf, one-eyed, toothless, the woman in isolation, the one whose limited earning power and consequent poverty had made her a social liability for the community'.[49] In this respect Meinhold's heroine Maria Schweidler is far from representative of the norm. She is depicted as a beautiful and gracious young woman, who differs from her fellow parishioners in terms of the erudition she has acquired through her father's tutelage. Her linguistic talent in particular works to her disadvantage, as her instinctive tendency to quote Latin hymns and prayers as a source of comfort in distress is misinterpreted as a facility with cursing and incantation. Perhaps it was not merely the innocence and naïve charm of the protagonist which attracted Duff Gordon to this text, but also a strong conviction, inculcated by her mother, of the importance of education for women of all classes and the centrality of foreign language acquisition to intercultural understanding.

---

46. Scott's work was translated into German by Georg Nikolaus Bärmann as *Briefe über Dämonologie und Hexerei* (Zwickau: Schumann, 1833).
47. See Marion George, 'Vom historischen Fakt zur Sinnfigur der Moderne. Zur Gestalt der Hexe in Tiecks Novelle *Hexensabbat* (1832)', in *Hexen: Historische Faktizität und fiktive Bildlichkeit / Sorcières: Faits historiques, imagerie et fiction*, ed. by Marion George and Andrea Rudolph (Dettelbach: Röll, 2004), pp. 253–70.
48. For example: Ludwig Bechstein, *Hexengeschichten* (1854), Wilhelm Heinrich Riehl, *Jörg Muckenhuber* (1860), Wilhelm Raabe, *Else von der Tanne* (1865), Theodor Storm, *Renate* (1878), Theodor Fontane, *Grete Minde* (1878) and his fragment *Sidonie von Borcke* (1879–82).
49. Olwen Hufton, *The Prospect Before Her: A History of Women in Western Europe, Vol. I: 1500–1800* (London: HarperCollins, 1995), p. 358.

If misconception and prejudice surrounding such matters were worth fighting, then an effective means of doing so was through disseminating Meinhold's thought-provoking novel to a new, English-speaking audience.

A further and more problematic way in which Meinhold's text differs from conventional narratives of witch trials is of course seen in the happy ending, akin to that of a fairy tale. The long-delayed young nobleman returns at the eleventh hour to rescue his beloved from her horrifying ordeal, and the two embark on a life of wedded harmony and affluence. Not only is this outcome simplistic, but its adherence to patriarchal paradigms of male authority and female submissiveness has inevitably attracted the criticism of modern commentators. The supposed witch, who represents a threat to the order of a male-dominated society, is, it is argued, domesticated and subsumed into the social framework that previously did not tolerate her.[50] Inviting though this interpretation may be for today's literary critics, it is coloured by the perspective of a more liberal era with a different view of marriage, and the implication that there is little here of ethical value overlooks Meinhold's integrity and achievement in challenging the evils of superstition, character-denunciation and persecution. In creating a happy ending, Meinhold may have been indulging the expectations of his mid-nineteenth-century readership, or indeed may have been seeking a conclusion which mitigated the harshness of the central theme, anticipating the aesthetic approach of the German Poetic Realists a few decades later. Even if the romantic ending is sentimental and improbable in the context of a tale about a witchcraft trial, for a theologically conservative writer of his time it is an intentionally optimistic choice which expresses a belief in the power of faith and moral principle.

For the twenty-first-century reader, *The Amber Witch* is a forgotten gem waiting to be rediscovered. Although Duff Gordon's English translation has remained in print ever since its first publication, Meinhold is no longer the household name he was in the Victorian era, and the lack of a modern edition with explanatory notes has served as a disincentive to engaging with a work described by Peter Skrine as 'this darkest of mid-century German masterpieces'.[51] Those who are new to the text will discover an instructive and poignant account of rural life during the Thirty Years' War, the most devastating conflict on European soil prior to the First World War. They will gain an insight into a time of superstition, fear and prejudice, of mob violence and fickleness, of poverty-driven desperation, of abuse of power and corruption, and of miscarriages of

---

50. See, for example, Waltraud Maierhofer, *Hexen — Huren — Heldenweiber. Bilder des Weiblichen in Erzähltexten über den Dreißigjährigen Krieg* (Cologne: Böhlau, 2005), pp. 229–30.
51. Peter Skrine, 'Historical Realism', in *Perspectives on German Realist Writing: Eight Essays*, ed. by Mark G. Ward (Lampeter: Mellen, 1995), pp. 113–124 (p. 123).

justice. These themes, though portrayed at a remove of several centuries, have a continuing resonance which enables a new generation to identify parallels and relevancies in their own world. But *The Amber Witch* is also an uplifting tale of resilience and resourcefulness, of courage and hope, which heartens the reader and restores faith in the possibility of a better society. The inner strength of the heroine, compared to the fearfulness and despair of her father, illustrates the capacity of youth to transcend inherited attitudes and hindrances, and conveys a message that is still fresh and progressive today.

We have a small but influential group of Victorian literati to thank for the preservation and promulgation of this obscure German text. Lady Duff Gordon was an exceptional woman, an intellectual with a bohemian lifestyle, a meticulous linguist and a natural translator, possessed of the gift of reinvigorating a text for a new audience. Her later writings from Egypt,[52] where she spent the last seven years of her relatively short life, bear witness to her tolerance and social awareness, reinforcing the likelihood that she did not choose *The Amber Witch* as a random translation project, but at least in part as an empathetic and enlightened response to its focus on injustice and oppression. Just as important as Duff Gordon herself, however, were the British devotees of Meinhold's stories who were also the artistic trend-setters of their day. They cared little about the theological controversy surrounding Strauss and the forgery scandal which had brought Meinhold into disrepute in Germany, and were more excited, as Joseph Jacobs put it in his Introduction to the handsome 1895 Nutt edition, by 'perhaps the most effective presentation of medieval thought and feeling which the whole Romantic movement produced'.[53] Sadly Meinhold, who died in 1851, caught little more than a glimpse of his nascent international success, and even Duff Gordon, who died in 1869, cannot have envisaged the full impact of her translation which secured the advancement of *The Amber Witch* through numerous editions and continues to keep it alive today.

---

52. Lucie Duff Gordon, *Letters from Egypt, 1863–1865*, ed. by Sarah Austin (London: Macmillan, 1865), and *Last Letters from Egypt*, ed. by Janet Ross (London: Macmillan, 1875).

53. Joseph Jacobs, 'Introduction', Wilhelm Meinhold, *The Amber Witch* (London: Nutt, 1895), p. xx.

EDITOR'S NOTE

In this volume the footnotes (indicated in Roman numerals) belong to the original German text, in which they are presented as editorial comments. The endnotes (indicated in Arabic numerals) have been added to provide explanatory information and are particular to this MHRA edition.

MARY SCHWEIDLER

THE AMBER WITCH

THE MOST INTERESTING TRIAL FOR WITCHCRAFT EVER KNOWN

PRINTED FROM AN IMPERFECT MANUSCRIPT BY HER FATHER ABRAHAM SCHWEIDLER, THE PASTOR OF COSEROW, IN THE ISLAND OF USEDOM

EDITED BY

WILHELM MEINHOLD

DOCTOR OF THEOLOGY

TRANSLATED FROM THE GERMAN BY

LADY DUFF GORDON

PREFACE

In laying before the public this deeply affecting and romantic trial, which I have not without reason called on the title-page the most interesting of all trials for witchcraft ever known, I will first give some account of the history of the manuscript.

At Coserow,[1] in the Island of Usedom, my former cure, the same which was held by our worthy author some two hundred years ago, there existed under a seat in the choir of the church[2] a sort of niche, nearly on a level with the floor. I had, indeed, often seen a heap of various writings in this recess; but owing to my short sight, and the darkness of the place, I had taken them for antiquated hymn-books, which were lying about in great numbers. But one day, while I was teaching in the church, I looked for a paper mark in the Catechism of one of the boys, which I could not immediately find; and my old sexton, who was past eighty (and who, although called Appelmann, was thoroughly unlike his namesake in our story, being a very worthy, although a most ignorant man), stooped down to the said niche, and took from it a folio volume which I had never before observed, out of which he, without the slightest hesitation, tore a strip of paper suited to my purpose, and reached it to me. I immediately seized upon the book, and, after a few minutes' perusal, I know not which was greater, my astonishment or my vexation at this costly prize. The manuscript, which was bound in vellum, was not only defective both at the beginning and at the end, but several leaves had even been torn out here and there in the middle. I scolded the old man as I had never done during the whole course of my life; but he excused himself, saying that one of my predecessors had given him the manuscript for waste paper, as it had lain about there ever since the memory of man, and he had often been in want of paper to twist round the altar candles, etc. The aged and half-blind pastor had mistaken the folio for old parochial accounts which could be of no more use to any one.[i]

No sooner had I reached home than I fell to work upon my new acquisition, and after reading a bit here and there with considerable trouble, my interest was powerfully excited by the contents.

I soon felt the necessity of making myself better acquainted with the nature and conduct of these witch trials, with the proceedings, nay, even with the history

---

[i] The original manuscript does indeed contain several accounts which at first sight may have led to this mistake; besides, the handwriting is extremely difficult to read, and in several places the paper is discoloured and decayed.

of the whole period in which these events occur. But the more I read of these extraordinary stories, the more was I confounded; and neither the trivial Beeker (*Die bezauberte Welt*, 'The Enchanted World'),[3] nor the more careful Horst (*Zauberbibliothek*, 'The Library of Magic'),[4] to which, as well as to several other works on the same subject,[5] I had flown for information, could resolve my doubts, but rather served to increase them.

Not alone is the demoniacal character, which pervades nearly all these fearful stories, so deeply marked, as to fill the attentive reader with feelings of alternate horror and dismay, but the eternal and unchangeable laws of human feeling and action are often arrested in a manner so violent and unforeseen, that the understanding is entirely baffled. For instance, one of the original trials which a friend of mine, a lawyer, discovered in our province, contains the account of a mother, who, after she had suffered the torture, and received the holy Sacrament, and was on the point of going to the stake, so utterly lost all maternal feeling, that her conscience obliged her to accuse as a witch her only dearly-loved daughter, a girl of fifteen, against whom no one had ever entertained a suspicion, in order, as she said, to save her poor soul. The court, justly amazed at an event which probably has never since been paralleled, caused the state of the mother's mind to be examined both by clergymen and physicians, whose original testimonies are still appended to the records, and are all highly favourable to her soundness of mind. The unfortunate daughter, whose name was Elizabeth Hegel, was actually executed on the strength of her mother's accusation.[ii]

The explanation commonly received at the present day, that these phenomena were produced by means of animal magnetism,[6] is utterly insufficient. How, for instance, could this account for the deeply demoniacal nature of old Lizzie Kolken as exhibited in the following pages? It is utterly incomprehensible, and perfectly explains why the old pastor, notwithstanding the horrible deceits practised on him in the person of his daughter, retained as firm a faith in the truth of witchcraft as in that of the Gospel.

During the earlier centuries of the middle ages little was known of witchcraft. The crime of magic, when it did occur, was leniently punished. For instance, the Council of Ancyra (314)[7] ordained the whole punishment of witches to consist in expulsion from the Christian community. The Visigoths punished them with stripes, and Charlemagne, by advice of his bishops, confined them in prison until such time as they should sincerely repent.[iii] It was not until very soon before the Reformation, that Innocent VIII. lamented that the complaints of universal Christendom against the evil practices of these women had become so general and so loud, that the most vigorous measures must be taken against them; and towards the end of the year 1489, he caused the notorious Hammer for Witches

---

[ii] It is my intention to publish this trial also, as it possesses very great psychological interest.
[iii] Horst, *Zauberbibliothek*, VI, p. 231.

(*Malleus Maleficarum*)[8] to be published, according to which proceedings were set on foot with the most fanatical zeal, not only in Catholic, but, strange to say, even in Protestant Christendom, which in other respects abhorred everything belonging to Catholicism. Indeed, the Protestants far outdid the Catholics in cruelty, until, among the latter, the noble-minded Jesuit, J. Spee,[9] and among the former, but not until seventy years later, the excellent Thomasius,[10] by degrees put a stop to these horrors.

After careful examination into the nature and characteristics of witchcraft, I soon perceived that among all these strange and often romantic stories, not one surpassed my 'amber witch' in lively interest; and I determined to throw her adventures into the form of a romance.[11] Fortunately, however, I was soon convinced that her story was already in itself the most interesting of all romances; and that I should do far better to leave it in its original antiquated form, omitting whatever would be uninteresting to modern readers, or so universally known as to need no repetition. I have therefore attempted, not indeed to supply what is missing at the beginning and end, but to restore those leaves which have been torn out of the middle, imitating, as accurately as I was able, the language and manner of the old biographer, in order that the difference between the original narrative and my own interpolations might not be too evident.

This I have done with much trouble, and after many ineffectual attempts; but I refrain from pointing out the particular passages which I have supplied, so as not to disturb the historical interest of the greater part of my readers. For modern criticism, which has now attained to a degree of acuteness never before equalled, such a confession would be entirely superfluous, as critics will easily distinguish the passages where Pastor Schweidler speaks from those written by Pastor Meinhold.[12]

I am, nevertheless, bound to give the public some account of what I have omitted, namely —

1st. Such long prayers as were not very remarkable for Christian unction.

2d. Well-known stories out of the Thirty Years' War.

3d. Signs and wonders in the heavens, which were seen here and there, and which are recorded by other Pomeranian writers of these fearful times; for instance, by Micraelius.[iv][13] But when these events formed part of the tale itself, as, for instance, the cross on the Streckelberg, I, of course, allowed them to stand.

4th. The specification of the whole income of the church at Coserow, before and during the terrible times of the Thirty Years' War.

5th. The enumeration of the dwellings left standing, after the devastations made by the enemy in every village throughout the parish.

[iv] *Vom Alten Pommerlande* (Of Old Pomerania), book V.

6th. The names of the districts to which this or that member of the congregation had emigrated.

7th. A ground plan and description of the old Manse.

I have likewise here and there ventured to make a few changes in the language, as my author is not always consistent in the use of his words or in his orthography. The latter I have, however, with very few exceptions, retained.

And thus I lay before the gracious reader a work, glowing with the fire of heaven, as well as with that of hell.

MEINHOLD

THE AMBER WITCH

THE AMBER WITCH

INTRODUCTION

The origin of our biographer cannot be traced with any degree of certainty, owing to the loss of the first part of his manuscript. It is, however, pretty clear that he was not a Pomeranian, as he says he was in Silesia in his youth, and mentions relations scattered far and wide, not only at Hamburg and Cologne, but even at Antwerp; above all, his south German language betrays a foreign origin, and he makes use of words which are, I believe, peculiar to Swabia. He must, however, have been living for a long time in Pomerania at the time he wrote, as he even more frequently uses Low-German expressions, such as occur in contemporary native Pomeranian writers.

Since he sprang from an ancient noble family, as he says on several occasions, it is possible that some particulars relating to the Schweidlers might be discovered in the family records of the seventeenth century which would give a clue to his native country; but I have sought for that name in all the sources of information accessible to me, in vain, and am led to suspect that our author, like many of his contemporaries, laid aside his nobility and changed his name when he took holy orders.

I will not, however, venture on any further conjectures; the manuscript, of which six chapters are missing, begins with the words "Imperialists plundered," and evidently the previous pages must have contained an account of the breaking out of the Thirty Years' War in the island of Usedom.[14] It goes on as follows: —

"Coffers, chests, and closets were all plundered and broken to pieces, and my surplice also was torn, so that I remained in great distress and tribulation. But my poor little daughter they did not find, seeing that I had hidden her in the stable, which was dark, without which I doubt not they would have made my heart heavy indeed. The lewd dogs would even have been rude to my old maid Ilse, a woman hard upon fifty, if an old cornet[15] had not forbidden them. Wherefore I gave thanks to my Maker when the wild guests were gone, that I had first saved my child from their clutches, although not one dust of flour, nor one grain of corn, one morsel of meat even of a finger's length was left, and I knew not how I should any longer support my own life, and my poor child's. *Item*,[16] I thanked God that I had likewise secured the *vasa sacra*,[17] which I had forthwith buried in the church in front of the altar, in presence of the two churchwardens, Hinrich Seden and Claus Bulken, of Uekeritze, commending them to the care of God. And now because, as I have already said, I was suffering the pangs of hunger, I wrote to his lordship the Sheriff Wittich V. Appelmann, at Pudgla,[v] [18] that for the love of God and his holy Gospel he should send me that which his highness' grace Philippus Julius[19] had allowed me as *praestanda*[20] from the convent at Pudgla, to wit, thirty bushels of barley and twenty-five marks of silver, which, howbeit his lordship had always withheld from me hitherto (for he was a very hard inhuman man, as he despised the holy Gospel and the preaching of the Word, and openly, without shame, reviled the servants of God, saying that they were useless feeders, and that Luther had but half cleansed the pigstye of the Church — God mend it!).[21] But he answered me nothing, and I should have perished for want if Hinrich Seden had not begged for me in the parish. May God reward the honest fellow for it in eternity! Moreover, he was then growing old, and was sorely plagued by his wicked wife Lizzie Kolken. Methought when I married them that it would not turn out over well, seeing that she was in common report of having long lived in unchastity with Wittich Appelmann, who had ever been an arch-rogue, and especially an arrant whoremaster, and such the Lord never blesses. This same Seden now brought me five loaves, two sausages, and a goose, which old goodwife Paal, at Loddin,[22] had given him; also a flitch of bacon from the farmer Jack Tewert. But he said I must shield him from his wife, who would have had half for herself, and when he denied her she cursed him, and wished him gout in his head, whereupon he straightway felt a pain in his right cheek, and it was quite hard and heavy already. At such shocking news I was affrighted, as became a good pastor, and asked whether peradventure he believed that she stood in evil communication with Satan, and could bewitch folks? But he said nothing, and shrugged his shoulders. So I sent for old Lizzie to come to me, who was a tall, meagre woman of about sixty, with squinting eyes,[23] so that she could not look any one in the face; likewise with quite red hair, and indeed her goodman had the same. But though I diligently admonished her out of God's Word, she made no answer until at last I said, 'Wilt thou unbewitch thy goodman (for I saw from the window how that he was raving in the street like a madman), or wilt thou that I should inform the magistrate of thy deeds?' Then, indeed, she gave in, and promised that he should soon be better (and so he was); moreover she begged that I would give her some bread and some bacon, inasmuch as it was three days since she had a bit of anything to put between her lips, saving always her tongue. So my daughter gave her half a loaf, and a piece of bacon about two handsbreadths large; but she did not think it enough, and muttered between

---

[v] A castle in Usedom, formerly a celebrated convent.

her teeth; whereupon my daughter said, 'If thou art not content, thou old witch, go thy ways and help thy goodman; see how he has laid his head on Zabel's fence, and stamps with his feet for pain.' Whereupon she went away, but still kept muttering between her teeth, 'Yea, forsooth, I will help him and thee too.'"

CHAPTER VII

How the Imperialists robbed me of all that was left, and likewise broke into the church and stole the vasa sacra; also what more befell us.

After a few days, when we had eaten almost all our food, my last cow fell down dead (the wolves had already devoured the others, as mentioned above),[24] not without a strong suspicion that Lizzie had a hand in it, seeing that the poor beast had eaten heartily the day before; but I leave that to a higher judge, seeing that I would not willingly calumniate any one; and it may have been the will of God, whose wrath I have well deserved. *Summa*,[25] I was once more in great need, and my daughter Mary pierced my heart with her sighs, when the cry was raised that another troop of Imperialists was come to Uekeritze, and was marauding there more cruelly than ever, and, moreover, had burnt half the village. Wherefore I no longer thought myself safe in my cottage; and after I had commended everything to the Lord in a fervent prayer, I went up with my daughter and old Ilse into the Streckelberg,[vi][26] where I already had looked out for ourselves a hole like a cavern, well grown over with brambles, against the time when the troubles should drive us thither. We therefore took with us all we had left to us for the support of our bodies, and fled into the woods, sighing and weeping, whither we soon were followed by the old men, and the women and children; these raised a great cry of hunger when they saw my daughter sitting on a log and eating a bit of bread and meat, and the little things came with their tiny hands stretched out and cried "Have some too, have some too." Therefore, being justly moved by such great distress, I hindered not my daughter from sharing all the bread and meat that remained among the hungry children. But first I made them pray — "The eyes of all wait upon thee";[vii] upon which words I then spake comfortably to the people, telling them that the Lord, who had now fed their little children, would find means to fill their own bellies, and that they must not be weary of trusting in him.

This comfort did not, however, last long; for after we had rested within and around the cavern for about two hours, the bells in the village began to ring so dolefully[27] that it went nigh to break all our hearts, the more as loud firing was heard between-whiles; *item*, the cries of men and the barking of dogs resounded,

---

[vi] A considerable mountain close to the sea near Coserow.
[vii] Psalm 145. 15–16.

so that we could easily guess that the enemy was in the village. I had enough to do to keep the women quiet, that they might not by their senseless lamentations betray our hiding-place to the cruel enemy; and more still when it began to smell smoky, and presently the bright flames gleamed through the trees. I therefore sent old Paasch up to the top of the hill, that he might look around and see how matters stood, but told him to take good care that they did not see him from the village, seeing that the twilight had but just begun.

This he promised, and soon returned with the news that about twenty horsemen had galloped out of the village towards the Damerow,[28] but that half the village was in flames. *Item*, he told us that by a wonderful dispensation of God a great number of birds had appeared in the juniper-bushes and elsewhere, and that if we could catch them they would be excellent food for us. I therefore climbed up the hill myself, and having found everything as he had said, and also perceived that the fire had, by the help of God's mercy, abated in the village; *item*, that my cottage was left standing, far beyond my merits and deserts; I came down again and comforted the people, saying, "The Lord hath given us a sign, and he will feed us, as he fed the people of Israel in the wilderness;[29] for he has sent us a fine flight of fieldfares across the barren sea, so that they whirr out of every bush as ye come near it. Who will now run down into the village, and cut off the mane and tail of my dead cow which lies out behind on the common?" (for there was no horsehair in all the village, seeing that the enemy had long since carried off or stabbed all the horses).[30] But no one would go, for fear was stronger even than hunger, till my old Ilse spoke, and said, "I will go, for I fear nothing, when I walk in the ways of God; only give me a good stick." When old Paasch had lent her his staff, she began to sing, "God the Father be with us,"[31] and was soon out of sight among the bushes. Meanwhile I exhorted the people to set to work directly, and to cut little wands for springes, and to gather berries while the moon still shone; there were a great quantity of mountain-ash and elder-bushes all about the mountain. I myself and my daughter Mary stayed to guard the little children, because it was not safe there from wolves. We therefore made a blazing fire, sat ourselves around it, and heard the little folks say the Ten Commandments, when there was a rustling and crackling behind us, and my daughter jumped up and ran into the cavern, crying, "*Proh dolor hostis!*"[viii] [32] But it was only some of the able-bodied men who had stayed behind in the village, and who now came to bring us word how things stood there. I therefore called to her directly, "*Emergas amici*"[33] whereupon she came skipping joyously out, and sat down again by the fire, and forthwith my warden Hinrich Seden related all that had happened, and how his life had only been saved by means of his wife Lizzie Kolken; but that Jurgen Flatow, Chim Burse, Claus Peer, and Chim Seideritz were killed, and the

---

[viii] Our author afterwards explains the learned education of the maiden.

last named of them left lying on the church steps. The wicked incendiaries had burned down twelve sheds, and it was not their fault that the whole village was not destroyed, but only in consequence of the wind not being in the quarter that suited their purpose. Meanwhile they tolled the bells in mockery and scorn, to see whether any one would come and quench the fire; and that when he and the three other young fellows came forward they fired off their muskets at them, but, by God's help, none of them were hit. Hereupon his three comrades jumped over the paling and escaped; but him they caught, and had already taken aim at him with their firelocks, when his wife Lizzie Kolken came out of the church with another troop and beckoned to them to leave him in peace. But they stabbed Lene Hebers as she lay in childbed, speared the child, and flung it over Claus Peer's hedge among the nettles, where it was yet lying when they came away. There was not a living soul left in the village, and still less a morsel of bread, so that unless the Lord took pity on their need they must all die miserably of hunger.

(Now who is to believe that such people can call themselves Christians!)

I next inquired, when he had done speaking (but with many sighs, as any one may guess), after my cottage; but of that they knew nought save that it was still standing. I thanked the Lord therefore with a quiet sigh; and having asked old Seden what his wife had been doing in the church, I thought I should have died for grief when I heard that the villains came out of it with both the chalices and patens in their hands.[34] I therefore spoke very sharply to old Lizzie, who now came slinking through the bushes; but she answered insolently that the strange soldiers had forced her to open the church, as her goodman had crept behind the hedge, and nobody else was there; that they had gone straight up to the altar, and seeing that one of the stones was not well fitted (which, truly, was an arch-lie), had begun to dig with their swords till they found the chalices and patens; or somebody else might have betrayed the spot to them, so I need not always to lay the blame on her, and rate her so hardly.

Meanwhile the old men and the women came with a good store of berries; *item*, my old maid, with the cow's tail and mane, who brought word that the whole house was turned upside down, the windows all broken, and the books and writings trampled in the dirt in the midst of the street, and the doors torn off their hinges. This, however, was a less sorrow to me than the chalices; and I only bade the people make springes and snares, in order next morning to begin our fowling, with the help of Almighty God. I therefore scraped the rods myself until near midnight; and when we had made ready a good quantity, I told old Seden to repeat the evening blessing, which we all heard on our knees; after which I wound up with a prayer, and then admonished the people to creep in under the bushes to keep them from the cold (seeing that it was now about the end of September, and the wind blew very fresh from the sea), the men apart, and the women also apart by themselves. I myself went up with my daughter and my maid into the cavern, where I had not slept long before I heard old Seden moaning bitterly because, as he said, he was seized with the colic. I therefore got up and gave him my place, and sat down again by the fire to cut springes, till I fell asleep for half an hour; and then morning broke, and by that time he had got better, and I woke the people to morning prayer. This time old Paasch had to say it, but could not get through with it properly, so that I had to help him. Whether he had forgot it, or whether he was frightened, I cannot say. *Summa*. After we had all prayed most devoutly, we presently set to work, wedging the springes into the trees, and hanging berries all around them; while my daughter took care of the children, and looked for blackberries for their breakfast. Now we wedged the snares right across the wood along the road to Uekeritze; and mark what a wondrous act of mercy befell from gracious God! As I stepped into the road with the hatchet in my hand (it was Seden his hatchet, which he had fetched out of the village early in the morning), I caught sight of a loaf as long as my arm, which a raven was pecking, and which doubtless one of the Imperial troopers had dropped out of his knapsack the day before, for there were fresh hoofmarks in the sand by it. So I secretly buttoned the breast of my coat over it, so that none should perceive anything, although the aforesaid Paasch was close behind me; *item*, all the rest followed at no great distance. Now, having set the springes so very early, towards noon we found such a great number of birds taken in them that Katy Berow, who went beside me while I took them out, scarce could hold them all in her apron; and at the other end old Pagels pulled nearly as many out of his doublet and coat pockets. My daughter then sat down with the rest of the womankind to pluck the birds; and as there was no salt (indeed it was long since most of us had tasted any), she desired two men to go down to the sea, and to fetch a little salt-water in an iron pot borrowed from Staffer Zuter; and so they did. In this water we first dipped the birds, and then roasted them at a large fire, while our mouths watered only at the sweet savour of them, seeing it was so long since we had tasted any food.

And now when all was ready, and the people seated on the earth, I said, "Behold how the Lord still feeds his people Israel in the wilderness with fresh quails: if now he did yet more, and sent us a piece of manna bread from heaven, what think ye? Would ye then ever weary of believing in him, and not rather willingly endure all want, tribulation, hunger and thirst, which he may hereafter lay upon you according to his gracious will?" Whereupon they all answered and said, "Yea, surely!" *Ego*: "Will you then promise me this in truth?" And they said again, "Yea, that will we!" Then with tears I drew forth the loaf from my breast, held it on high, and cried, "Behold, then, thou poor believing little flock, how sweet a manna loaf your faithful Redeemer hath sent ye through me!" Whereupon they all wept, sobbed and groaned; and the little children again came running up and held out their hands, crying, "See, bread, bread!" But as I myself could not pray for heaviness of soul, I bade Paasch his little girl say the *Gratias* the while my Mary cut up the loaf and gave to each his share. And now we all joyfully began to eat our meat from God in the wilderness.

Meanwhile I had to tell in what manner I had found the blessed manna bread, wherein I neglected not again to exhort them to lay to heart this great sign and wonder, how that God in his mercy had done to them as of old to the prophet Elijah, to whom a raven brought bread in his great need in the wilderness;[35] as likewise this bread had been given to me by means of a raven, which showed it to me, when otherwise I might have passed it by in my heaviness without ever seeing it.

When we were satisfied with food, I said the thanksgiving from Luke 12. 24, where the Lord saith, "Consider the ravens: for they neither sow nor reap; which neither have storehouse nor barn; and God feedeth them: how much more are ye better than the fowls?" But our sins stank before the Lord. For old Lizzie, as I afterwards heard, would not eat her birds because she thought them unsavoury, but threw them among the juniper-bushes; whereupon the wrath of the Lord was kindled against us as of old against the people of Israel, and at night we found but seven birds in the snares, and next morning but two. Neither did any raven come again to give us bread. Wherefore I rebuked old Lizzie, and admonished the people to take upon themselves willingly the righteous chastisement of the Most High God, to pray without ceasing, to return to their desolate dwellings, and to see whether the all-merciful God would peradventure give them more on the sea.[36] That I also would call upon him with prayer night and day, remaining for a time in the cavern with my daughter and the maid to watch the springs, and see whether his wrath might be turned from us. That they should meanwhile put my manse to rights to the best of their power, seeing that the cold was become very irksome to me. This they promised me, and departed with many sighs. What a little flock! I counted but twenty-five souls where there used to be above eighty: all the rest had been slain by hunger, pestilence, or the sword.[ix] I then abode a while alone and sorrowing in the cave, praying to God, and sent my daughter with the maid into the village to see how things stood at the manse; *item*, to gather together the books and papers, and also to bring me word whether Hinze the carpenter, whom I had straightway sent back to the village, had knocked together some coffins for the poor corpses, so that I might bury them next day. I then went to look at the springs, but found only one single little bird, whereby I saw that the wrath of God had not yet passed away. Howbeit, I found a fine blackberry bush, from which I gathered nearly a pint of berries, and put them, together with the bird, in Staffer Zuter his pot, which the honest fellow had left with us for a while, and set them on the fire for supper against my child and the maid should return. It was not long before they came through the coppice and told me of the fearful devastation which Satan had made in the village and manse by the

---

[ix] This took place in the year 1628, after the horrors of the Thirty Years' War were spread most fearfully over this island; pity that the description of the old vicar, which he doubtless gave in the preceding pages, has been lost.

permission of all-righteous God. My child had gathered together a few books, which she brought with her, above all, a *Virgilius*[37] and a Greek Bible. And after she had told me that the carpenter would not have done till next day, and we had satisfied the cravings of hunger, I made her read to me again, for the greater strengthening of my faith, the *locus* about the blessed raven from the Greek of Luke, at the twelfth chapter; also, the beautiful *locus parallelus*,[38] Matthew 6. After which the maid said the evening blessing, and we all went into the cave to rest for the night. When I awoke next morning, just as the blessed sun rose out the sea and peeped over the mountain, I heard my poor hungry child already standing outside the cave reciting the beautiful verses about the joys of paradise which St. Augustine wrote and I had taught her.[x][39] She sobbed for grief as she spoke the words: —

> Uno pane vivunt cives utriusque patriae;
> Avidi et semper pleni, quod habent desiderant.
> Non societas fastidit, neque fames cruciat;
> Inhiantes semper edunt, et edentes inhiant.
> Flos perpetuus rosarum ver agit perpetuum;
> Candent lilia, rubescit crocus, sudat balsamum,
> Virent prata, vernant sata, rivi mellis influunt;
> Pigmentorum spirat odor liquor et aromatum,
> Pendent poma floridorum non lapsura nemorum.
> Non alternat luna vices, sol vel cursus syderum.
> Agnus est faelicis urbis lumen inocciduum.[xi]

At these words my own heart was melted; and when she ceased from speaking, I asked, "What art thou doing, my child?" Whereupon she answered, "Father, I am eating." Thereat my tears now indeed began to flow, and I praised her for feeding her soul, as she had no meat for her body. I had not, however, spoken long, before she cried to me to come and look at the great wonder that had risen

---

[x] This is an error. The following verses are written by the Cardinal Bishop of Ostia, Peter Damianus (d. 23 Feb. 1072), after Augustine's prose.
[xi] The following version is from the pen of a friend. — *Trans.*

> "In that far land the citizens all share one equal bread.
> And keep desire and hunger still, although to fullness fed:
> Unwearied by satiety, unracked by hunger's strife,
> The air they breathe is nourishment, and spiritual life!
> Around them, bright with endless Spring, perpetual roses bloom;
> Warm balsams gratefully exude luxurious perfume;
> Red crocuses, and lilies white, shine dazzling in the sun;
> Green meadows yield them harvests green, and streams with honey run;
> Unbroken droop the laden boughs, with heavy fruitage bent,
> Of incense and of odours strange the air is redolent;
> And neither sun, not moon, nor stars, dispense their changeful light,
> But the Lamb's eternal glory makes the happy city bright!"

out of the sea, and already appeared over the cave. For behold a cloud, in shape just like a cross, came over us, and let great heavy drops, as big or bigger than large peas, fall on our heads, after which it sank behind the coppice. I presently arose and ran up the mountain with my daughter to look after it. It floated on towards the Achterwater,[xii] where it spread itself out into a long blue streak, whereon the sun shone so brightly that it seemed like a golden bridge on which, as my child said, the blessed angels danced. I fell on my knees with her and thanked the Lord that our cross had passed away from us; but, alas! our cross was yet to come, as will be told hereafter.

CHAPTER VIII

How our need waxed sorer and sorer, and how I sent old Ilse with another letter to Pudgla, and how heavy a misfortune this brought upon me.

Next day, when I had buried the poor corpses amid the lamentations of the whole village (by the same token that they were all buried under where the lime-tree overhangs the wall[xiii]), I heard with many sighs that neither the sea nor the Achterwater would yield anything. It was now ten days since the poor people had caught a single fish. I therefore went out into the field, musing how the wrath of the just God might be turned from us, seeing that the cruel winter was now at hand, and neither corn, apples, fish nor flesh to be found in the village, nor even throughout all the parish. There was indeed plenty of game in the forests of Coserow and Uekeritze; but the old forest ranger, Zabel Nehring, had died last year of the plague, and there was no new one in his place. Nor was there a musket nor a grain of powder to be found in all the parish; the enemy had robbed and broken everything: we were therefore forced, day after day, to see how the stags and the roes, the hares and the wild boars, *et cet.*, ran past us, when we would so gladly have had them in our bellies, but had no means of getting at them: for they were too cunning to let themselves be caught in pit-falls. Nevertheless, Claus Peer succeeded in trapping a roe, and gave me a piece of it, for which may God reward him. *Item*, of domestic cattle there was not a head left; neither was there a dog, nor a cat, which the people had not either eaten in their extreme hunger, or knocked on the head or drowned long since. Albeit old farmer Paasch still owned two cows; *item*, an old man in Uekeritze was said to have one little pig: — this was all. Thus, then, nearly all the people lived on blackberries and other wild fruits: the which also soon grew to be scarce, as may easily be guessed. Besides all this, a boy of fourteen was missing (old Labahn his son) and was never more heard of, so that I shrewdly think that the wolves devoured him.

[xii] A wash formed by the river Peene in the neighbourhood.
[xiii] This exists no longer.

And now let any Christian judge by his own heart in what sorrow and heaviness I took my staff in my hand, seeing that my child fell away like a shadow from pinching hunger; although I myself, being old, did not, by the help of God's mercy, find any great failing in my strength. While I thus went continually weeping before the Lord, on the way to Uekeritze, I fell in with an old beggar with his wallet, sitting on a stone, and eating a piece of God's rare gift, to wit, a bit of bread. Then truly did my poor mouth so fill with water that I was forced to bow my head and let it run upon the earth before I could ask, "Who art thou? and whence comest thou? seeing that thou hast bread." Whereupon he answered that he was a poor man of Bannemin,[40] from whom the enemy had taken all; and as he had heard that the Lieper Winkel[xiv] had long been in peace, he had travelled thither to beg.[41] I straightway answered him, "Oh, poor beggar-man, spare to me, a sorrowful servant of Christ, who is poorer even than thyself, one little slice of bread for his wretched child; for thou must know that I am the pastor of this village, and that my daughter is dying of hunger. I beseech thee by the living God not to let me depart without taking pity on me, as pity also hath been shown to thee!" But the beggar-man would give me none, saying that he himself had a wife and four children, who were likewise staggering towards death's door under the bitter pangs of hunger; that the famine was sorer far in Bannemin than here, where we still had berries; whether I had not heard that but a few days ago a woman (he told me her name, but horror made me forget it) had there killed her own child, and devoured it from hunger?[xv] [42] That he could not therefore help me, and I might go to the Lieper Winkel myself.

I was horror-stricken at his tale, as is easy to guess, for we in our own trouble had not yet heard of it, there being little or no traffic between one village and another; and thinking on Jerusalem,[xvi] and sheer despairing because the Lord had visited us, as of old that ungodly city, although we had not betrayed or crucified him, I almost forgot all my necessities, and took my staff in my hand to depart. But I had not gone more than a few yards when the beggar called me to stop, and when I turned myself round he came towards me with a good hunch of bread which he had taken out of his wallet, and said, "There! but pray for me also, so that I may reach my home; for if on the road they smell that I have bread, my own brother would strike me dead, I believe." This I promised with joy, and instantly turned back to take to my child the gift hidden in my pocket. And behold, when I came to the road which leads to Loddin, I could scarce trust my eyes (before I had overlooked it in my distress) when I saw my glebe, which could produce seven bushels, ploughed, sown, and in stalk; the blessed crop of rye had already shot lustily out of the earth a finger's length in height. I could not choose

---

[xiv] A remote part of the island of Usedom.
[xv] Micraelius also mentions this horrible event in his History of Pomerania.
[xvi] Where, according to Josephus, the same thing occurred.

but think that the Evil One had deceived me with a false show, yet, however hard I rubbed my eyes, rye it was and rye it remained. And seeing that old Paasch his piece of land which joined mine was in like manner sown, and that the blades had shot up to the same height, I soon guessed that the good fellow had done this deed, seeing that all the other land lay waste. Wherefore, I readily forgave him for not knowing the morning prayer; and thanking the Lord for so much love from my flock, and earnestly beseeching him to grant me strength and faith to bear with them steadfastly and patiently all the troubles and adversities which it might please him henceforward to lay upon us, according to his divine pleasure, I ran rather than walked back into the village to old Paasch his farm, where I found him just about to kill his cow, which he was slaughtering from grim hunger. "God bless thee," said I, "worthy friend, for sowing my field; how shall I reward thee?" But the old man answered, "Let that be, and do you pray for us"; and when I gladly promised this and asked him how he had kept his corn safe from the savage enemy, he told me that he had hidden it secretly in the caves of the Streckelberg, but that now all his store was used up. Meanwhile he cut a fine large piece of meat from the top of the loin, and said, "There is something for you, and when that is gone you can come again for more." As I was then about to go with many thanks, his little Mary, a child nearly seven years old, the same who had said the *Gratias*[43] on the Streckelberg, seized me by the hand and wanted to go to school to my daughter; for since my *Custos*,[44] as above mentioned, departed this life in the plague, she had to teach the few little ones there were in the village; this, however, had long been abandoned. I could not, therefore, deny her, although I feared that my child would share her bread with her, seeing that she dearly loved the little maid, who was her godchild; and so indeed it happened; for when the child saw me take out the bread, she shrieked for joy, and began to scramble up on the bench. Thus she also got a piece of the slice, our maid got another, and my child put the third piece into her own mouth, as I wished for none, but said that I felt no signs of hunger and would wait until the meat was boiled, the which I now threw upon the bench. It was a goodly sight to see the joy which my poor child felt when I then also told her about the rye. She fell upon my neck, wept, sobbed, then took the little one up in her arms, danced about the room with her, and recited as she was wont, all manner of Latin *versus*, which she knew by heart. Then she would prepare a right good supper for us, as a little salt was still left in the bottom of a barrel of meat which the Imperialists had broken up. I let her take her own way, and having scraped some soot from the chimney and mixed it with water, I tore a blank leaf out of *Virgilius*, and wrote to the *Pastor Liepensis*, his reverence Abraham Tiburtius, praying that for God his sake he would take our necessities to heart, and would exhort his parishioners to save us from dying of grim hunger, and charitably to spare to us some meat and drink, according as the all-merciful God had still left some to them, seeing that a beggar had told me that they had long been in peace from the terrible enemy. I knew not, however, wherewithal to seal the letter, until I found in the church a little wax still sticking to a wooden altar-candlestick, which the Imperialists had not thought it worth their while to steal, for they had only taken the brass ones. I sent three fellows in a boat with Hinrich Seden, the churchwarden, with this letter to Liepe.

First, however, I asked my old Ilse, who was born in Liepe, whether she would not rather return home, seeing how matters stood, and that I, for the present at least, could not give her a stiver of her wages (mark that she had already saved up a small sum, seeing that she had lived in my service above twenty years, but the soldiers had taken it all). Howbeit, I could nowise persuade her to this, but she wept bitterly, and besought me only to let her stay with the good damsel whom she had rocked in her cradle. She would cheerfully hunger with us if it needs must be, so that she were not turned away. Whereupon I yielded to her, and the others went alone.

Meanwhile the broth was ready, but scarce had we said the *Gratias*, and were about to begin our meal, when all the children of the village, seven in number, came to the door, and wanted bread, as they had heard we had some from my daughter her little godchild. Her heart again melted, and notwithstanding I besought her to harden herself against them, she comforted me with the message to Liepe, and poured out for each child a portion of broth on a wooden platter (for these also had been despised by the enemy), and put into their little hands a bit of meat, so that all our store was eaten up at once. We were, therefore, left fasting next morning, till towards mid-day, when the whole village gathered together in a meadow on the banks of the river to see the boat return. But, God be merciful to us, we had cherished vain hopes! six loaves and a sheep, *item*, a quarter of apples, was all they had brought. His reverence Abraham Tiburtius wrote to me that after the cry of their wealth had spread throughout the island, so many beggars had flocked thither that it was impossible to be just to all, seeing that they themselves did not know how it might fare with them in these heavy troublous times. Meanwhile he would see whether he could raise any more. I therefore with many sighs had the small pittance carried to the manse, and though two loaves were, as *Pastor Liepensis* said in his letter, for me alone, I gave them up to be shared among all alike, whereat all were content save Seden his squint-eyed wife, who would have had somewhat *extra* on the score of her husband's journey, which, however, as may be easily guessed, she did not get; wherefore she again muttered certain words between her teeth as she went away, which, however, no one understood. Truly she was an ill woman, and not to be moved by the word of God.

Any one may judge for himself that such a store could not last long; and as all my parishioners felt an ardent longing after spiritual food, and as I and the churchwardens could only get together about sixteen farthings in the whole parish, which was not enough to buy bread and wine, the thought struck me once more to inform my lord the Sheriff of our need. With how heavy a heart I did this may be easily guessed, but necessity knows no law. I therefore tore the last blank leaf out of *Virgilius*, and begged that, for the sake of the Holy Trinity, his lordship would mercifully consider mine own distress and that of the whole parish, and bestow a little money to enable me to administer the holy sacrament for the comfort of afflicted souls; also, if possible, to buy a cup, were it only of tin, since the enemy had plundered us of ours, and I should otherwise be forced to consecrate the sacred elements in an earthen vessel. *Item*, I besought him to have pity on our bodily wants, and at last to send me the first-fruits which had stood over for so many years. That I did not want it for myself alone, but would willingly share it with my parishioners, until such time as God in his mercy should give us more.

Here a huge blot fell upon my paper; for the windows being boarded up, the room was dark, and but little light came through two small panes of glass which I had broken out of the church, and stuck in between the boards; this, perhaps, was the reason why I did not see better. However, as I could not anywhere get another piece of paper, I let it pass, and ordered the maid, whom I sent with the letter to Pudgla, to excuse the same to his lordship the Sheriff, the which she promised to do, seeing that I could not add a word more on the paper, as it was written all over. I then sealed it as I had done before.

But the poor creature came back trembling for fear and bitterly weeping, and said that his lordship had kicked her out of the castle-gate, and had threatened to set her in the stocks if she ever came before him again. "Did the parson think that he was as free with his money as I seemed to be with my ink? I surely had water enough to celebrate the Lord's supper wherewithal. For if the Son of God had once changed the water into wine,[45] he could surely do the like again. If I had no cup, I might water my flock out of a bucket, as he did himself"; with many more blasphemies, such as he afterwards wrote to me, and by which, as may easily be guessed, I was filled with horror. Touching the first-fruits, as she told me he said nothing at all. In such great spiritual and bodily need the blessed Sunday came round, when nearly all the congregation would have come to the Lord's table, but could not. I therefore spoke on the words of St. Augustine, *crede et manducasti*,[46] and represented that the blame was not mine, and truly told what had happened to my poor maid at Pudgla, passing over much in silence, and only praying God to awaken the hearts of magistrates for our good. Peradventure I may have spoken more harshly than I meant. I know not, only that I spoke that which was in my heart. At the end I made all the congregation stay on their knees for nearly an hour, and call upon the Lord for his holy sacrament; *item*, for the relief of their bodily wants, as had been done every Sunday, and at all the daily prayers I had been used to read ever since the heavy time of the plague. Last of all I led the glorious hymn, "When in greatest need we be,"[47] which was no sooner finished than my new churchwarden, Claus Bulk of Uekeritze, who had formerly been a groom with his lordship, and whom he had now put into a farm, ran off to Pudgla, and told him all that had taken place in the church. Whereat his lordship was greatly angered, insomuch that he summoned the whole parish, which still numbered about 150 souls, without counting the children, and dictated *ad protocollum*[48] whatsoever they could remember of the sermon, seeing that he meant to inform his princely grace the Duke of Pomerania of the blasphemous lies which I had vomited against him, and which must sorely offend every Christian heart. *Item*, what an avaricious wretch I must be to be always wanting something of him, and to be daily, so to say, pestering him in these hard times with my filthy letters, when he had not enough to eat himself. This he said should break the parson his neck, since his princely grace did all that he asked of him, and that no one in the parish need give me anything more, but only let me go my ways. He would soon take care that they should have quite a different sort of parson from what I was.

(Now I would like to see the man who could make up his mind to come into the midst of such wretchedness at all.)

This news was brought to me in the selfsame night, and gave me a great fright, as I now saw that I should not have a gracious master in his lordship, but should all the time of my miserable life, even if I could anyhow support it, find in him an ungracious lord. But I soon felt some comfort, when Chim Krüger from Uekeritze, who brought me the news, took a little bit of his sucking-pig out of his pocket and gave it to me. Meanwhile old Paasch came in and said the same, and likewise brought me a piece of his old cow; *item*, my other warden, Hinrich Seden, with a slice of bread, and a fish which he had taken in his net, all saying they wished for no better priest than me, and that I was only to pray to the merciful Lord to bestow more upon them, whereupon I should want for nothing. Meanwhile I must be quiet and not betray them. All this I promised, and my daughter Mary took the blessed gifts of God off the table and carried them into the inner chamber. But, alas! next morning, when she would have put the meat into the caldron, it was all gone. I know not who prepared this new sorrow for me, but much believe it was Hinrich Seden his wicked wife, seeing he can never hold his tongue, and most likely told her everything. Moreover, Paasch his little daughter saw that she had meat in her pot next day; *item*, that she had quarrelled with her husband, and had flung the fish-board at him, whereon some fresh fish-scales were sticking: she had, however, presently recollected herself when she saw the child. (Shame on thee, thou old witch, it is true enough, I dare say!) Hereupon nought was left us but to feed our poor souls with the word of God. But even our souls were so cast down that they could receive nought, any more than our bellies; my poor child, especially, from day to day grew paler, greyer, and yellower, and always threw up all her food, seeing she ate it without salt or bread. I had long wondered that the bread from Liepe was not yet done, but that every day at dinner I still had a morsel. I had often asked, "Whence comes all this blessed bread? I believe, after all, you save the whole for me, and take none for yourself or the maid." But they both then lifted to their mouths a piece of fir-tree bark, which they had cut to look like bread, and laid by their plates; and as the room was dark, I did not find out their deceit, but thought that they, too, were eating bread. But at last the maid told me of it, so that I should allow it no longer, as my daughter would not listen to her. It is not hard to guess how my heart was wrung when I saw my poor child lying on her bed of moss struggling with grim hunger. But things were to go yet harder with me, for the Lord in his anger would break me in pieces like a potter's vessel.[49] For behold, on the evening of the same day, old Paasch came running to me, complaining that all his and my corn in the field had been pulled up and miserably destroyed, and that it must have been done by Satan himself, as there was not a trace either of oxen or horses. At these words my poor child screamed aloud and fainted. I would have run to help her, but could not reach her bed, and fell on the ground myself for bitter grief. The loud cries of the maid and old Paasch soon brought us both to our senses. But I could not rise from the ground alone, for the Lord had bruised all my bones. I besought them, therefore, when they would have helped me, to leave me where I was; and when they would not, I cried out that I must again fall on the ground to pray, and begged them all save my daughter to depart out of the room. This they did, but the prayer would not come. I fell into heavy doubting and despair, and murmured against the Lord that he plagued me more sorely than Lazarus or Job.[50] Wretch that I was, I cried, "Thou didst leave to Lazarus at least the crumbs and the pitiful dogs, but to me thou hast left nothing, and I myself am less in thy sight even than a dog; and Job thou didst not afflict until thou hadst mercifully taken away his children, but to me thou hast left my poor little daughter, that her torments may increase mine own a thousandfold. Behold, then, I can only pray that thou wilt take her from the earth, so that my grey head may gladly follow her to the grave! Woe is me, ruthless father, what have I done? I have eaten bread, and suffered my child to hunger! Oh, Lord Jesu, who hast said, 'What man is there of you, whom if his son ask bread will he give him a stone?'[51] Behold I am that man! — behold I am that ruthless father! I have eaten bread and have given wood to my child! Punish me; I will bear it and lie still. Oh, righteous Jesu, I have eaten bread, and have given wood to my child!" As I did not speak, but rather shrieked these words, wringing my hands the while, my child fell upon my neck, sobbing, and chid me for murmuring against the Lord, seeing that even she, a weak and frail woman, had never doubted his mercy, so that with shame and repentance I presently came to myself, and humbled myself before the Lord for such heavy sin.

Meanwhile the maid had run into the village with loud cries to see if she could get anything for her poor young mistress, but the people had already eaten their noontide meal, and most of them were gone to sea to seek their blessed supper; thus she could find nothing, seeing that old wife Seden, who alone had any victuals, would give her none, although she prayed her by Jesu's wounds.

She was telling us this when we heard a noise in the chamber, and presently Lizzie her worthy old husband, who had got in at the window by stealth, brought us a pot of good broth, which he had taken off the fire whilst his wife was gone for a moment into the garden. He well knew that his wife would make him pay for it, but that he did not mind, so the young mistress would but drink it, and she would find it salted and all. He would make haste out of the window again, and see that he got home before his wife, that she might not find out where he had been. But my daughter would not touch the broth, which sorely vexed him, so that he set it down on the ground cursing, and ran out of the room. It was not long before his squint-eyed wife came in at the front door, and when she saw the pot still steaming on the ground, she cried out, "Thou thief, thou cursed thieving carcass!" and would have flown at the face of my maid. But I threatened her, and told her all that had happened, and that if she would not believe me she might go into the chamber and look out of the window, whence she might still, belike, see her good man running home. This she did, and presently we heard her calling after him, "Wait, and the devil shall tear off thine arms; only wait till thou art home again!" After this she came back, and, muttering something, took the pot off the ground. I begged her, for the love of God, to spare a little to my child; but she mocked at me and said, "You can preach to her, as you did to me," and walked towards the door with the pot. My child indeed besought me to let her go, but I could not help calling after her, "For the love of God, one good sup, or my poor child must give up the ghost: wilt thou that at the day of judgment God should have mercy on thee, so show mercy this day to me and mine!" But she scoffed at us again, and cried out, "Let her cook herself some bacon," and went out at the door. I then sent the maid after her with the hour-glass which stood before me on the table, to offer it to her for a good sup out of the pot; but the maid brought it back, saying that she would not have it. Alas, how I wept and sobbed, as my poor dying child with a loud sigh buried her head again in the moss! Yet the merciful God was more gracious to me than my unbelief had deserved; for when the hard-hearted woman bestowed a little broth on her neighbour, old Paasch, he presently brought it to my child, having heard from the maid how it stood with her; and I believe that this broth, under God, alone saved her life, for she raised her head as soon as she had supped it, and was able to go about the house again in an hour. May God reward the good fellow for it! Thus I had some joy in the midst of my trouble. But while I sat by the fireside in the evening musing on my fate, my grief again broke forth, and I made up my mind to leave my house, and even my cure, and to wander through the wide world with my daughter as a beggar. God knows I had cause enough for it; for now that all my hopes were dashed, seeing that my field was quite ruined, and that the Sheriff had become my bitter enemy; moreover, that it was five years since I had had a wedding, *item*, but two christenings during the past year, I saw my own and my daughter's death staring me in the face, and no prospect of better times at hand. Our want was increased by the great fears of the congregation; for although by God's wondrous mercy they had already begun to take good draughts of fish both in the sea and the Achterwater, and many of the people in the other villages had already gotten bread, salt, oatmeal, etc., from the Polters and Quatzners, of Anklam and Lassan[xvii][52] in exchange for their fish; nevertheless, they brought me nothing, fearing lest it might be told at Pudgla, and make his lordship ungracious to them. I therefore beckoned my daughter to me, and told her what was in my thoughts, saying that God in his mercy could any day bestow on me another cure if I was found worthy in his sight of such a favour, seeing that these terrible days of pestilence and war had called away many of the servants of his word, and that I had not fled like a hireling from his flock, but on the contrary, till *datum* shared sorrow and death with it. Whether she were able to walk five or ten miles a day; for that then we would beg our way to Hamburg, to my departed wife her step-brother, Martin Behring, who is a great merchant in that city.

This at first sounded strange to her, seeing that she had very seldom been out of our parish, and that her departed mother and her little brother lay in our churchyard. She asked, "Who was to make up their graves and plant flowers on them? *Item*, as the Lord had given her a smooth face, what I should do if in these wild and cruel times she were attacked on the highways by marauding soldiers or other villains, seeing that I was a weak old man and unable to defend her; *item*, wherewithal should we shield ourselves from the frost, as the winter was setting in and the enemy had robbed us of our clothes, so that we had scarce enough left to cover our nakedness?" All this I had not considered, and was forced to own that she was right; so after much discussion we determined to leave it this night to the Lord, and to do whatever he should put into our hearts next morning. At any rate, we saw that we could in nowise keep the old maid any longer; I therefore called her out of the kitchen, and told her she had better go early next morning to Liepe, as there still was food there, whereas here she must starve, seeing that perhaps we ourselves might leave the parish and the country to-morrow. I thanked her for the love and faith she had shown us, and begged her at last, amid the loud sobs of my poor daughter, to depart forthwith privately, and not to make our hearts still heavier by leave-taking; that old Paasch was going a-fishing to-night on the Achterwater, as he had told me, and no doubt would readily set her on shore at Grüssow,[53] where she had friends, and could eat her fill even to-day. She could not say a word for weeping, but when she saw that I was really in earnest she went out of the room. Not long after we heard the house-door shut to, whereupon my daughter moaned, "She is gone already," and ran straight to the window to look after her. "Yes," cried she, as she saw her through the little panes, "she is really gone"; and she wrung her hands and would not be comforted.

[xvii] These people still go about the Achterwater every day in small boats called Polten and Quatzen, and buy from the boors any fish they may have caught.

At last, however, she was quieted when I spoke of the maid Hagar, whom Abraham had likewise cast off, but on whom the Lord had nevertheless shown mercy in the wilderness;[54] and hereupon we commended ourselves to the Lord, and stretched ourselves on our couches of moss.

CHAPTER IX

How the old maid-servant humbled me by her faith,
and the Lord yet blessed me His unworthy servant.

"Bless the Lord, O my soul; and all that is within me, bless his holy name. Bless the Lord, O my soul, and forget not all his benefits. Who forgiveth all thine iniquities; who healeth all thy diseases; who redeemeth thy life from destruction; who crowneth thee with loving kindness and tender mercies" (Psalm 103).

Alas! wretched man that I am, how shall I understand all the benefits and mercies which the Lord bestowed upon me the very next day? I now wept for joy, as of late I had done for sorrow; and my child danced about the room like a young roe, and would not go to bed, but only cry and dance, and between-whiles repeat the 103rd Psalm, then dance and cry again until morning broke. But as she was still very weak, I rebuked her presumption, seeing that this was tempting the Lord; and now mark what had happened.

After we had both woke in the morning with deep sighs, and called upon the Lord to manifest to us in our hearts what we should do, we still could not make up our minds. I therefore called to my child, if she felt strong enough, to leave her bed and light a fire in the stove herself, as our maid was gone; that we would then consider the matter further. She accordingly got up, but came back in an instant with cries of joy, because the maid had privately stolen back into the house, and had already made a fire. Hereupon I sent for her to my bedside, and wondered at her disobedience, and asked what she now wanted here but to torment me and my daughter still more, and why she did not go yesterday with old Paasch? But she lamented and wept so sore that she scarce could speak, and I understood only thus much — that she had eaten with us, and would likewise starve with us, for that she could never part from her young mistress, whom she had known from her cradle. Such faithful love moved me so, that I said almost with tears, "But hast thou not heard that my daughter and I have determined to wander as beggars about the country; where, then, wilt thou remain?" To this she answered that neither would she stay behind, seeing it was more fitting for her to beg than for us; but that she could not yet see why I wished to go out into the wide world; whether I had already forgotten that I had said in my induction sermon that I would abide with my flock in affliction and in death? That I should stay yet a little longer where I was, and send her to Liepe, as she hoped to get something worth having for us there from her friends and others. These words, especially those about my induction sermon, fell heavy on my conscience, and I was ashamed of my want of faith, since not my daughter only, but yet more even my maid, had stronger faith than I, who nevertheless professed to be a servant of God's word. I believed that the Lord — to keep me, poor fearful hireling, and at the same time to humble me — had awakened the spirit of this poor maid-servant to prove me, as the maid in the palace of the high-priest had also proved the fearful St. Peter.[55] Wherefore I turned my face towards the wall, like Hezekiah,[56] and humbled myself before the Lord, which scarce had I done before my child ran into the room again, with a cry of joy; for behold, some Christian heart had stolen quietly into the house in the night, and had laid in the chamber two loaves, a good piece of meat, a bag of oatmeal, *item*, a bag of salt, holding near a pint. Any one may guess what shouts of joy we all raised. Neither was I ashamed to confess my sins before my maid; and in our common morning prayer, which we said on our knees, I made fresh vows to the Lord of obedience and faith. Thus we had that morning a grand breakfast, and sent something to old Paasch besides; *item*, my daughter again sent for all the little children to come, and kindly fed them with our store before they said their tasks; and when in my heart of little faith I sighed thereat, although I said nought, she smiled, and said, "Take therefore no thought for the morrow, for the morrow shall take thought for the things of itself."[xviii]

The Holy Ghost spoke by her, as I cannot but believe, nor thou either, beloved reader: for mark what happened. In the afternoon she (I mean my child) went up the Streckelberg to seek for blackberries, as old Paasch had told her, through the maid, that a few bushes were still left. The maid was chopping wood in the yard, to which end she had borrowed old Paasch his axe, for the Imperialist thieves had thrown away mine, so that it could nowhere be found; and I myself was pacing up and down in the room, meditating my sermon; when my child, with her apron full, came quickly in at the door, quite red and with beaming eyes, and scarce able for joy to say more than "Father, father, what have I got?" "Well," quoth I, "what hast thou got, my child?" Whereupon she opened her apron, and I scarce trusted my eyes when I saw, instead of the blackberries which she had gone to seek, two shining pieces of amber, each nearly as big as a man's head, not to mention the small pieces, some of which were as large as my hand, and that, God knows, is no small one. "Child of my heart," cried I, "how camest thou by this blessing from God?" As soon as she could fetch her breath, she told me as follows: —

That while she was seeking for blackberries in a dell near the shore she saw somewhat glistening in the sun, and on coming near she found this wondrous godsend, seeing that the wind had blown the sand away from off a black vein of

---

[xviii] Matthew 6. 34.

amber.[xix] [57] That she straightway had broken off these pieces with a stick, and that there was plenty more to be got, seeing that it rattled about under the stick when she thrust it into the sand, neither could she force it farther than, at most, a foot deep into the ground; *item*, she told me that she had covered the place all over again with sand, and swept it smooth with her apron, so as to leave no traces.

Moreover, that no stranger was at all likely to go thither, seeing that no blackberries grew very near, and she had gone to the spot, moved by curiosity and a wish to look upon the sea, rather than from any need; but that she could easily find the place again herself, inasmuch as she had marked it with three little stones. What was our first act after the all-merciful God had rescued us out of such misery, nay, even, as it seemed, endowed us with great riches, any one may guess. When we at length got up off our knees, my child would straightway have run to tell the maid our joyful news. But I forbade her, seeing that we could not be sure that the maid might not tell it again to her friends, albeit in all other things she was a faithful woman and feared God; but that if she did that, the Sheriff would be sure to hear of it, and to seize upon our treasure for his princely highness the Duke — that is to say, for himself; and that nought would be left to us but the sight thereof, and our want would begin all over again; that we therefore would say, when folks asked about the luck that had befallen us, that my deceased brother, who was a councillor at Rotterdam, had left us a good lump of money; and, indeed, it was true that I had inherited near two hundred florins from him a year ago, which, however, the soldiery (as mentioned above) cruelly robbed me of; *item*, that I would go to Wolgast[58] myself next day and sell the little bits as best I might, saying that thou hadst picked them up by the seaside; thou mayest tell the maid the same, if thou wilt, but show the larger pieces to no one, and I will send them to thy uncle at Hamburg to be turned into money for us; perchance I may be able to sell one of them at Wolgast, if I find occasion, so as to buy clothes enough for the winter for thee and for me, wherefore thou, too, mayst go with me. We will take the few farthings which the congregation have brought together to pay the ferry, and thou canst order the maid to wait for us till eventide at the water-side to carry home the victuals. She agreed to all this, but said we had better first break off some more amber, so that we might get a good round sum for it at Hamburg; and I thought so too, wherefore we stopped at home next day, seeing that we did not want for food, and that my child, as well as myself, both wished to refresh ourselves a little before we set out on our journey; *item*, we likewise bethought us that old Master Rothoog, of Loddin, who is a cabinetmaker, might knock together a little box for us to put the amber in,

---

[xix] This happens frequently even now, and has occurred to the editor himself. The small dark vein held indeed a few pieces of amber, mixed with charcoal, a sure proof of its vegetable origin, of which we may observe in passing there is now scarce any doubt, since whole trees of amber have been found in Prussia, and are preserved in the museum at Königsberg.

wherefore I sent the maid to him in the afternoon. Meanwhile we ourselves went up the Streckelberg, where I cut a young fir-tree with my pocket-knife, which I had saved from the enemy, and shaped it like a spade, so that I might be better able to dig deep therewith. First, however, we looked about us well on the mountain, and, seeing nobody, my daughter walked on to the place, which she straightway found again. Great God! what a mass of amber was there! The vein was hard upon twenty feet long, as near as I could feel, and the depth of it I could not sound. Nevertheless, save four good-sized pieces, none, however, so big as those of yesterday, we this day only broke out little splinters, such as the apothecaries bruise for incense. After we had most carefully covered and smoothed over the place, a great mishap was very near befalling us; for we met Witthan her little girl, who was seeking blackberries, and she asked what my daughter carried in her apron, who straightway grew red, and stammered so that our secret would have been betrayed if I had not presently said, "What is that to thee? She has got fir-apples for firing,"[59] which the child believed. Wherefore we resolved in future only to go up the mountain at night by moonlight, and we went home and got there before the maid, and hid our treasure in the bedstead, so that she should not see it.

CHAPTER X

How we journeyed to Wolgast, and made good barter there.

Two days after, so says my daughter, but old Ilse thinks it was three (and I myself know not which is true), we at last went to the town, seeing that Master Rothoog had not got the box ready before. My daughter covered it over with a piece of my departed wife her wedding-gown, which the Imperialists had indeed torn to pieces, but as they had left it lying outside, the wind had blown it into the orchard, where we found it. It was very shabby before, otherwise I doubt not they would have carried it off with them. On account of the box, we took old Ilse with us, who had to carry it, and, as amber is very light ware, she readily believed that the box held nothing but eatables. At daybreak, then, we took our staves in our hands and set out with God. Near Zitze,[xx] a hare ran across the road before us, which they say bodes no good. Well-a-day! When we came near Bannemin I asked a fellow if it was true that here a mother had slaughtered her own child from hunger, as I had heard. He said it was, and that the old woman's name was Zisse; but that God had been wroth at such a horrid deed, and she had got no good by it, seeing that she vomited so much upon eating it that she forthwith gave up the ghost. On the whole, he thought things were already going rather better with the parish, as Almighty God had richly blessed them with fish, both out of the sea

---

[xx] A village half way between Coserow and Wolgast, now called Zinnowitz.

and the Achterwater. Nevertheless a great number of people had died of hunger here also. He told us that their vicar, his reverence Johannes Lampius,[xxi] had had his house burnt down by the Imperialists, and was lying in a hovel near the church. I sent him my greeting, desiring that he would soon come to visit me (which the fellow promised he would take care to deliver to him), for the reverend Johannes is a pious and learned man, and has also composed sundry Latin *Chronosticha* on these wretched times, in *metrum heroicum*, which, I must say, pleased me greatly.[xxii] [60] When we had crossed the ferry we went in at Sehms his house, on the Castle Green, who keeps an ale-house; he told us that the pestilence had not yet altogether ceased in the town; whereat I was much afraid, more especially as he described to us so many other horrors and miseries of these fearful times, both here and in other places, *e.g.* of the great famine in the island of Rügen, where a number of people had grown as black as Moors from hunger; a wondrous thing if it be true, and one might almost gather therefrom how the first blackamoors came about.[xiii] [61] But be that as it may. *Summa*. When Master Sehms had told us all the news he had heard, and we had thus learnt, to our great comfort, that the Lord had not visited us only in these times of heavy need, I called him aside into a chamber and asked him whether I could not here find means to get money for a piece of amber which my daughter had found by the sea. At first he said "No"; but then recollecting, he began, "Stay, let me see, at Nicolas Graeke's, the inn at the castle, there are two great Dutch merchants — Dieterich von Pehnen and Jacob Kiekebusch — who are come to buy pitch and boards, *item* timber for ships and beams; perchance they may like to cheapen your amber too; but you had better go up to the castle yourself, for I do not know for certain whether they still are there." This I did, although I had not yet eaten anything in the man's house, seeing that I wanted to know first what sort of bargain I might make, and to save the farthings belonging to the church until then. So I went into the castle-yard. Gracious God! what a desert had even his Princely Highness' house become within a short time! The Danes had ruined the

---

[xxi] The present parish archives contain several short and incomplete notices of his sufferings during these dreadful wars.

[xxii] The old vicar has introduced them among the still existing parochial accounts, and we will here give a specimen of them: —

For 1620.
VsqVe qVo Do MIne IrasCerIs, sIs nobIs pater!

For 1628.
InqVe tVa DeXtra fer operaM tV ChrIste benIgne!

[xxiii] Micraelius also, in his "Ancient Pomerania" (vol. 71. 2), mentions this circumstance, but only says: "Those who came over to Stralsund were quite black from the hunger they had suffered." This accounts for the strange exaggeration of mine host, and the still stranger conclusion of our author.

stables and hunting-lodge, Anno 1628; *item*, destroyed several rooms in the castle; and in the *locamentum*[62] of his Princely Highness Duke Philippus, where, Anno 22, he so graciously entertained me and my child, as will be told further on, now dwelt the innkeeper Nicolas Graeke; and all the fair tapestries, whereon was represented the pilgrimage to Jerusalem of his Princely Highness Bogislaus X,[63] were torn down and the walls left grey and bare.[xxiv] At this sight my heart was sorely grieved; but I presently inquired for the merchants, who sat at the table drinking their parting cup, with their travelling equipments already lying by them, seeing that they were just going to set out on their way to Stettin; straightway one of them jumped up from his liquor — a little fellow with a right noble paunch and a black plaster on his nose — and asked me what I would of them? I took him aside into a window, and told him I had some fine amber, if he had a mind to buy it of me, which he straightway agreed to do. And when he had whispered somewhat into the ear of his fellow, he began to look very pleasant, and reached me the pitcher before we went to my inn. I drank to him right heartily, seeing that (as I have already said) I was still fasting, so that I felt my very heart warmed by it in an instant. (Gracious God, what can go beyond a good draught of wine taken within measure!) After this we went to my inn, and told the maid to carry the box on one side into a small chamber. I had scarce opened it and taken away the gown, when the man (whose name was Dieterich von Pehnen, as he had told me by the way) held up both hands for joy, and said he had never seen such wealth of amber, and how had I come by it? I answered that my child had found it on the sea-shore; whereat he wondered greatly that we had so much amber here, and offered me three hundred florins for the whole box. I was quite beside myself for joy at such an offer, but took care not to let him see it, and bargained with him till I got five hundred florins, and I was to go with him to the castle and take the money forthwith. Hereupon I ordered mine host to make ready at once a mug of beer and a good dinner for my child, and went back to the castle with the man and the maid, who carried the box, begging him, in order to avoid common talk, to say nothing of my good fortune to mine host, nor, indeed, to any one else in the town, and to count out the money to me privately, seeing that I could not be sure that the thieves might not lay in wait for me on the road home if they heard of it, and this the man did; for he whispered something into the ear of his fellow, who straightway opened his leathern surcoat, *item* his doublet and hose, and unbuckled from his paunch a well-filled purse, which he gave to him. *Summa*. Before long I had my riches in my pocket, and, moreover, the man begged me to

---

[xxiv] Compare Heller's "Chronicle of the Town of Wolgast," p. 42, &c. The riots were caused by the successor of Philippus Julius (d. 6 February 1625), who was also the last Duke of Pomerania, Bogislaus XIV., choosing to reside in Stettin. At the present time the castle is a mere ruin, and only several large vaulted cellars remain, wherein some of the tradesmen of the present day keep their shops.

write to him at Amsterdam whenever I found any more amber, the which I promised to do. But the worthy fellow (as I have since heard) died of the plague at Stettin, together with his companion — truly I wish it had happened otherwise.[xxv] [64] Shortly after I was very near getting into great trouble; for, as I had an extreme longing to fall on my knees, so that I could not wait until such time as I should have got back to my inn, I went up three or four steps of the castle stairs and entered into a small chamber, where I humbled myself before the Lord. But the host, Nicolas Graeke, followed me, thinking I was a thief, and would have stopped me, so that I knew not how to excuse myself by saying that I had been made drunken by the wine which the strange merchants had given to me (for he had seen what a good pull I had made at it), seeing I had not broken my fast that morning, and that I was looking for a chamber wherein I might sleep a while, which lie he believed (if, in truth, it were a lie, for I was really drunken, though not with wine, but with love and gratitude to my Maker), and accordingly he let me go.

But I must now tell my story of his Princely Highness, as I promised above. Anno 22, as I chanced to walk with my daughter, who was then a child of about twelve years old, in the castle-garden at Wolgast, and was showing her the beautiful flowers that grew there, it chanced that as we came round from behind some bushes we espied my gracious lord the Duke Philippus Julius, with his Princely Highness the Duke Bogislaff,[65] who lay here on a visit, standing on a mount and conversing, wherefore we were about to return. But as my gracious lords presently walked on toward the drawbridge, we went to look at the mount where they had stood; of a sudden my little girl shouted loudly for joy, seeing that she found on the earth a costly signet-ring, which one of their Princely Highnesses doubtless had dropped. I therefore said, "Come and we will follow our gracious lords with all speed, and thou shall say to them in Latin, '*Serenissimi principes, quis vestrum hunc annulum deperdidit?*'[66] (for, as I have mentioned above, I had instructed her in the Latin tongue ever since her seventh year); and if one of them says '*Ego*,' give to him the ring. Item. — Should he ask thee in Latin to whom thou belongest, be not abashed, and say '*Ego sum filia pastoris Coserowiensis*';[67] for thou wilt thus find favour in the eyes of their Princely Highnesses, for they are both gracious gentlemen, more especially the taller one, who is our gracious ruler, Philippus Julius himself." This she promised to do; but as she trembled sorely as she went, I encouraged her yet more and promised her a new gown if she did it, seeing that even as a little child she would have given a great deal for fine clothes. As soon, then, as we were come into the courtyard, I stood by the statue of his

---

[xxv] Micraelius mentions these Dutch merchants, p. 171, but asserts that the cause of their death was doubtful, and that the town physician, Dr. Laurentius Eichstadius, in Stettin, had written a special medical paper on the subject. However, he calls one of them Kiekepost, instead of Kiekebusch.

Princely Highness Ernest Ludewig,[xxvi] and whispered her to run boldly after them, as their Princely Highnesses were only a few steps before us, and had already turned toward the great entrance. This she did, but of a sudden she stood still, and would have turned back, because she was frightened by the spurs of their Princely Highnesses, as she afterwards told me, seeing that they rattled and jingled very loudly.

But my gracious lady the Duchess Agnes saw her from the open window wherein she lay, and called to his Princely Highness, "My lord, there is a little maiden behind you, who, it seems, would speak with you," whereupon his Princely Highness straightway turned him round, smiling pleasantly, so that my little maid presently took courage, and, holding up the ring, spoke in Latin as I had told her. Hereat both the princes wondered beyond measure, and after my gracious Duke Philippus had felt his finger, he answered, "*Dulcissima puella, ego perdidi*";[68] whereupon she gave it to him. Then he patted her cheek, and again asked, "*Sed quaenam es, et unde venis?*"[69] whereupon she boldly gave her answer, and at the same time pointed with her finger to where I stood by the statue; whereupon his Princely Highness motioned me to draw near. My gracious lady saw all that passed from the window, but all at once she left it. She, however, came back to it again before I had time even humbly to draw near to my gracious lord, and beckoned to my child, and held a cake out of the window for her. On my telling her, she ran up to the window, but her Princely Highness could not reach so low nor she so high above her as to take it, wherefore my gracious lady commanded her to come up into the castle, and as she looked anxiously round after me, motioned me also, as did my gracious lord himself, who presently took the timid little maid by the hand and went up with his Princely Highness the Duke Bogislaff. My gracious lady came to meet us at the door, and caressed and embraced my little daughter, so that she soon grew quite bold and ate the cake. When my gracious lord had asked me my name, *item*, why I had in so singular a manner taught my daughter the Latin tongue, I answered that I had heard much from a cousin at Cologne of Maria Schurman,[xxvii] [70] and as I had observed a very

---

[xxvi] The father of Philippus Julius, died at Wolgast 17 June 1592.

[xxvii] Anna Maria Schurman, born at Cologne on the 5 Nov. 1607, died at Wiewardin the 5 May 1678, was, according to the unanimous testimony of her contemporaries, a prodigy of learning, and perhaps the most learned woman that ever lived. The Frenchman Naudé says of her, "You find in her alone all that the hand can fashion or the mind conceive. No one paints better, no one works better in brass, wax and wood. In needlework she excels all women past or present. It is impossible to say in what branch of knowledge she is most distinguished. Not content with the European languages, she understands Hebrew, Arabic, Syriac, and writes Latin so well that no one who has devoted his whole life to it can do it better." The celebrated Netherlander Spanheim calls her a teacher of the Graces and the Muses; the still more celebrated Salmasius confesses that he knows not in which branch of learning to say she excels: and the Pole Rotyer calls her "The sole example of all wondrous works in one single learned

excellent *ingenium*[71] in my child, and also had time enough in my lonely cure, I did not hesitate to take her in hand, and teach her from her youth up, seeing I had no boy alive. Hereat their Princely Highnesses marvelled greatly, and put some more questions to her in Latin, which she answered without any prompting from me. Whereupon my gracious lord Duke Philippus said in the vulgar tongue, "When thou art grown up and art one day to be married, tell it to me, and thou shall then have another ring from me, and whatsoever else pertains to a bride, for thou hast this day done me good service, seeing that this ring is a precious jewel to me, as I had it from my wife." Hereupon I whispered her to kiss his Princely Highness' hand for such a promise, and so she did.

(But alas! most gracious God, it is one thing to promise, and quite another to hold. Where is his Princely Highness at this time? Wherefore let me ever keep in mind that "thou only art faithful, and that which thou hast promised thou wilt surely hold." Psalm 33. 4. Amen.[xxviii][72])

Item. When his Princely Highness had also inquired concerning myself and my cure, and heard that I was of ancient and noble family, and my *salarium*[73] very small, he called from the window to his chancellor, D. Rungius, who stood without, looking at the sun-dial, and told him that I was to have an addition from the convent at Pudgla, *item* from the crown-lands at Ernsthoff, as I mentioned above; but, more's the pity, I never have received the same, although the *instrumentum donationis*[74] was sent me soon after by his Princely Highness' chancellor.

Then cakes were brought for me also, *item*, a glass of foreign wine in a glass painted with armorial bearings, whereupon I humbly took my leave, together with my daughter.

However, to come back to my bargain, anybody may guess what joy my child felt when I showed her the fair ducats and florins I had gotten for the amber. To the maid, however, we said that we had inherited such riches from my brother in Holland; and after we had again given thanks to the Lord on our knees, and eaten our dinner, we bought in a great store of bread, salt, meat, and stock-fish: *item*, of clothes, seeing that I provided what was needful for us three throughout the winter from the cloth-merchant. Moreover, for my daughter I bought a hair-net and a scarlet silk bodice, with a black apron and white petticoat, *item*, a fine pair

---

person, and a perfect *monstrum* of her sex, yet without fault or blame." For, in truth, with all her extraordinary knowledge she was marvellously humble, although she herself confesses that the immoderate praises of the learned even yet at times blinded her to her own defects. In her later years she went over to the sect of the Labadists, which appears to have some points in common with that of the Muckers. She died unmarried, as an early love affair in her fifteenth year with the Dutchman Caets had been broken off. It is related of her, as a strange fancy, that she liked to eat spiders. The celebrated Spanheim was the first to publish an edition of her works under the title of Annae Mariae a Schurman Opuscula. Leyden, 1648.

[xxviii] Luther's version.

of earrings, as she begged hard for them; and as soon as I had ordered the needful from the cordwainer we set out on our way homewards, as it began to grow very dark; but we could not carry nearly all we had bought. Wherefore we were forced to get a peasant from Bannemin to help us, who likewise was come into the town; and as I found out from him that the fellow who gave me the piece of bread was a poor cotter called Pantermehl, who dwelt in the village by the roadside, I shoved a couple of loaves in at his house-door without his knowing it, and we went on our way by the bright moonlight, so that by the help of God we got home about ten o'clock at night. I likewise gave a loaf to the other fellow, though truly he deserved it not, seeing that he would go with us no further than to Zitze. But I let him go, for I, too, had not deserved that the Lord should so greatly bless me.

CHAPTER XI

How I fed all the congregation: item, how I journeyed to the horse fair at Gützkow, and what befell me there.

Next morning my daughter cut up the blessed bread, and sent to every one in the village a good large piece. But as we saw that our store would soon run low, we sent the maid with a truck, which we bought of Adam Lempken, to Wolgast to buy more bread, which she did. *Item*, I gave notice throughout the parish that on Sunday next I should administer the blessed sacrament, and in the meantime I bought up all the large fish that the people of the village had caught. And when the blessed Sunday was come I first heard the confessions of the whole parish, and after that I preached a sermon on Matthew 15. 32 — "I have compassion on the multitude … for they have nothing to eat." I first applied the same to spiritual food only, and there arose a great sighing from both the men and the women, when, at the end, I pointed to the altar, whereon stood the blessed food for the soul, and repeated the words, "I have compassion on the multitude … for they have nothing to eat." (N.B. — The pewter cup I had borrowed at Wolgast, and bought there a little earthenware plate for a paten till such time as Master Bloom should have made ready the silver cup and paten I had bespoke.) Thereupon as soon as I had consecrated and administered the blessed sacrament, *item*, led the closing hymn, and every one had silently prayed his "Our Father" before going out of church, I came out of the confessional again, and motioned the people to stay yet a while, as the blessed Saviour would feed not only their souls, but their bodies also, seeing that he still had the same compassion on his people as of old on the people at the Sea of Galilee, as they should presently see.[75] Then I went into the tower and fetched out two baskets which the maid had bought at Wolgast, and which I had hidden there in good time; set them down in front of the altar, and took off the napkins with which they were covered, whereupon a very loud shout arose, inasmuch as they saw one filled with broiled fish and the other with bread, which we had put into them privately. Hereupon, like our Saviour, I gave thanks and brake it, and gave it to the churchwarden Hinrich Seden, that he might distribute it among the men, and to my daughter for the women. Whereupon I made application of the text, "I have compassion on the multitude ... for they have nothing to eat," to the food of the body also; and walking up and down in the church, amid great outcries from all, I exhorted them alway to trust in God's mercy, to pray without ceasing, to work diligently, and to consent to no sin. What was left I made them gather up for their children and the old people who were left at home.

After church, when I had scarce put off my surplice, Hinrich Seden his squint-eyed wife came and impudently asked for more for her husband's journey to Liepe; neither had she had anything for herself, seeing she had not come to church. This angered me sore, and I said to her, "Why wast thou not at church? Nevertheless, if thou hadst come humbly to me thou shouldst have gotten somewhat even now, but as thou comest impudently, I will give thee nought: think on what thou didst to me and to my child." But she stood at the door and glowered impudently about the room till my daughter took her by the arm and led her out, saying, "Hear'st thou, thou shalt come back humbly before thou gett'st anything, but when thou comest thus, thou also shalt have thy share, for we will no longer reckon with thee an eye for an eye, and a tooth for a tooth;[76] let the Lord do that if such be his will, but we will gladly forgive thee!" Hereupon she at last went out at the door, muttering to herself as she was wont; but she spat several times in the street,[77] as we saw from the window.

Soon after I made up my mind to take into my service a lad, near upon twenty years of age, called Claus Neels, seeing that his father, old Neels of Loddin, begged hard that I would do so, besides which the lad pleased me well in manners and otherwise. Then, as we had a good harvest this year, I resolved to buy me a couple of horses forthwith, and to sow my field again; for although it was now late in the year, I thought that the most merciful God might bless the crop with increase if it seemed good to him.

Neither did I feel much care with respect to food for them, inasmuch as there was a great plenty of hay in the neighbourhood, seeing that all the cattle had been killed or driven away (as related above). I therefore made up my mind to go in God's name with my new ploughman to Gützkow, whither a great many Mecklenburg horses were brought to the fair, seeing that times were not yet so bad there as with us.[xxix] Meanwhile I went a few more times up the Streckelberg with my daughter at night, and by moonlight, but found very little; so that we began to think our luck had come to an end, when, on the third night, we broke off some pieces of amber bigger even than those the two Dutchmen had bought.

[xxix] The fief of Mecklenburg was given by the Emperor to Wallenstein, who spared the country as much as he could.

These I resolved to send to my wife's brother, Martin Behring, at Hamburg, seeing that the schipper Wulff of Wolgast intends, as I am told, to sail thither this very autumn, with pitch and wood for shipbuilding. I accordingly packed it all up in a strong chest, which I carried with me to Wolgast when I started with my man on my journey to Gützkow. Of this journey I will only relate thus much, that there were plenty of horses and very few buyers in the market. Wherefore I bought a pair of fine black horses for twenty florins apiece; *item*, a cart for five florins; *item*, twenty-five bushels of rye, which also came from Mecklenburg, at one florin the bushel, whereas it is hardly to be had now at Wolgast for love or money, and costs three florins or more the bushel. I might therefore have made a good bargain in rye at Gützkow if it had become my office, and had I not, moreover, been afraid lest the robbers, who swarm in these evil times, should take away my corn, and ill-use and perchance murder me into the bargain, as has happened to sundry people already. For, at this time especially, such robberies were carried on after a strange and frightful fashion on Strellin heath at Gützkow; but by God's help it all came to light just as I journeyed thither with my man-servant to the fair, and I will here tell how it happened. Some months before a man had been broken on the wheel at Gützkow,[78] because, being tempted of Satan, he murdered a travelling workman. The man, however, straightway began to walk after so fearful a fashion, that in the evening and night-season he sprang down from the wheel in his gallows' dress whenever a cart passed by the gallows, which stands hard by the road to Wolgast, and jumped up behind the people, who in horror and dismay flogged on their horses, and thereby made a great rattling on the log embankment which leads beside the gallows into a little wood called the Kraulin. And it was a strange thing that on the same night the travellers were almost always robbed or murdered on Strellin heath. Hereupon the magistrates had the man taken down from the wheel and buried under the gallows, in hopes of laying his ghost. But it went on just as before, sitting at night snow-white on the wheel, so that none durst any longer travel the road to Wolgast. Until at last it happened that, at the time of the above-named fair, young Rüdiger von Nienkerken of Mellenthin,[79] in Usedom, who had been studying at Wittenberg and elsewhere, and was now on his way home, came this road by night with his carriage. Just before, at the inn, I myself had tried to persuade him to stop the night at Gützkow on account of the ghost, and to go on his journey with me next morning, but he would not. Now as soon as this young lord drove along the road, he also espied the apparition sitting on the wheel, and scarcely had he passed the gallows when the ghost jumped down and ran after him. The driver was horribly afraid, and lashed on the horses, as everybody else had done before, and they, taking fright, galloped away over the log-road with a marvellous clatter. Meanwhile, however, the young nobleman saw by the light of the moon how that the apparition flattened a ball of horse-dung whereon it trod, and straightway felt sure within himself that it was no ghost. Whereupon he called to the driver to stop; and as the man would not hearken to him, he sprang out of the carriage, drew his rapier, and hastened to attack the ghost. When the ghost saw this he would have turned and fled, but the young nobleman gave him such a blow on the head with his fist that he fell upon the ground with a loud wailing. *Summa*: the young lord, having called back his driver, dragged the ghost into the town again, where he turned out to be a shoemaker called Schwelm.

I also, on seeing such a great crowd, ran thither with many others to look at the fellow. He trembled like an aspen leaf; and when he was roughly told to make a clean breast, whereby he might peradventure save his own life, if it appeared that he had murdered no one, he confessed that he had got his wife to make him a gallows' dress, which he had put on, and had sat on the wheel before the dead man, when, from the darkness and the distance, no one could see that the two were sitting there together; and this he did more especially when he knew that a cart was going from the town to Wolgast. When the cart came by, and he jumped down and ran after it, all the people were so affrighted that they no longer kept their eyes upon the gallows, but only on him, flogged the horses, and galloped with much noise and clatter over the log embankment. This was heard by his fellows in Strellin and Dammbecke (two villages which are about three-fourths on the way), who held themselves ready to unyoke the horses and to plunder the travellers when they came up with them. That after the dead man was buried he could play the ghost more easily still, etc. That this was the whole truth, and that he himself had never in his life robbed, still less murdered, any one; wherefore he begged to be forgiven: that all the robberies and murders which had happened had been done by his fellows alone. Ah, thou cunning knave! But I heard afterwards that he and his fellows were broken on the wheel together, as was but fair.

And now to come back to my journey. The young nobleman abode that night with me at the inn, and early next morning we both set forth; and as we had grown into good-fellowship together, I got into his coach with him, as he offered me, so as to talk by the way, and my Claus drove behind us. I soon found that he was a well-bred, honest, and learned gentleman, seeing that he despised the wild student life, and was glad that he had now done with their scandalous drinking-bouts: moreover, he talked his Latin readily. I had therefore much pleasure with him in the coach. However, at Wolgast the rope of the ferry-boat broke, so that we were carried down the stream to Zeuzin,[xxx] and at length we only got ashore with great trouble. Meanwhile it grew late, and we did not get into Coserow till nine, when I asked the young lord to abide the night with me, which he agreed to do. We found my child sitting in the chimney-corner, making a petticoat for her little god-daughter out of her own old clothes. She was greatly frighted, and changed

---

[xxx] Now Sauzin.

colour when she saw the young lord come in with me, and heard that he was to lie there that night, seeing that as yet we had no more beds than we had bought for our own need from old Zabel Nehring the forest ranger his widow, at Uekeritze. Wherefore she took me aside: What was to be done? My bed was in an ill plight, her little god-child having lain on it that morning; and she could nowise put the young nobleman into hers, although she would willingly creep in by the maid herself. And when I asked her why not? she blushed scarlet and began to cry, and would not show herself again the whole evening, so that the maid had to see to everything, even to the putting white sheets on my child's bed for the young lord, as she would not do it herself. I only tell this to show how maidens are. For next morning she came into the room with her red silk bodice, and the net on her hair, and the apron; *summa*, dressed in all the things I had bought her at Wolgast, so that the young lord was amazed, and talked much with her over the morning meal. Whereupon he took his leave, and desired me to visit him at his castle.

CHAPTER XII

What further joy and sorrow befell us: item, how Wittich Appelmann rode to Damerow to the wolf-hunt, and what he proposed to my daughter.

The Lord blessed my parish wonderfully this winter, inasmuch as not only a great quantity of fish were caught and sold in all the villages, but in Coserow they even killed four seals: *item*, the great storm of the 12th of December threw a goodly quantity of amber on the shore, so that many found amber, although no very large pieces, and they began to buy cows and sheep from Liepe and other places, as I myself also bought two cows; *item*, my grain which I had sown, half on my own field and half on old Paasch's, sprang up bravely and gladly, as the Lord had till *datum* bestowed on us an open winter; but so soon as it had shot up a finger's length, we found it one morning again torn up and ruined, and this time also by the devil's doings, since now, as before, not the smallest trace of oxen or of horses was to be seen in the field. May the righteous God, however, reward it, as indeed he already has done. Amen.

Meanwhile, however, something uncommon happened. For one morning, as I have heard, when Lord Wittich saw out of the window that the daughter of his fisherman, a child of sixteen, whom he had diligently pursued, went into the coppice to gather dry sticks, he went thither too; wherefore, I will not say, but every one may guess for himself. When he had gone some way along the convent mound, and was come to the first bridge, where the mountain-ash stands, he saw two wolves coming towards him; and as he had no weapon with him, save a staff, he climbed up into a tree; whereupon the wolves trotted round it, blinked at him with their eyes, licked their lips, and at last jumped with their fore-paws up against the tree, snapping at him; he then saw that one was a he-wolf, a great fat brute with only one eye. Hereupon in his fright he began to scream, and the long-suffering of God was again shown to him, without, however, making him wiser; for the maiden, who had crept behind a juniper-bush in the field when she saw the Sheriff coming, ran back again to the castle and called together a number of people, who came and drove away the wolves, and rescued his lordship. He then ordered a great wolf-hunt to be held next day in the convent wood, and he who brought the one-eyed monster, dead or alive, was to have a barrel of beer for his pains. Still they could not catch him, albeit they that day took four wolves in their nets, and killed them. He therefore straightway ordered a wolf-hunt to be held in my parish. But when the fellow came to toll the bell for a wolf-hunt, he did not stop a while, as is the wont for wolf-hunts, but loudly rang the bell on, *sine morâ*,[80] so that all the folk thought a fire had broken out, and ran screaming out of their houses. My child also came running out (I myself had driven to visit a sick person at Zempin, seeing that walking began to be wearisome to me, and that I could now afford to be more at mine ease); but she had not stood long, and was asking the reason of the ringing, when the Sheriff himself, on his grey charger, with three cart-loads of toils and nets following him, galloped up and ordered the people straightway to go into the forest and to drive the wolves with rattles. Hereupon he, with his hunters and a few men whom he had picked out of the crowd, were to ride on and spread the nets behind Damerow, seeing that the island is wondrous narrow there,[xxxi] and the wolf dreads the water. When he saw my daughter he turned his horse round, chucked her under the chin, and graciously asked her who she was, and whence she came? When he had heard it, he said she was as fair as an angel, and that he had not known till now that the parson here had so beauteous a girl. He then rode off, looking round at her two or three times. At the first beating they found the one-eyed wolf, who lay in the rushes near the water. Hereat his lordship rejoiced greatly, and made the grooms drag him out of the net with long iron hooks, and hold him there for near an hour, while my lord slowly and cruelly tortured him to death, laughing heartily the while, which is a *prognosticon*[81] of what he afterwards did with my poor child, for wolf or lamb is all one to this villain. Just God! But I will not be beforehand with my tale.

Next day came old Seden his squint-eyed wife, limping like a lame dog, and put it to my daughter whether she would not go into the service of the Sheriff; praised him as a good and pious man; and vowed that all the world said of him were foul lies, as she herself could bear witness, seeing that she had lived in his service for above ten years. *Item*, she praised the good cheer they had there, and the handsome beer-money that the great lords who often lay there gave the servants which waited upon them; that she herself had more than once received

---

[xxxi] The space, which is constantly diminishing, now scarcely measures a bow-shot across.

a rose-noble[82] from his Princely Highness Duke Ernest Ludewig; moreover, many pretty fellows came there, which might make her fortune, inasmuch as she was a fair woman, and might take her choice of a husband; whereas here in Coserow, where nobody ever came, she might wait till she was old and ugly before she got a curch on her head, etc. Hereat my daughter was beyond measure angered, and answered, "Ah! thou old witch, and who has told thee that I wish to go into service to get a curch[83] on my head? Go thy ways, and never enter the house again, for I have nought to do with thee." Whereupon she walked away again, muttering between her teeth.

Scarce had a few days passed, and I was standing in the chamber with the glazier, who was putting in new windows, when I heard my daughter scream in the kitchen. Whereupon I straightway ran in thither, and was shocked and affrighted when I saw the Sheriff himself standing in the corner with his arm round my child her neck; he, however, presently let her go, and said: "Aha, reverend Abraham, what a coy little fool you have for a daughter! I wanted to greet her with a kiss, as I always use to do, and she struggled and cried out as if I had been some young fellow who had stolen in upon her, whereas I might be her father twice over." As I answered nought, he went on to say that he had done it to encourage her, seeing that he desired to take her into his service, as indeed I knew, with more excuses of the same kind which I have forgot. Hereupon I pressed him to come into the room, seeing that after all he was the ruler set over me by God, and humbly asked what his lordship desired of me. Whereupon he answered me graciously that it was true he had just cause for anger against me, seeing that I had preached at him before the whole congregation, but that he was ready to forgive me, and to have the complaint he had sent in *contra me*[84] to his Princely Highness at Stettin, and which might easily cost me my place, returned to him if I would but do his will. And when I asked what his Lordship's will might be, and excused myself as best I might with regard to the sermon, he answered that he stood in great need of a faithful housekeeper whom he could set over the other women-folk; and as he had learnt that my daughter was a faithful and trustworthy person, he would that I should send her into his service. "See there," said he to her, and pinched her cheek the while, "I want to lead you to honour, though you are such a young creature, and yet you cry out as if I were going to bring you to dishonour. Fie upon you!" (My child still remembers all this *verbotenus*;[85] I myself should have forgot it a hundred times over in all the wretchedness I since underwent.) But she was offended at his words, and, jumping up from her seat, she answered shortly, "I thank your lordship for the honour, but will only keep house for my papa, which is a better honour for me"; whereupon he turned to me and asked what I said to that. I must own that I was not a little affrighted, inasmuch as I thought of the future and of the credit in which the Sheriff stood with his Princely Highness. I therefore answered with all humility that I could not force my child, and that I loved to have her about me, seeing that my dear huswife had departed this life during the heavy pestilence, and I had no child but only her. That I hoped therefore his lordship would not be displeased with me that I could not send her into his lordship's service. This angered him sore, and after disputing some time longer in vain he took leave, not without threats that he would make me pay for it. *Item*, my man, who was standing in the stable, heard him say as he went round the corner, "I will have her yet, in spite of him!"

I was already quite disheartened by all this, when, on the Sunday following, there came his huntsman Johannes Kurt, a tall, handsome fellow, and smartly dressed. He brought a roebuck tied before him on his horse, and said that his lordship had sent it to me for a present, in hopes that I would think better of his offer, seeing that he had been ever since seeking on all sides for a housekeeper in vain. Moreover, that if I changed my mind about it his lordship would speak for me to his Princely Highness, so that the dotation of Duke Philippus Julius should be paid to me out of the princely *aerarium*,[86] etc. But the young fellow got the same answer as his master had done, and I desired him to take the roebuck away with him again. But this he refused to do; and as I had by chance told him at first that game was my favourite meat, he promised to supply me with it abundantly, seeing that there was plenty of game in the forest, and that he often went a-hunting on the Streckelberg; moreover, that I (he meant my daughter) pleased him uncommonly, the more because I would not do his master's will, who, as he told me in confidence, would never leave any girl in peace, and certainly would not let my damsel alone. Although I had rejected his game, he brought it notwithstanding, and in the course of three weeks he was sure to come four or five times, and grew more and more sweet upon my daughter. He talked a vast deal about his good place, and how he was in search of a good huswife, whence we soon guessed what quarter the wind blew from. *Ergo*, my daughter told him that if he was seeking for a huswife she wondered that he lost his time in riding to Coserow to no purpose, for that she knew of no huswife for him there, which vexed him so sore that he never came again.

And now any one would think that the grapes were sour even for the Sheriff; nevertheless he came riding to us soon after, and without more ado asked my daughter in marriage for his huntsman. Moreover, he promised to build him a house of his own in the forest; *item*, to give him pots and kettles, crockery, bedding, etc., seeing that he had stood god-father to the young fellow, who, moreover, had ever borne himself well during seven years he had been in his service. Hereupon my daughter answered that his lordship had already heard that she would keep house for nobody but her papa, and that she was still much too young to become a huswife.

This, however, did not seem to anger him, but after he had talked a long time to no purpose, he took leave quite kindly, like a cat which pretends to let a mouse go, and creeps behind the corners, but she is not in earnest, and presently springs out upon it again. For doubtless he saw that he had set to work stupidly; wherefore he went away in order to begin his attack again after a better fashion, and Satan went with him, as whilom with Judas Iscariot.[87]

CHAPTER XIII

What more happened during the winter: Item, how in the spring witchcraft began in the village.

Nothing else of note happened during the winter, save that the merciful God bestowed a great plenty of fish, both from the Achterwater and the sea, and the parish again had good food; so that it might be said of us, as it is written, "For a small moment have I forsaken thee; but with great mercies will I gather thee."[xxxii] Wherefore we were not weary of praising the Lord; and the whole congregation did much for the church, buying new pulpit and altar cloths, seeing that the enemy had stolen the old ones. *Item*, they desired to make good to me the money I had paid for the new cups, which, however, I would not take.

There were still, however, about ten peasants in the parish who had not been able to buy their seed-corn for the spring, inasmuch as they had spent all their earnings on cattle and corn for bread. I therefore made an agreement with them that I would lend them the money for it, and that if they could not repay me this year, they might the next, which offer they thankfully took; and we sent seven waggons to Friedland, in Mecklenburg, to fetch seed-corn for us all. For my beloved brother-in-law, Martin Behring, in Hamburg, had already sent me by the schipper Wulf, who had sailed home by Christmas, 700 florins for the amber: may the Lord prosper it with him!

Old Thiemcke died this winter in Loddin, who used to be the midwife in the parish, and had also brought my child into the world. Of late, however, she had had but little to do, seeing that in this year I only baptized two children, namely, Jung his son in Uekeritze, and Lene Hebers her little daughter, the same whom the Imperialists afterwards speared. *Item*, it was now full five years since I had married the last couple. Hence any one may guess that I might have starved to death had not the righteous God so mercifully considered and blessed me in other ways. Wherefore to him alone be all honour and glory. Amen.

Meanwhile, however, it so happened that, not long after the Sheriff had last been here, witchcraft began in the village. I sat reading with my child the second book of *Virgilius* of the fearful destruction of the city of Troy,[88] which was more terrible even than that of our own village, when a cry arose that our old neighbour Zabel his red cow, which he had bought only a few days before, had stretched out all-fours and seemed about to die; and this was the more strange as she had fed

---

[xxxii] Isaiah 54. 7.

heartily but half an hour before. My child was therefore begged to go and pluck three hairs from its tail, and bury them under the threshold of the stall; for it was well known that if this was done by a pure maid the cow would get better.[89] My child then did as they would have her, seeing that she is the only maid in the whole village (for the others are still children); and the cow got better from that very hour, whereat all the folks were amazed. But it was not long before the same thing befell Witthahn her pig, whilst it was feeding heartily. She too came running to beg my child for God's sake to take compassion on her, and to do something for her pig, as ill men had bewitched it. Hereupon she had pity on her also, and it did as much good as it had done before. But the woman, who was *gravida*,[90] was straightway taken in labour from the fright; and my child was scarce out of the pigsty when the woman went into her cottage, wailing and holding by the wall, and called together all the woman of the neighbourhood, seeing that the proper midwife was dead, as mentioned above; and before long something shot to the ground from under her; and when the women stooped down to pick it up, the devil's imp,[91] which had wings like a bat, flew up off the ground, whizzed and buzzed about the room, and then shot out of the window with a great noise, so that the glass clattered down into the street. When they looked after it nothing was to be found. Any one may judge for himself what a great noise this made in all the neighbourhood; and the whole village believed that it was no one but old Seden his squint-eyed wife that had brought forth such a devil's brat.

But the people soon knew not what to believe. For that woman her cow got the same thing as all the other cows; wherefore she too came lamenting, and begged my daughter to take pity on her, as on the rest, and to cure her poor cow for the love of God. That if she had taken it ill of her that she had said anything about going into service with the Sheriff, she could only say she had done it for the best, etc. *Summa*, she talked over my unhappy child to go and cure her cow.

Meanwhile I was on my knees every Sunday before the Lord with the whole congregation, praying that he would not allow the Evil One to take from us that which his mercy had once more bestowed upon us after such extreme want. *Item*, that he would bring to light the *auctor*[92] of such devilish works, so that he might receive the punishment he deserved.

But all was of no avail. For a very few days had passed when the mischief befell Stoffer Zuter his spotted cow, and he, too, like all the rest, came running to fetch my daughter; she accordingly went with him, but could do no good, and the beast died under her hands.

Item, Katy Berow had bought a little pig with the money my daughter had paid her in the winter for spinning, and the poor woman kept it like a child, and let it run about her room. This little pig got the mischief, like all the rest, in the twinkling of an eye; and when my daughter was called it grew no better, but also died under her hands; whereupon the poor woman made a great outcry and tore her hair for grief, so that my child was moved to pity her, and promised her another pig next time my sow should litter. Meantime another week passed over, during which I went on, together with the whole congregation, to call upon the Lord for his merciful help, but all in vain, when the same thing happened to old wife Seden her little pig. Whereupon she again came running for my daughter with loud outcries, and although my child told her that she must have seen herself that nothing she could do for the cattle cured them any longer, she ceased not to beg and pray her and to lament till she went forth to do what she could for her with the help of God. But it was all to no purpose, inasmuch as the little pig died before she left the sty.

What think you this devil's whore then did? After she had run screaming through the village she said that any one might see that my daughter was no longer a maid, else why could she now do no good to the cattle, whereas she had formerly cured them? She supposed my child had lost her maiden honour on the Streckelberg, whither she went so often this spring, and that God only knew who had taken it! But she said no more then, and we did not hear the whole until afterwards. And it is indeed true that my child had often walked on the Streckelberg this spring, both with me and also alone, in order to seek for flowers and to look upon the blessed sea, while she recited aloud, as she was wont, such verses out of *Virgilius* as pleased her best (for whatever she read a few times, that she remembered).

Neither did I forbid her to take these walks, for there were no wolves now left on the Streckelberg, and even if there had been they always fly before a human creature in the summer season. Howbeit, I forbade her to dig for amber. For as it now lay deep, and we knew not what to do with the earth we threw up, I resolved to tempt the Lord no further, but to wait till my store of money grew very scant before we would dig any more.

But my child did not do as I had bidden her, although she had promised she would, and of this her disobedience came all our misery. (Oh, blessed Lord, how grave a matter is thy holy fourth[xxxiii] commandment!)[93] For as his reverence Johannes Lampius, of Crummin, who visited me this spring, had told me that the Cantor of Wolgast wanted to sell the *Opp. St. Augustini*,[94] and I had said before her that I desired above all things to buy that book, but had not money enough left, she got up in the night without my knowledge to dig for amber, meaning to sell it as best she might at Wolgast, in order secretly to present me with the *Opp. St. Augustini* on my birthday, which falls on the 28th *mensis Augusti*. She had always covered over the earth she cast up with twigs of fir, whereof there were plenty in the forest, so that no one should perceive anything of it.

Meanwhile, however, it befell that the young *nobilis*[95] Rüdiger of Nienkerken came riding one day to gather news of the terrible witchcraft that went on in the

---

[xxxiii] In Luther's version.

village. When I had told him all about it he shook his head doubtingly, and said he believed that all witchcraft was nothing but lies and deceit; whereat I was struck with great horror, inasmuch as I had hitherto held the young lord to be a wiser man, and now could not but see that he was an Atheist. He guessed what my thoughts were, and with a smile he answered me by asking whether I had ever read Johannes Wierus,[xxxiv][96] who would hear nothing of witchcraft, and who argued that all witches were melancholy persons who only imagined to themselves that they had a *pactum* with the devil; and that to him they seemed more worthy of pity than of punishment? Hereupon I answered that I had not indeed read any such book (for say, who can read all that fools write?), but that the appearances here and in all other places proved that it was a monstrous error to deny the reality of witchcraft, inasmuch as people might then likewise deny that there were such things as murder, adultery, and theft.

But he called my *argumentum* a *dilemma*, and after he had discoursed a great deal of the devil, all of which I have forgotten, seeing it savoured strangely of heresy, he said he would relate to me a piece of witchcraft which he himself had seen at Wittenberg.

It seems that one morning, as an Imperial captain mounted his good charger at the Elstergate in order to review his company, the horse presently began to rage furiously, reared, tossed his head, snorted, kicked, and roared, not as horses used to neigh, but with a sound as though the voice came from a human throat, so that all the folks were amazed, and thought the horse bewitched. It presently threw the captain, and crushed his head with its hoof, so that he lay writhing on the ground, and straightway set off at full speed. Hereupon a trooper fired his carabine at the bewitched horse, which fell in the midst of the road, and presently died. That he, Rüdiger, had then drawn near, together with many others, seeing that the colonel had forthwith given orders to the surgeon of the regiment to cut open the horse and see in what state it was inwardly. However, that everything was quite right, and both the surgeon and army physician testified that the horse was thoroughly sound; whereupon all the people cried out more than ever about witchcraft. Meanwhile he himself (I mean the young *nobilis*) saw a thin smoke coming out from the horse's nostrils, and on stooping down to look what it might be, he drew out a match as long as my finger, which still smouldered, and which some wicked fellow had privately thrust into its nose with a pin. Hereupon all thoughts of witchcraft were at an end, and search was made for the culprit, who

---

[xxxiv] A Netherland physician, who, long before Spee or Thomasius, attacked the wicked follies of the belief in witchcraft prevalent in his time in the paper *confutatio de magorum Daemonia*, Frankfort, 1590, and was therefore denounced by Bodinus and others as one of the worst magicians. It is curious that this liberal man had in another book, *De praestigiis Daemonum*, taught the method of raising devils, and described the whole of hell, with the names and surnames of its 572 princes.

was presently found to be no other than the captain's own groom. For one day that his master had dusted his jacket for him he swore an oath that he would have his revenge, which indeed the provost-marshal himself had heard as he chanced to be standing in the stable. *Item*, another soldier bore witness that he had seen the fellow cut a piece off the fuse not long before he led out his master's horse. And thus thought the young lord, would it be with all witchcraft if it were sifted to the bottom; like as I myself had seen at Gützkow, where the devil's apparition turned out to be a cordwainer, and that one day I should own that it was the same sort of thing here in our village. By reason of this speech I liked not the young nobleman from that hour forward, believing him to be an Atheist. Though, indeed, afterwards, I have had cause to see that he was in the right, more's the pity; for had it not been for him what would have become of my daughter?

But I will say nothing beforehand. — *Summa*: I walked about the room in great displeasure at his words, while the young lord began to argue with my daughter upon witchcraft, now in Latin, and now in the vulgar tongue, as the words came into his mouth, and wanted to hear her mind about it. But she answered that she was a foolish thing, and could have no opinion on the matter; but that, nevertheless, she believed that what happened in the village could not be by natural means. Hereupon the maid called me out of the room (I forget what she wanted of me); but when I came back again my daughter was as red as scarlet, and the nobleman stood close before her. I therefore asked her, as soon as he had ridden off, whether anything had happened, which she at first denied, but afterwards owned that he had said to her while I was gone that he knew but one person who could bewitch; and when she asked him who that person was, he caught hold of her hand and said, "It is yourself, sweet maid; for you have thrown a spell upon my heart, as I feel right well!" But that he said nothing further, but only gazed on her face with eager eyes, and this it was that made her so red.

But this is the way with maidens; they ever have their secrets if one's back is turned but for a minute; and the proverb

"To drive a goose and watch a maid
Needs the devil himself to aid,"

is but too true, as will be shown hereafter, more's the pity!

CHAPTER XIV

How old Seden disappeared all on a sudden: Item, how the great Gustavus Adolphus came to Pomerania, and took the fort at Peenemünde.

We were now left for some time in peace from witchcraft; unless, indeed, I reckon the caterpillars, which miserably destroyed my orchard, and which truly were a strange thing; for the trees blossomed so fair and sweetly that one day as we were walking under them, and praising the almighty power of the most merciful God, my child said, "If the Lord goes on to bless us so abundantly, it will be Christmas Eve with us every night of next winter!" But things soon fell out far otherwise; for all in a moment the trees were covered with such swarms of caterpillars (great and small, and of every shape and colour) that one might have measured them by the bushel, and before long my poor trees looked like brooms, and the blessed fruit — which was so well set — all fell off, and was scarce good enough for the pigs. I do not choose to lay this to any one, though I had my own private thoughts upon the matter, and have them yet. However, my barley, whereof I had sown about three bushels out on the common, shot up bravely. On my field I had sown nothing, seeing that I dreaded the malice of Satan. Neither was corn at all plentiful throughout the parish — in part because they had sown no winter crops, and in part because the summer crops did not prosper. However, in all the villages a great supply of fish was caught by the mercy of God, especially herring; but they were very low in price. Moreover, they killed many seals; and at Whitsuntide I myself killed one as I walked by the sea with my daughter. The creature lay on a rock close to the water, snoring like a Christian. Thereupon I pulled off my shoes and drew near him softly, so that he heard me not, and then struck him over his nose with my staff (for a seal cannot bear much on his nose), so that he tumbled over into the water; but he was quite stunned, and I could easily kill him outright. It was a fat beast, though not very large; and we melted forty pots of train-oil out of his fat, which we put by for a winter store.

Meanwhile, however, something seized old Seden all at once, so that he wished to receive the holy sacrament. When I went to him he could give no reason for it; or perhaps he would give none for fear of his old Lizzie, who was always watching him with her squinting eyes, and would not leave the room. However, Zuter his little girl, a child near twelve years old, said that a few days before, while she was plucking grass for the cattle under the garden-hedge by the road, she heard the husband and wife quarrelling violently again, and that the goodman threw in her teeth that he now knew of a certainty that she had a familiar spirit, and that he would straightway go and tell it to the priest. Albeit this is only a child's tale, it may be true for all that, seeing that children and fools, they say, speak the truth.

But be that as it may. *Summa*, my old warden grew worse and worse; and though I visited him every morning and evening — as I use to do to my sick — in order to pray with him, and often observed that he had somewhat on his mind, nevertheless he could not disburthen himself of it, seeing that old Lizzie never left her post.

This went on for a while, when at last one day, about noon, he sent to beg me to scrape a little silver off the new sacramental cup, because he had been told that he should get better if he took it mixed with the dung of fowls. For some time I would not consent, seeing that I straightway suspected that there was some devilish mischief behind it; but he begged and prayed, till I did as he would have me.

And lo and behold, he mended from that very hour; so that when I went to pray with him at evening, I found him already sitting on the bench with a bowl between his knees, out of which he was supping broth. However, he would not pray (which was strange, seeing that he used to pray so gladly, and often could not wait patiently for my coming, insomuch that he sent after me two or three times if I was not at hand, or elsewhere employed); but he told me he had prayed already, and that he would give me the cock whose dung he had taken for my trouble, as it was a fine large cock, and he had nothing better to offer for my Sunday's dinner. And as the poultry was by this time gone to roost, he went up to the perch which was behind the stove, and reached down the cock, and put it under the arm of the maid, who was just come to call me away.

Not for all the world, however, would I have eaten the cock, but I turned it out to breed. I went to him once more, and asked whether I should give thanks to the Lord next Sunday for his recovery; whereupon he answered that I might do as I pleased in the matter. Hereat I shook my head, and left the house, resolving to send for him as soon as ever I should hear that his old Lizzie was from home (for she often went to fetch flax to spin from the Sheriff). But mark what befell within a few days! We heard an outcry that old Seden was missing, and that no one could tell what had become of him. His wife thought he had gone up into the Streckelberg, whereupon the accursed witch ran howling to our house and asked my daughter whether she had not seen anything of her goodman, seeing that she went up the mountain every day. My daughter said she had not; but, woe is me, she was soon to hear enough of him; for one morning, before sunrise, as she came down into the wood on her way back from her forbidden digging after amber, she heard a woodpecker (which no doubt was old Lizzie herself)[97] crying so dolefully, close beside her, that she went in among the bushes to see what was the matter. There was the woodpecker sitting on the ground before a bunch of hair, which was red, and just like what old Seden's had been, and as soon as it espied her it flew up, with its beak full of the hair and slipped into a hollow tree. While my daughter still stood looking at this devil's work, up came old Paasch — who also had heard the cries of the woodpecker, as he was cutting roofing shingles on the mountain, with his boy — and was likewise struck with horror when he saw the hair on the ground. At first they thought a wolf must have eaten him, and searched all about, but could not find a single bone. On looking up they fancied they saw something red at the very top of the tree, so they made the boy climb up, and he forthwith cried out that here, too, there was a great bunch of red hair stuck to some leaves as if with pitch, but that it was not pitch, but something speckled red and white, like fishguts; *item*, that the leaves all around, even where there was no hair, were stained and spotted, and had a very ill smell. Hereupon the lad, at his master's bidding, threw down the clotted branch, and they two below straightway judged that this was the hair and brains of old Seden, and that the devil had carried him off bodily, because he would not pray nor give thanks to the Lord for his recovery. I myself believed the same, and told it on the Sunday as a warning to the congregation. But further on it will be seen that the Lord had yet greater cause for giving him into the hands of Satan, inasmuch as he had been talked over by his wicked wife to renounce his Maker in the hopes of getting better. Now, however, this devil's whore did as if her heart was broken, tearing out her red hair by whole handsful when she heard about the woodpecker from my child and old Paasch, and bewailing that she was now a poor widow, and who was to take care of her for the future, etc.

Meanwhile we celebrated on this barren shore, as best we could and might, together with the whole Protestant Church, the 25th day *mensis Junii*, whereon, one hundred years ago, the Estates of the holy Roman Empire laid their confession before the most high and mighty Emperor Carolus V., at Augsburg;[98] and I preached a sermon on Matthew 10. 32, of the right confession of our Lord and Saviour Jesus Christ, whereupon the whole congregation came to the Sacrament. Now, towards the evening of the selfsame day, as I walked with my daughter by the sea-shore, we saw several hundred sail of ships, both great and small, round about Ruden, and plainly heard firing, whereupon we judged forthwith that this must be the most high and mighty King Gustavus Adolphus,[99] who was now coming, as he had promised, to the aid of poor persecuted Christendom. While we were still debating, a boat sailed towards us from Oie,[xxxv] wherein was Kate Berow her son, who is a farmer there, and was coming to see his old mother. The same told us that it really was the king, who had this morning run before Ruden with his fleet from Rügen; that a few men of Oie were fishing there at the time, and saw how he went ashore with his officers, and straightway bared his head and fell upon his knees.[xxxvi][100]

Thus, then, most gracious God, did I thy unworthy servant enjoy a still greater happiness and delight that blessed evening than I had done on the blessed morn; and any one may think that I delayed not for a moment to fall on my knees with my child, and to follow the example of the king. And God knows I never in my life prayed so fervently as that evening, whereon the Lord showed such a wondrous sign upon us as to cause the deliverer of his poor Christian people to come among them on the very day when they had everywhere called upon him, on their knees, for his gracious help against the murderous wiles of the Pope and the devil. That night I could not sleep for joy, but went quite early in the morning to Damerow, where something had befallen Vithe his boy. I supposed that he, too, was bewitched; but this time it was not witchcraft, seeing that the boy had eaten something unwholesome in the forest. He could not tell what kind of berries

---

[xxxv] Ruden and Oie, two small islands between Usedom and Rügen.
[xxxvi] See also the *Theatrum Europeum*, p. 226 ff.

they were; but the *malum*, which turned all his skin bright scarlet, soon passed over. As I therefore was returning home shortly after, I met a messenger from Peenemünde, whom his Majesty the high and mighty King Gustavus Adolphus had sent to tell the Sheriff that on the 29th of June, at ten o'clock in the morning, he was to send three guides to meet his Majesty at Coserow, and to guide him through the woods to Swine, where the Imperialists were encamped. *Item*, he related how his Majesty had taken the fort at Peenemünde yesterday (doubtless the cause of the firing we heard last evening), and that the Imperialists had run away as fast as they could, and played the bushranger properly; for after setting their camp on fire they all fled into the woods and coppices, and part escaped to Wolgast and part to Swine.

Straightway I resolved in my joy to invent a *carmen gratulatorium*[101] to his Majesty, whom, by the grace of Almighty God, I was to see, the which my little daughter might present to him.

I accordingly proposed it to her as soon as I got home, and she straightway fell on my neck for joy, and then began to dance about the room. But when she had considered a little, she thought her clothes were not good enough to wear before his Majesty, and that I should buy her a blue silk gown, with a yellow apron, seeing that these were the Swedish colours, and would please his Majesty right well. For a long time I would not, seeing that I hate this kind of pride; but she teased me with her kisses and coaxing words, till I, like an old fool, said yes, and ordered my ploughman to drive her over to Wolgast to-day to buy the stuff. Wherefore I think that the just God, who hateth the proud, and showeth mercy on the humble, did rightly chastise me for such pride. For I myself felt a sinful pleasure when she came back with two women who were to help her to sew, and laid the stuff before me. Next day she set to work at sunrise to sew, and I composed my *carmen* the while. I had not got very far in it when the young Lord Rüdiger of Nienkerken came riding up, in order, as he said, to inquire whether his Majesty were indeed going to march through Coserow. And when I told him all I knew of the matter, *item* informed him of our plan, he praised it exceedingly, and instructed my daughter (who looked more kindly upon him to-day than I altogether liked) how the Swedes use to pronounce the Latin, as *ratscho* pro *ratio*, *uet* pro *ut*, *schis* pro *scis*, etc., so that she might be able to answer his Majesty with all due readiness. He said, moreover, that he had held much converse with Swedes at Wittenberg, as well as at Griepswald,[102] wherefore if she pleased they might act a short *colloquium*,[103] wherein he would play the king. Hereupon he sat down on the bench before her, and they both began chattering together, which vexed me sore, especially when I saw that she made but small haste with her needle the while. But say, dear reader, what was I to do? Wherefore I went my ways, and let them chatter till near noon, when the young lord at last took leave. But he promised to come again on Tuesday, when the king was here, and believed that the whole island would flock together at Coserow. As soon as he was gone, seeing that my *vena poetica*[104] (as may be easily guessed) was still stopped up, I had the horses put to and drove all over the parish, exhorting the people in every village to be at the Giant's Stone by Coserow at nine o'clock on Tuesday, and that they were all to fall on their knees as soon as they should see the king coming and that I knelt down; *item*, to join at once in singing the Ambrosian hymn of praise,[105] which I should lead off as soon as the bells began to ring. This they all promised to do; and after I had again exhorted them to it on Sunday in church, and prayed to the Lord for his Majesty out of the fulness of my heart, we scarce could await the blessed Tuesday for joyful impatience.

CHAPTER XV

*Of the arrival of the high and mighty
King Gustavus Adolphus and what befell thereat.*

Meanwhile I finished my *carmen* in *metrum elegiacum*,[106] which my daughter transcribed (seeing that her handwriting is fairer than mine) and diligently learned, so that she might say it to his Majesty. *Item*, her clothes were gotten ready, and became her purely; and on Monday she went up to the Streckelberg, although the heat was such that the crows gasped on the hedges; for she wanted to gather flowers for a garland she designed to wear, and which was also to be blue and yellow. Towards evening she came home with her apron filled with all manner of flowers; but her hair was quite wet, and hung all matted about her shoulders. (My God, my God, was everything to come together to destroy me, wretched man that I am!) I asked, therefore, where she had been that her hair was so wet and matted: whereupon she answered that she had gathered flowers round the Kölpin,[xxxvii] and from thence she had gone down to the sea-shore, where she had bathed in the sea, seeing that it was very hot and no one could see her. Thus, said she, jesting, she should appear before his Majesty to-morrow doubly a clean maid. This displeased me at the time, and I looked grave, although I said nought.

Next morning at six o'clock all the people were already at the Giant's Stone, men, women, and children. *Summa*, everybody that was able to walk was there. At eight o'clock my daughter was already dressed in all her bravery, namely, a blue silken gown, with a yellow apron and kerchief, and a yellow hair-net, with a garland of blue and yellow flowers round her head. It was not long before my young lord arrived, finely dressed, as became a nobleman. He wanted to inquire, as he said, by which road I should go up to the Stone with my daughter, seeing that his father, Hans von Nienkerken, *item* Wittich Appelmann and the Lepels of Gnitze, were also going, and that there was much people on all the high roads,

---

[xxxvii] A small lake near the sea.

as though a fair was being held. But I straightway perceived that all he wanted was to see my daughter, inasmuch as he presently occupied himself about her, and began chattering with her in the Latin again. He made her repeat to him the *carmen* to his Majesty; whereupon he, in the person of the king, answered her: "*Dulcissima et venustissima puella, quae mihi in coloribus caeli, ut angelus Domini appares utinam semper mecum esses, nunquam mihi male caderet*";[107] whereupon she grew red, as likewise did I, but from vexation, as may be easily guessed. I therefore begged that his lordship would but go forward toward the Stone, seeing that my daughter had yet to help me on with my surplice; whereupon, however, he answered that he would wait for us the while in the chamber, and that we might then go together. *Summa*, I blessed myself from this young lord; but what could I do? As he would not go, I was forced to wink at it all; and before long we went up to the Stone, where I straight-way chose three sturdy fellows from the crowd, and sent them up the steeple, that they might begin to ring the bells as soon as they should see me get up upon the Stone and wave my napkin. This they promised to do, and straightway departed; whereupon I sat down on the Stone with my daughter, thinking that the young lord would surely stand apart, as became his dignity; albeit he did not, but sat down with us on the Stone. And we three sat there all alone, and all the folk looked at us, but none drew near to see my child's fine clothes, not even the young lasses, as is their wont to do; but this I did not observe till afterwards, when I heard how matters stood with us even then. Towards nine o'clock Hans von Nienkerken and Wittich Appelmann galloped up, and old Nienkerken called to his son in an angry voice: and seeing that the young lord heard him not, he rode up to the Stone, and cried out so loud that all the folk might hear, "Canst thou not hearken, boy, when thy father calls thee?" Whereupon Rüdiger followed him in much displeasure, and we saw from a distance how the old lord seemed to threaten his son, and spat out before him; but knew not what this might signify: we were to learn it soon enough, though, more's the pity! Soon after the two Lepels of Gnitze[xxxviii] came from the Damerow; and the noblemen saluted one other on the green sward close beside us, but without looking on us. And I heard the Lepels say that nought could yet be seen of his Majesty, but that the coastguard fleet around Ruden was in motion, and that several hundred ships were sailing this way. As soon as this news was known, all the folk ran to the sea-shore (which is but a step from the Stone); and the noblemen rode thither too, all save Wittich, who had dismounted, and who, when he saw that I sent old Paasch his boy up into a tall oak-tree to look out for the king, straightway busied himself about my daughter again, who now sat all alone upon the Stone: "Why had she not taken his huntsman? and whether she would not change her mind on the matter and have him now, or else come into service

---

[xxxviii] A peninsula in Usedom.

with him (the Sheriff) himself? for that if she would not, he believed she might be sorry for it one day." Whereupon she answered him (as she told me), that there was but one thing she was sorry for, namely, that his lordship would take so much useless pains upon her; whereupon she rose with all haste and came to where I stood under the tree, looking after the lad who was climbing up it. But our old Ilse said that he swore a great curse when my daughter turned her back upon him, and went straightway into the alder-grove close by the high road, where stood the old witch Lizzie Kolken.

Meanwhile I went with my daughter to the sea-shore, and found it quite true that the whole fleet was sailing over from Ruden and Oie towards Wollin, and several ships passed so close before us that we could see the soldiers standing upon them and the flashing of their arms. *Item*, we heard the horses neigh and the soldiery laugh. On one ship, too, they were drumming, and on another cattle lowed and sheep bleated. Whilst we yet gazed we saw smoke come out from one of the ships, followed by a great noise, and presently we were aware of the ball bounding over the water, which foamed and splashed on either side, and coming straight towards us. Hereupon the crowd ran away on every side with loud cries, and we plainly heard the soldiery in the ships laugh thereat. But the ball flew up and struck into the midst of an oak hard by Paasch his boy, so that nearly two cartloads of boughs fell to the earth with a great crash, and covered all the road by which his Majesty was to come. Hereupon the boy would stop no longer in the tree, however much I exhorted him thereto, but cried out to us as he came down that a great troop of soldiers was marching out of the forest by Damerow, and that likely enough the king was among them. Hereupon the Sheriff ordered the road to be cleared forthwith, and this was some time a-doing, seeing that the thick boughs were stuck fast in the trees all around; the nobles, as soon as all was made ready, would have ridden to meet his Majesty, but stayed still on the little green sward, because we already heard the noise of horses, carriages, and voices close to us in the forest.

It was not long before the cannons broke through the brushwood with the three guides seated upon them. And seeing that one of them was known to me (it was Stoffer Krauthahn of Peenemünde), I drew near and begged him that he would tell me when the king should come. But he answered that he was going forward with the cannon to Coserow, and that I was only to watch for a tall dark man, with a hat and feather and a gold chain round his neck, for that that was the king, and that he rode next after the great standard whereon was a yellow lion.

Wherefore I narrowly watched the procession as it wound out of the forest. And next after the artillery came the Finnish and Lapland bowmen, who went clothed all in furs, although it was now the height of summer, whereat I greatly wondered. After these there came much people, but I know not what they were. Presently I espied over the hazel-tree which stood in my way so that I could not see everything as soon as it came forth out of the coppice, the great flag with the lion on it, and behind that the head of a very dark man with a golden chain round his neck, whereupon straightway I judged this must be the king. I therefore waved my napkin toward the steeple, whereupon the bells forthwith rang out, and while the dark man rode nearer to us, I pulled off my skull-cap, fell upon my knees, and led the Ambrosian hymn of praise, and all the people plucked their hats from their heads and knelt down on the ground all around, singing after me; men, women, and children, save only the nobles, who stood still on the green sward, and did not take off their hats and behave with attention until they saw that his Majesty drew in his horse. (It was a coal-black charger, and stopped with its two fore-feet right upon my field, which I took as a sign of good fortune.) When we had finished, the Sheriff quickly got off his horse, and would have approached the king with his three guides, who followed after him; *item*, I had taken my child by the hand, and would also have drawn near to the king. Howbeit, his Majesty motioned away the Sheriff and beckoned us to approach, whereupon I wished his Majesty joy in the Latin tongue, and extolled his magnanimous heart, seeing that he had deigned to visit German ground for the protection and aid of poor persecuted Christendom; and praised it as a sign from God that such had happened on this the high festival of our poor church, and I prayed his Majesty graciously to receive what my daughter desired to present to him; whereupon his Majesty looked on her and smiled pleasantly. Such gracious bearing made her bold again, albeit she trembled visibly just before, and she reached him a blue and yellow wreath, whereon lay the *carmen*, saying, "*Accipe hanc vilem coronam et haec*"[108] whereupon she began to recite the *carmen*. Meanwhile his Majesty grew more and more gracious, looking now on her and now on the *carmen*, and nodded with especial kindness towards the end, which was as follows: —

> Tempus erit, quo tu reversus ab hostibus ultor
> Intrabis patriae libera regna meae;
> Tunc meliora student nostrae tibi carmina musae,
> Tunc tua, maxime rex, Martia facta canam.
> Tu modo versiculis ne spernas vilibus ausum
> Auguror et res est ista futura brevi!
> Sis foelix, fortisque diu, vive optime princeps,
> Omnia, et ut possis vincere, dura. Vale![xxxix] 90

[xxxix] Thou shalt return chastiser of the foe,
  To the freed kingdoms of my native land!
  Then shall our song with loftier cadence flow,
  Boasting the deeds of thy heroic hand!
  Scorn not, meanwhile, the feeble lines which thus
  Thy future glory and success foretell.
  Live, prince beloved! be brave, be prosperous;
  Conquer, howe'er opposed – and fare thee well!

As soon as she held her peace, his Majesty said, "*Propius accedas, patria virgo, ut te osculer*";[110] whereupon she drew near to his horse, blushing deeply. I thought he would only have kissed her forehead, as potentates commonly use to do, but not at all! he kissed her lips with a loud smack, and the long feathers on his hat drooped over her neck, so that I was quite afraid for her again. But he soon raised up his head, and taking off his gold chain, whereon dangled his own effigy, he hung it round my child's neck with these words: "*Hocce tuce pulchritudim! et si favente Deo redux fuero victor, promissum carmen et praeterea duo oscula exspecto.*"[111]

Hereupon the Sheriff with his three men again came forward and bowed down to the ground before his Majesty. But as he knew no Latin, *item* no Italian nor French, I had to act as interpreter. For his Majesty inquired how far it was to Swine, and whether there was still much foreign soldiery there: And the Sheriff thought there were still about 200 Croats in the camp; whereupon his Majesty spurred on his horse, and nodding graciously, cried "*Valete!*"[112] And now came the rest of the troops, about 3000 strong, out of the coppice, which likewise had a valiant bearing, and attempted no fooleries, as troops are wont to do, when they passed by us and the women, but marched on in honest quietness, and we followed the train until the forest beyond Coserow, where we commended it to the care of the Almighty, and every one went on his way home.

CHAPTER XVI

*How little Mary Paasch was sorely plagued of the devil,
and the whole parish fell off from me.*

Before I proceed any further I will first mark that the illustrious King Gustavus Adolphus, as we presently heard, had cut down the 300 Croats at Swine, and was thence gone by sea to Stettin. May God be for ever gracious to him! Amen.

But my sorrows increased from day to day, seeing that the devil now played pranks such as he never had played before. I had begun to think that the ears of God had hearkened to our ardent prayers, but it pleased him to try us yet more hardly than ever. For, a few days after the arrival of the most illustrious King Gustavus Adolphus, it was bruited about that my child her little god-daughter was possessed of the Evil One, and tumbled about most piteously on her bed, insomuch that no one was able to hold her. My child straightway went to see her little god-daughter, but presently came weeping home. Old Paasch would not suffer her even to come near her, but railed at her very angrily, and said that she should never come within his doors again, as his child had got the mischief from the white roll which she had given her that morning. It was true that my child had given her a roll, seeing that the maid had been the day before to Wolgast and had brought back a napkin full of them.

Such news vexed me sore, and after putting on my cassock I went to old Paasch his house to exorcise the foul fiend and to remove such disgrace from my child. I found the old man standing on the floor by the cockloft steps weeping; and after I had spoken "The peace of God," I asked him first of all whether he really believed that his little Mary had been bewitched by means of the roll which my child had given her? He said, "Yes!" And when I answered that in that case I also must have been bewitched, *item* Pagel his little girl, seeing that we both had eaten of the rolls, he was silent, and asked me with a sigh, whether I would not go into the room and see for myself how matters stood. I then entered with "The peace of God," and found six people standing round little Mary her bed; her eyes were shut, and she was as stiff as a board; wherefore Kit Wells (who was a young and sturdy fellow) seized the little child by one leg and held her out like a hedgestake, so that I might see how the devil plagued her. I now said a prayer, and Satan, perceiving that a servant of Christ was come, began to tear the child so fearfully that it was pitiful to behold; for she flung about her hands and feet so that four strong men were scarce able to hold her: *item* she was afflicted with extraordinary risings and fallings of her belly, as if a living creature were therein, so that at last the old witch Lizzie Kolken sat herself upon her belly, whereupon the child seemed to be somewhat better, and I told her to repeat the Apostles' Creed, so as to see whether it really were the devil who possessed her.[xl] She straightway grew worse than before, and began to gnash her teeth, to roll her eyes, and to strike so hard with her hands and feet that she flung her father, who held one of her legs, right into the middle of the room, and then struck her foot so hard against the bedstead that the blood flowed, and Lizzie Kolken was thrown about on her belly as though she had been in a swing. And as I ceased not, but exorcised Satan that he should leave her, she began to howl and to bark like a dog, *item* to laugh, and spoke at last, with a gruff bass voice, like an old man's, "I will not depart." But he should soon have been forced to depart out of her, had not both father and mother besought me by God's holy Sacrament to leave their poor child in peace, seeing that nothing did her any good, but rather made her worse. I was therefore forced to desist, and only admonished the parents to seek for help, like the Canaanitish woman, in true repentance and incessant prayer, and with her to sigh in constant faith, "Have mercy upon me, O Lord, Thou Son of David, my daughter is grievously vexed of a devil," (Matthew 15); that the heart of our Lord would then melt, so that he would have mercy on their child, and command Satan to depart from her. *Item*, I promised to pray for the little child on the following Sunday with the whole congregation, and told them to bring her, if it were any

---

[xl] It was imagined in those fearful times that when the sick person could repeat the three articles of belief, and especially some passages from the Bible bearing particular reference to the work of redemption, he was not possessed, since "no man can say that Jesus is the Lord, but by the Holy Ghost" (I Corinthians 12. 3).

ways possible, to the church, seeing that the ardent prayer of the whole congregation has power to rise beyond the clouds. This they promised to do, and I then went home sorely troubled, where I soon learned that she was somewhat better; thus it still is sure that Satan hates nothing so much, after the Lord Jesus, as the servants of the Gospel. But wait, and I shall even yet "bruise thy head with my heel" (Genesis 3); nought shall avail thee.

Howbeit before the blessed Sunday came, I perceived that many of my people went out of my way, both in the village and elsewhere in the parish, where I went to visit sundry sick folks. When I went to Uekeritze to see young Tittlewitz, there even befell me as follows: — Claus Pieper the peasant stood in his yard chopping wood, and on seeing me he flung the axe out of his hand so hastily that it stuck in the ground, and he ran towards the pigsty, making the sign of the cross. I motioned him to stop, and asked why he thus ran from me, his confessor? Whether, peradventure, he also believed that my daughter had bewitched her little god-child? "*Ille.* Yes, he believed it, because the whole parish did. *Ego.* Why, then, had she been so kind to her formerly, and kept her like a sister through the worst of the famine? *Ille.* This was not the only mischief she had done. *Ego.* What, then, had she done besides? *Ille.* That was all one to me. *Ego.* He should tell me, or I would complain to the magistrate. *Ille.* That I might do, if I pleased." Whereupon he went his way insolently. Any one may guess that I was not slow to inquire everywhere what people thought my daughter had done; but no one would tell me anything, and I might have grieved to death at such evil reports. Moreover not one child came during this whole week to school to my daughter; and when I sent out the maid to ask the reason she brought back word that the children were ill, or that the parents wanted them for their work. I thought and thought, but all to no purpose, until the blessed Sunday came round when I meant to have held a great Sacrament, seeing that many people had made known their intention to come to the Lord's table. It seemed strange to me that I saw no one standing (as was their wont) about the church door; I thought, however, that they might have gone into the houses. But when I went into the church with my daughter, there were not more than six people assembled, among whom was old Lizzie Kolken; and the accursed witch no sooner saw my daughter follow me than she made the sign of the cross and ran out of the door under the steeple; whereupon the five others, among them mine own church-warden Claus Bulken (I had not appointed any one in the room of old Seden), followed her. I was so horror-struck that my blood curdled, and I began to tremble, so that I fell with my shoulder against the confessional. My child, to whom I had as yet told nothing, in order to spare her, then asked me, "Father, what is the matter with all the people; are they, too, bewitched?" Whereupon I came to myself again and went into the churchyard to look after them. But all were gone save my church-warden, Claus Bulken, who stood under the lime-tree, whistling to himself. I stepped up to him and asked what had come to the people? Whereupon he answered he could not tell; and when I asked him again why, then, he himself had left the church, he said, What was he to do there alone, seeing that no collection could be made? I then implored him to tell me the truth, and what horrid suspicion had arisen against me in the parish? But he answered, I should very soon find it out for myself; and he jumped over the wall and went into old Lizzie her house, which stands close by the churchyard.

My child had made ready some veal broth for dinner, for which I mostly use to leave everything else; but I could not swallow one spoonful, but sat resting my head on my hand, and doubted whether I should tell her or no. Meanwhile the old maid came in ready for a journey, and with a bundle in her hand, and begged me with tears to give her leave to go. My poor child turned pale as a corpse, and asked in amaze what had come to her? but she merely answered, "Nothing!" and wiped her eyes with her apron. When I recovered my speech, which had well-nigh left me at seeing that this faithful old creature was also about to forsake me, I began to question her why she wished to go; she who had dwelt with me so long, and who would not forsake us even in the great famine, but had faithfully borne up against it, and, indeed, had humbled me by her faith, and had exhorted me to stand out gallantly to the last, for which I should be grateful to her as long as I lived. Hereupon she merely wept and sobbed yet more, and at length brought out that she still had an old mother of eighty living in Liepe, and that she wished to go and nurse her till her end. Hereupon my daughter jumped up and answered with tears, "Alas, old Ilse, why wilt thou leave us, for thy mother is with thy brother? Do but tell me why thou wilt forsake me, and what harm have I done thee, that I may make it good to thee again." But she hid her face in her apron and sobbed and could not get out a single word; whereupon my child drew away the apron from her face, and would have stroked her cheeks to make her speak. But when Ilse saw this she struck my poor child's hand and cried, "Ugh!" spat out before her,[113] and straightway went out at the door. Such a thing she had never done even when my child was a little girl, and we were both so shocked that we could neither of us say a word.

Before long my poor child gave a loud cry, and cast herself upon the bench, weeping and wailing, "What has happened, what has happened?" I therefore thought I ought to tell her what I had heard — namely, that she was looked upon as a witch. Whereat she began to smile instead of weeping any more, and ran out of the door to overtake the maid, who had already left the house, as we had seen. She returned after an hour, crying out that all the people in the village had run away from her when she would have asked them whither the maid was gone. *Item*, the little children, for whom she had kept school, had screamed, and had hidden themselves from her; also no one would answer her a single word, but all spat out before her, as the maid had done. On her way home she had seen a boat on the water, and had run as fast as she could to the shore, and called with might and main after old Ilse, who was in the boat. But she had taken no notice of her, not even once to look round after her, but had motioned her to be gone. And now she went on to weep and to sob the whole day and the whole night, so that I was more miserable than even in the time of the great famine. But the worst was yet to come, as will be shown in the following chapter.

CHAPTER XVII

How my poor child was taken up for a witch, and carried to Pudgla.

The next day, Monday, the 12th July, at about eight in the morning, while we sat in our grief, wondering who could have prepared such great sorrow for us, and speedily agreed that it could be none other than the accursed witch Lizzie Kolken, a coach with four horses drove quickly up to the door, wherein sat six fellows, who straightway all jumped out. Two went and stood at the front, two at the back door, and two more, one of whom was the constable Jacob Knake, came into the room, and handed me a warrant from the Sheriff for the arrest of my daughter, as in common repute of being a wicked witch, and for her examination before the criminal court.[114] Any one may guess how my heart sank within me when I read this. I dropped to the earth like a felled tree, and when I came to myself my child had thrown herself upon me with loud cries, and her hot tears ran down over my face. When she saw that I came to myself, she began to praise God therefor with a loud voice, and essayed to comfort me, saying that she was innocent, and should appear with a clean conscience before her judges. *Item*, she repeated to me the beautiful text from Matthew, chapter five: "Blessed are ye when men shall revile you, and persecute you, and shall say all manner of evil against you falsely for my sake."

And she begged me to rise and to throw my cassock over my doublet, and go with her, for that without me she would not suffer herself to be carried before the Sheriff. Meanwhile, however, all the village — men, women, and children — had thronged together before my door; but they remained quiet, and only peeped in at the windows, as though they would have looked right through the house. When we had both made us ready, and the constable, who at first would not take me with them, had thought better of it, by reason of a good fee which my daughter gave him, we walked to the coach; but I was so helpless that I could not get up into it.

Old Paasch, when he saw this, came and helped me up into the coach, saying, "God comfort ye! Alas, that you should ever see your child to come to this!" and he kissed my hand to take leave.

A few others came up to the coach, and would have done likewise; but I besought them not to make my heart still heavier, and to take Christian charge of my house and my affairs until I should return. Also to pray diligently for me and my daughter, so that the Evil One, who had long gone about our village like a roaring lion,[115] and who now threatened to devour me, might not prevail against us, but might be forced to depart from me and from my child as from our guileless Saviour in the wilderness.[116] But to this none answered a word; and I heard right well, as we drove away, that many spat out after us, and one said (my child thought it was Berow her voice), "We would far sooner lay fire under thy coats than pray for thee." We were still sighing over such words as these when we came near to the churchyard, and there sat the accursed witch Lizzie Kolken at the door of her house with her hymn-book in her lap, screeching out at the top of her voice, "God the Father, dwell with us,"[117] as we drove past her; the which vexed my poor child so sore that she swounded, and fell like one dead upon me. I begged the driver to stop, and called to old Lizzie to bring us a pitcher of water; but she did as though she had not heard me, and went on to sing so that it rang again. Whereupon the constable jumped down, and at my request ran back to my house to fetch a pitcher of water; and he presently came back with it, and the people after him, who began to say aloud that my child's bad conscience had stricken her, and that she had now betrayed herself. Wherefore I thanked God when she came to life again, and we could leave the village. But at Uekeritze it was just the same, for all the people had flocked together, and were standing on the green before Labahn his house when we went by.

Nevertheless, they were quiet enough as we drove past, albeit some few cried, "How can it be, how can it be?" I heard nothing else. But in the forest near the watermill the miller and all his men ran out and shouted, laughing, "Look at the witch, look at the witch!" Whereupon one of the men struck at my poor child with the sack which he held in his hand, so that she turned quite white, and the flour flew all about the coach like a cloud. When I rebuked him, the wicked rogue laughed and said, that if no other smoke than that ever came under her nose, so much the better for her. *Item*, it was worse in Pudgla than even at the mill. The people stood so thick on the hill, before the castle, that we could scarce force our way through, and the Sheriff caused the death-bell in the castle-tower to toll as an *avisum*.[118] Whereupon more and more people came running out of the ale-houses and cottages. Some cried out, "Is that the witch?" Others, again, "Look at the parson's witch! the parson's witch!" and much more, which for very shame I may not write. They scraped up the mud out of the gutter which ran from the castle-kitchen and threw it upon us; *item*, a great stone, the which struck one of the horses so that it shied, and belike would have upset the coach had not a man sprung forward and held it in. All this happened before the castle-gates, where the Sheriff stood smiling and looking on, with a heron's feather stuck in his grey hat. But so soon as the horse was quiet again, he came to the coach and mocked at my child, saying, "See, young maid, thou wouldst not come to me, and here thou art nevertheless!" Whereupon she answered, "Yea, I come; and may you one day come before your judge as I come before you"; whereunto I said, Amen, and asked him how his lordship could answer before God and man for what he had done to a wretched man like myself and to my child? But he answered, saying,

Why had I come with her? And when I told him of the rude people here, *item*, of the churlish miller's man, he said that it was not his fault, and threatened the people all around with his fist, for they were making a great noise. Thereupon he commanded my child to get down and to follow him, and went before her into the castle; motioned the constable, who would have gone with them, to stay at the foot of the steps, and began to mount the winding staircase to the upper rooms alone with my child.

But she whispered me privately, "Do not leave me, father"; and I presently followed softly after them. Hearing by their voices in which chamber they were, I laid my ear against the door to listen. And the villain offered to her that if she would love him nought should harm her, saying he had power to save her from the people; but that if she would not, she should go before the court next day, and she might guess herself how it would fare with her, seeing that he had many witnesses to prove that she had played the wanton with Satan, and had suffered him to kiss her. Hereupon she was silent, and only sobbed, which the arch-rogue took as a good sign, and went on: "If you have had Satan himself for a sweetheart, you surely may love me." And he went to her and would have taken her in his arms, as I perceived; for she gave a loud scream, and flew to the door; but he held her fast, and begged and threatened as the devil prompted him. I was about to go in when I heard her strike him in the face, saying, "Get thee behind me, Satan,"[119] so that he let her go. Whereupon she ran out at the door so suddenly that she threw me on the ground, and fell upon me with a loud cry. Hereat the Sheriff, who had followed her, started, but presently cried out, "Wait, thou prying parson, I will teach thee to listen!" and ran out and beckoned to the constable who stood on the steps below. He bade him first shut me up in one dungeon, seeing that I was an eavesdropper, and then return and thrust my child into another. But he thought better of it when we had come halfway down the winding-stair, and said he would excuse me this time, and that the constable might let me go, and only lock up my child very fast, and bring the key to him, seeing she was a stubborn person, as he had seen at the very first hearing which he had given her.

Hereupon my poor child was torn from me, and I fell in a swound upon the steps. I know not how I got down them; but when I came to myself, I was in the constable his room, and his wife was throwing water in my face. There I passed the night sitting in a chair, and sorrowed more than I prayed, seeing that my faith was greatly shaken, and the Lord came not to strengthen it.

CHAPTER XVIII

Of the first trial, and what came thereof.

Next morning, as I walked up and down in the court, seeing that I had many times asked the constable in vain to lead me to my child (he would not even tell me where she lay), and for very disquietude I had at last begun to wander about there; about six o'clock there came a coach from Uzdom,[xli] wherein sat his worship, Master Samuel Pieper, *consul dirigens*,[120] *item*, the *camerarius*[121] Gebhard Wenzel, and a *scriba*,[122] whose name, indeed, I heard, but have forgotten it again; and my daughter forgot it too, albeit in other things she has an excellent memory, and, indeed, told me most of what follows, for my old head well-nigh burst, so that I myself could remember but little. I straightway went up to the coach, and begged that the worshipful court would suffer me to be present at the trial, seeing that my daughter was yet in her nonage, but which the Sheriff, who meanwhile had stepped up to the coach from the terrace, whence he had seen all, had denied me. But his worship Master Samuel Pieper, who was a little round man, with a fat paunch, and a beard mingled with grey hanging down to his middle, reached me his hand, and condoled with me like a Christian in my trouble: I might come into court in God's name; and he wished with all his heart that all whereof my daughter was filed might prove to be foul lies. Nevertheless I had still to wait two hours before their worships came down the winding stair again. At last towards nine o'clock I heard the constable moving about the chairs and benches in the judgment-chamber; and as I conceived that the time was now come, I went in and sat myself down on a bench. No one, however, was yet there, save the constable and his young daughter, who was wiping the table, and held a rosebud between her lips. I was fain to beg her to give it me, so that I might have it to smell to; and I believe that I should have been carried dead out of the room that day if I had not had it. God is thus able to preserve our lives even by means of a poor flower, if so he wills it!

At length their worships came in and sat round the table, whereupon *Dom. Consul*[124] motioned the constable to fetch in my child. Meanwhile he asked the Sheriff whether he had put *Rea*[125] in chains, and when he said No, he gave him such a reprimand that it went through my very marrow. But the Sheriff excused himself, saying that he had not done so from regard to her quality, but had locked her up in so fast a dungeon that she could not possibly escape therefrom. Whereupon *Dom. Consul* answered that much is possible to the devil, and that they would have to answer for it should *Rea* escape. This angered the Sheriff, and he replied that if the devil could convey her through walls seven feet thick, and through three doors, he could very easily break her chains too. Whereupon *Dom. Consul* said that hereafter he would look at the prison himself; and I think that the Sheriff had been so kind only because he yet hoped (as, indeed, will hereafter be shown) to talk over my daughter to let him have his will of her.

And now the door opened, and my poor child came in with the constable, but

---

[xli] Or Usedom, a small town which gives its name to the whole island.

walking backwards,[xlii] and without her shoes, the which she was forced to leave without. The fellow had seized her by her long hair, and thus dragged her up to the table, when first she was to turn round and look upon her judges. He had a vast deal to say in the matter, and was in every way a bold and impudent rogue, as will soon be shown. After *Dom. Consul* had heaved a deep sigh, and gazed at her from head to foot, he first asked her her name, and how old she was; *item*, if she knew why she was summoned before them? On the last point she answered that the Sheriff had already told her father the reason; that she wished not to wrong any one, but thought that the Sheriff himself had brought upon her the repute of a witch, in order to gain her to his wicked will. Hereupon she told all his ways with her, from the very first, and how he would by all means have had her for his housekeeper; and that when she would not (although he had many times come himself to her father his house), one day, as he went out of the door, he had muttered in his beard, "I will have her, despite of all!" which their servant Claus Neels had heard, as he stood in the stable; and he had also sought to gain his ends by means of an ungodly woman, one Lizzie Kolken, who had formerly been in his service; that this woman, belike, had contrived the spells which they laid to her charge: she herself knew nothing of witchcraft; *item*, she related what the Sheriff had done to her the evening before, when she had just come, and when he for the first time spoke out plainly, thinking that she was then altogether in his power: nay, more, that he had come to her that very night again, in her dungeon, and had made her the same offers, saying that he would set her free if she would let him have his will of her; and that when she denied him, he had struggled with her, whereupon she had screamed aloud, and had scratched him across the nose, as might yet be seen, whereupon he had left her; wherefore she would not acknowledge the Sheriff as her judge, and trusted in God to save her from the hand of her enemies, as of old he had saved the chaste Susannah.[125]

When she now held her peace amid loud sobs, *Dom. Consul* started up after he had looked, as we all did, at the Sheriff's nose, and had in truth espied the scar upon it, and cried out in amaze, "Speak, for God his sake, speak, what is this that I hear of your lordship?" Whereupon the Sheriff, without changing colour, answered that although, indeed, he was not called upon to say anything to their worships, seeing that he was the head of the court, and that *Rea*, as appeared from numberless *indicia*,[126] was a wicked witch, and therefore could not bear witness against him or any one else; he, nevertheless, would speak, so as to give no cause of scandal to the court; that all the charges brought against him by this person were foul lies; it was, indeed, true, that he would have hired her for a housekeeper, whereof he stood greatly in need, seeing that his old Dorothy was already growing

---

[xlii] This ridiculous proceeding always took place at the first examination of a witch, as it was imagined that she would otherwise bewitch the judges with her looks. On this occasion indeed such an event was not unlikely.

infirm; it was also true that he had yesterday questioned her in private, hoping to get her to confess by fair means, whereby her sentence would be softened, inasmuch as he had pity on her great youth; but that he had not said one naughty word to her, nor had he been to her in the night; and that it was his little lap-dog, called Below, which had scratched him, while he played with it that very morning; that his old Dorothy could bear witness to this, and that the cunning witch had only made use of this wile to divide the court against itself, thereby and with the devil's help, to gain her own advantage, inasmuch as she was a most cunning creature, as the court would soon find out.

Hereupon I plucked up a heart, and declared that all my daughter had said was true, and that the evening before I myself had heard, through the door, how his lordship had made offers to her, and would have done wantonness with her; *item*, that he had already sought to kiss her once at Coserow; *item*, the troubles which his lordship had formerly brought upon me in the matter of the first-fruits.

Howbeit the Sheriff presently talked me down, saying, that if I had slandered him, an innocent man, in church, from the pulpit, as the whole congregation could bear witness, I should doubtless find it easy to do as much here, before the court; not to mention that a father could, in no case, be a witness for his own child.

But *Dom. Consul* seemed quite confounded, and was silent, and leaned his head on the table, as in deep thought. Meanwhile the impudent constable began to finger his beard from under his arm; and *Dom. Consul* thinking it was a fly, struck at him with his hand, without even looking up; but when he felt the constable his hand, he jumped up and asked him what he wanted? Whereupon the fellow answered, "Oh, only a louse was creeping there, and I would have caught it."

At such impudence his worship was so exceeding wroth that he struck the constable on the mouth, and ordered him, on pain of heavy punishment, to leave the room.

Hereupon he turned to the Sheriff, and cried, angrily, "Why, in the name of all the ten devils, is it thus your lordship keeps the constable in order? and truly, in this whole matter, there is something which passes my understanding." But the Sheriff answered, "Not so; should you not understand it all when you think upon the eels?"

Hereat *Dom. Consul* of a sudden turned ghastly pale, and began to tremble, as it appeared to me, and called the Sheriff aside into another chamber. I have never been able to learn what that about the eels could mean. —

Meanwhile *Dominus Camerarius* Gebhard Wenzel sat biting his pen, and looking furiously — now at me, and now at my child, but said not a word; neither did he answer *Scriba*, who often whispered somewhat into his ear, save by a growl. At length both their worships came back into the chamber together, and *Dom. Consul*, after he and the Sheriff had seated themselves, began to reproach my poor child violently, saying that she had sought to make a disturbance in the worshipful court; that his lordship had shown him the very dog which had scratched his nose, and that, moreover, the fact had been sworn to by the old housekeeper.

(Truly *she* was not likely to betray him, for the old harlot had lived with him for years, and she had a good big boy by him, as will be seen hereafter.)

Item, he said that so many *indicia* of her guilt had come to light, that it was impossible to believe anything she might say; she was therefore to give glory to God, and openly to confess everything, so as to soften her punishment; whereby she might perchance, in pity for her youth, escape with life, etc.

Hereupon he put his spectacles on his nose, and began to cross-question her, during near four hours, from a paper which he held in his hand. These were the main articles, as far as we both can remember:

Quaestio. Whether she could bewitch?

Responsio. No; she knew nothing of witchcraft.

Q. Whether she could charm?

R. Of that she knew as little.

Q. Whether she had ever been on the Blocksberg?[127]

R. That was too far off for her; she knew few hills save the Streckelberg, where she had been very often.

Q. What had she done there?

R. She had looked out over the sea, or gathered flowers; *item*, at times carried home an apronful of dry brushwood.

Q. Whether she had ever called upon the devil there?

R. That had never come into her mind.

Q. Whether, then, the devil had appeared to her there, uncalled?

R. God defend her from such a thing.

Q. So she could not bewitch?

R. No.

Q. What, then, befell Kit Zuter his spotted cow, that it suddenly died in her presence?

R. She did not know; and that was a strange question.

Q. Then it would be as strange a question, why Katie Berow her little pig had died?

R. Assuredly; she wondered what they would lay to her charge.

Q. Then she had not bewitched them?

R. No; God forbid it.

Q. Why, then, if she were innocent, had she promised old Katie another little pig, when her sow should litter?

R. She did that out of kind-heartedness. (And hereupon she began to weep bitterly, and said she plainly saw that she had to thank old Lizzie Kolken for all this, inasmuch as she had often threatened her when she would not fulfil all her greedy desires, for she wanted everything that came in her way; moreover, that

Lizzie had gone all about the village when the cattle were bewitched, persuading the people that if only a pure maid pulled a few hairs out of the beasts' tails they would get better. That she pitied them, and knowing herself to be a maid, went to help them; and indeed, at first it cured them, but latterly not.)

Q. What cattle had she cured?

R. Zabel his red cow; *item*, Witthan her pig, and old Lizzie's own cow.

Q. Why could she afterwards cure them no more?

R. She did not know, but thought — albeit she had no wish to fyle any one — that old Lizzie Kolken, who for many a long year had been in common repute as a witch, had done it all, and bewitched the cows in her name and then charmed them back again, as she pleased, only to bring her to misfortune.

Q. Why, then, had old Lizzie bewitched her own cow, *item*, suffered her own pig to die, if it was she that had made all the disturbance in the village, and could really charm?

R. She did not know; but belike there was some one (and here she looked at the Sheriff) who paid her double for it all.

Q. It was in vain that she sought to shift the guilt from off herself; had she not bewitched old Paasch his crop, nay, even her own father's, and caused it to be trodden down by the devil, *item*, conjured all the caterpillars into her father's orchard?

R. The question was almost as monstrous as the deed would have been. There sat her father, and his worship might ask him whether she ever had shown herself an undutiful child to him. (Hereupon I would have risen to speak, but *Dom. Consul* suffered me not to open my mouth, but went on with his examination; whereupon I remained silent and downcast.)

Q. Whether she did likewise deny that it was through her malice that the woman Witthan had given birth to a devil's imp, which straight-way started up and flew out at the window, so that when the midwife sought for it it had disappeared?

R. Truly she did; and indeed she had all the days of her life done good to the people instead of harm, for during the terrible famine she had often taken the bread out of her own mouth to share it among the others, especially the little children. To this the whole parish must needs bear witness, if they were asked; whereas witches and warlocks always did evil and no good to men, as our Lord Jesus taught (Matthew 12), when the Pharisees blasphemed him, saying that he cast out devils by Beelzebub the prince of the devils; hence his worship might see whether she could in truth be a witch.

Q. He would soon teach her to talk of blasphemies; he saw that her tongue was well hung; but she must answer the questions he asked her, and say nothing more. The question was not *what* good she had done to the poor, but *wherewithal* she had done it; she must now show how she and her father had of a sudden grown so rich that she could go pranking about in silken raiment, whereas she used to be so very poor?

Hereupon she looked towards me, and said, "Father, shall I tell?" Whereupon I answered, "Yes, my child, now thou must openly tell all, even though we thereby become beggars." She accordingly told how, when our need was sorest, she had found the amber, and how much we had gotten for it from the Dutch merchants.

Q. What were the names of these merchants?

R. Dieterich von Pehnen and Jakob Kiekebusch; but, as we have heard from a schipper, they since died of the plague at Stettin.

Q. Why had we said nothing of such a godsend?

R. Out of fear of our enemy the Sheriff, who, as it seemed, had condemned us to die of hunger, inasmuch as he forbade the parishioners, under pain of heavy displeasure, to supply us with anything, saying, that he would send them a better parson.

Hereupon *Dom. Consul* again looked the Sheriff sharply in the face, who answered that it was true he had said this, seeing that the parson had preached at him in the most scandalous manner from the pulpit; but that he knew very well, at the time, that they were far enough from dying of hunger.

Q. How came so much amber on the Streckelberg? She had best confess at once that the devil had brought it to her.

R. She knew nothing about that. But there was a great vein of amber there, as she could show to them all that very day; and she had broken out the amber, and covered the hole well over with fir-twigs, so that none should find it.

Q. When had she gone up the Streckelberg; by day or by night?

R. Hereupon she blushed, and for a moment held her peace; but presently made answer, "Sometimes by day, and sometimes by night."

Q. Why did she hesitate? She had better make a full confession of all, so that her punishment might be less heavy. Had she not there given over old Seden to Satan, who had carried him off through the air, and left only a part of his hair and brains sticking to the top of an oak?

R. She did not know whether that was his hair and brains at all, nor how it came there. She went to the tree one morning because she heard a woodpecker cry so dolefully. *Item*, old Paasch, who also had heard the cries, came up with his axe in his hand.

Q. Whether the woodpecker was not the devil himself, who had carried off old Seden?

R. She did not know: but he must have been dead some time, seeing that the blood and brains which the lad fetched down out of the tree were quite dried up.

Q. How and when, then, had he come by his death?

R. That Almighty God only knew. But Zuter his little girl had said, that one day, while she gathered nettles for the cows under Seden his hedge, she heard the goodman threaten his squint-eyed wife that he would tell the parson that he now knew of a certainty that she had a familiar spirit; whereupon the goodman had presently disappeared. But that this was a child's tale, and she would fyle no one on the strength of it.

Hereupon *Dom. Consul* again looked the Sheriff steadily in the face, and said, "Old Lizzie Kolken must be brought before us this very day": whereto the Sheriff made no answer; and he went on to ask,

Q. Whether, then, she still maintained that she knew nothing of the devil?

R. She maintained it now, and would maintain it until her life's end.

Q. And nevertheless, as had been seen by witnesses, she had been re-baptized by him in the sea in broad daylight. — Here again she blushed, and for a moment was silent.

Q. Why did she blush again? She should for God his sake think on her salvation, and confess the truth.

R. She had bathed herself in the sea, seeing that the day was very hot; that was the whole truth.

Q. What chaste maiden would ever bathe in the sea? Thou liest; or wilt thou even yet deny that thou didst bewitch old Paasch his little girl with a white roll?

R. Alas! alas! she loved the child as though it were her own little sister; not only had she taught her as well as all the other children without reward, but during the heavy famine she had often taken the bit from her own mouth to put it into the little child's. How, then, could she have wished to do her such grievous harm?

Q. Wilt thou even yet deny? — Reverend Abraham, how stubborn is your child! See here, is this no witches' salve,[xliii] which the constable fetched out of thy coffer last night? Is this no witches' salve, eh?

R. It was a salve for the skin, which would make it soft and white, as the apothecary at Wolgast had told her, of whom she bought it.

Q. Hereupon he shook his head, and went on: How! wilt thou then lastly deny that on this last Saturday the both July, at twelve o'clock at night, thou didst on the Streckelberg call upon thy paramour the devil in dreadful words, whereupon he appeared to thee in the shape of a great hairy giant,[128] and clipped thee and toyed with thee?

At these words she grew more pale than a corpse, and tottered so that she was forced to hold by a chair: and I, wretched man, who would readily have sworn away my life for her, when I saw and heard this, my senses forsook me, so that I fell down from the bench, and *Dom. Consul* had to call in the constable to help me up.

When I had come to myself a little, and the impudent varlet saw our common consternation, he cried out, grinning at the court the while, 'Is it all out? is it all

---

[xliii] It was believed that the devil gave the witches a salve, by the use of which they made themselves invisible, changed themselves into animals, flew through the air &c.

out? has she confessed?' Whereupon *Dom. Consul* again showed him the door with a sharp rebuke, as might have been expected; and it is said that this knave played the pimp for the Sheriff, and indeed I think he would not otherwise have been so bold.

Summa: I should well-nigh have perished in my distress, but for the little rose, which by the help of God's mercy kept me up bravely; and now the whole court rose and exhorted my poor fainting child, by the living God, and as she would save her soul, to deny no longer, but in pity to herself and her father to confess the truth.

Hereupon she heaved a deep sigh, and grew as red as she had been pale before, insomuch that even her hand upon the chair was like scarlet, and she did not raise her eyes from the ground.

R. She would now then confess the simple truth, as she saw right well that wicked people had stolen after and watched her at nights. That she had been to seek for amber on the mountain, and that to drive away fear she had, as she was wont to do at her work, recited the Latin *carmen* which her father had made on the illustrious King Gustavus Adolphus: when young Rüdiger of Nienkerken, who had ofttimes been at her father's house and talked of love to her, came out of the coppice, and when she cried out for fear, spoke to her in Latin, and clasped her in his arms. That he wore a great wolf's-skin coat, so that folks should not know him if they met him, and tell the lord his father that he had been on the mountain by night.

At this her confession I fell into sheer despair, and cried in great wrath, "O thou ungodly and undutiful child, after all, then, thou hast a paramour! Did not I forbid thee to go up the mountain by night? What didst thou want on the mountain by night?" and I began to moan and weep and wring my hands, so that *Dom. Consul* even had pity on me, and drew near to comfort me. Meanwhile she herself came towards me, and began to defend herself, saying, with many tears, that she had gone up the mountain by night, against my commands, to get so much amber that she might secretly buy for me, against my birthday, the *Opera Sancti Augustini*, which the Cantor at Wolgast wanted to sell. That it was not her fault that the young lord lay in wait for her one night; and that she would swear to me, by the living God, that nought that was unseemly had happened between them there, and that she was still a maid.

And herewith the first hearing was at end, for after *Dom. Consul* had whispered somewhat into the ear of the Sheriff, he called in the constable again, and bade him keep good watch over *Rea*; *item*, not to leave her at large in her dungeon any longer, but to put her in chains. These words pierced my very heart, and I besought his worship to consider my sacred office, and my ancient noble birth, and not to do me such dishonour as to put my daughter in chains. That I would answer for her to the worshipful court with my own head that she would not escape. Whereupon *Dom. Consul*, after he had gone to look at the dungeon himself, granted me my request, and commanded the constable to leave her as she had been hitherto.

CHAPTER XIX

How Satan, by the permission of the most righteous God, sought altogether to ruin us, and how we lost all hope.

The same day, at about three in the afternoon, when I was gone to Conrad Seep his alehouse to eat something, seeing that it was now nearly two days since I had tasted aught save my tears, and he had placed before me some bread and sausage, together with a mug of beer, the constable came into the room and greeted me from the Sheriff, without, however, so much as touching his cap, asking whether I would not dine with his lordship; that his lordship had not remembered till now that I belike was still fasting, seeing the trial had lasted so long. Hereupon I made answer to the constable that I already had my dinner before me, as he saw himself, and desired that his lordship would hold me excused. Hereat the fellow wondered greatly, and answered; did I not see that his lordship wished me well, albeit I had preached at him as though he were a Jew? I should think on my daughter, and be somewhat more ready to do his lordship's will, whereby peradventure all would yet end well. For his lordship was not such a rough ass as *Dom. Consul*, and meant well by my child and me, as beseemed a righteous magistrate.

After I had with some trouble rid myself of this impudent fox, I tried to eat a bit, but nothing would go down save the beer. I therefore soon sat and thought again whether I would not lodge with Conrad Seep, so as to be always near my child; *item*, whether I should not hand over my poor misguided flock to M. Vigelius, the pastor of Benz, for such time as the Lord still should prove me. In about an hour I saw through the window how that an empty coach drove to the castle, and the Sheriff and *Dom. Consul* straightway stepped thereinto with my child; *item*, the constable climbed up behind. Hereupon I left everything on the table and ran to the coach, asking humbly whither they were about to take my poor child; and when I heard they were going to the Streckelberg to look after the amber, I begged them to take me also, and to suffer me to sit by my child, for who could tell how much longer I might yet sit by her! This was granted to me, and on the way the Sheriff ordered me to take up my abode in the castle and to dine at his table as often as I pleased, and that he would, moreover, send my child her meat from his own table. For that he had a Christian heart, and well knew that we were to forgive our enemies. But I refused his kindness with humble thanks, as my child did also, seeing we were not yet so poor that we could not maintain ourselves. As we passed by the watermill the ungodly varlet there again thrust his head out of a hole and pulled wry faces at my child; but, dear reader, he got something to remember it by; for the Sheriff beckoned to the constable to fetch the fellow out, and after he had reproached him with the tricks he had twice played my child, the constable had to take the coachman his new whip and to give him fifty lashes, which, God knows, were not laid on with a feather. He bellowed like a bull, which, however, no one heard for the noise of the mill-wheels, and when at last he did as though he could not stir, we left him lying on the ground and went on our way.

As we drove through Uekeritze a number of people flocked together, but were quiet enough, save one fellow who, *salvâ veniâ*,[129] mocked at us with unseemly gestures in the midst of the road when he saw us coming. The constable had to jump down again, but could not catch him, and the others would not give him up, but pretended that they had only looked at our coach and had not marked him. May be this was true! And I am therefore inclined to think that it was Satan himself who did it to mock at us; for mark, for God's sake, what happened to us on the Streckelberg! Alas! through the delusions of the foul fiend, we could not find the spot where we had dug for the amber. For when we came to where we thought it must be, a huge hill of sand had been heaped up as by a whirlwind, and the fir-twigs which my child had covered over it were gone. She was near falling in a swound when she saw this, and wrung her hands and cried out with her Saviour, "My God, my God! why hast thou forsaken me!"[130]

Howbeit, the constable and the coachman were ordered to dig, but not one bit of amber was to be found, even so big as a grain of corn, whereupon *Dom. Consul* shook his head and violently upbraided my child. And when I answered that Satan himself, as it seemed, had filled up the hollow in order to bring us altogether into his power, the constable was ordered to fetch a long stake out of the coppice which we might thrust still deeper into the sand. But no hard *objectum* was anywhere to be felt, notwithstanding the Sheriff, *Dom. Consul*, and myself in my anguish did try everywhere with the stake.

Hereupon my child besought her judges to go with her to Coserow, where she still had much amber in her coffer which she had found here, and that if it were the gift of the devil it would all be changed, since it was well known that all the presents the devil makes to witches straightway turn to mud and ashes.

But, God be merciful to us, God be merciful to us! when we returned to Coserow, amid the wonderment of all the village, and my daughter went to her coffer, the things therein were all tossed about, and the amber gone. Hereupon she shrieked so loud that it would have softened a stone, and cried out: "The wicked constable hath done this! when he fetched the salve out of my coffer, he stole the amber from me, unhappy maid." But the constable, who stood by, would have torn her hair, and cried out, "Thou witch, thou damned witch, is it not enough that thou hast belied my lord, but thou must now belie me too?" But *Dom. Consul* forbade him, so that he did not dare lay hands upon her. *Item*, all the money was gone which she had hoarded up from the amber she had privately sold, and which she thought already came to about ten florins.

But the gown which she had worn at the arrival of the most illustrious King Gustavus Adolphus, as well as the golden chain with his effigy which he had given her, I had locked up, as though it were a relic, in the chest in the vestry, among the altar and pulpit cloths, and there we found them still; and when I excused myself therefore, saying that I had thought to have saved them up for her there against her bridal day, she gazed with fixed and glazed eyes into the box, and cried out, "Yes, against the day when I shall be burnt; O Jesu, Jesu, Jesu!" Hereat *Dom. Consul* shuddered and said, "See how thou still dost smite thyself with thine own words! For the sake of God and thy salvation, confess, for if thou knowest thyself to be innocent, how, then, canst thou think that thou wilt be burnt?" But she still looked him fixedly in the face, and cried aloud in Latin, "*Innocentia, quid est innocentia? Ubi libido dominatur, innocentia leve praesidium est.*"[xliv] 131

Hereupon *Dom. Consul* again shuddered, so that his beard wagged, and said, "What, dost thou indeed know Latin? Where didst thou learn the Latin?" And when I answered this question as well as I was able for sobbing, he shook his head and said, "I never in my life heard of a woman that knew Latin." Upon this he knelt down before her coffer, and turned over everything therein, drew it away from the wall, and when he found nothing he bade us show him her bed, and did the same with that. This, at length, vexed the Sheriff, who asked him whether they should not drive back again, seeing that night was coming on. But he answered, "Nay, I must first have the written paction which Satan has given her"; and he went on with his search until it was almost dark.[xlv] But they found nothing at all, although *Dom. Consul*, together with the constable, passed over no hole or corner, even in the kitchen and cellar. Hereupon he got up again into the coach, muttering to himself, and bade my daughter sit so that she should not look upon him.

And now we once more had the same *spectaculum* with the accursed old witch Lizzie Kolken, seeing that she again sat at her door as we drove by, and began to sing at the top of her voice, "We praise thee, O Lord."[132] But she screeched like a stuck pig, so that *Dom. Consul* was amazed thereat, and when he had heard who she was, he asked the Sheriff whether he would not that she should be seized by the constable and be tied behind the coach to run after it, as we had no room for her elsewhere; for that he had often been told that all old women who had red squinting eyes and sharp voices were witches, not to mention the suspicious things which *Rea* had declared against her. But he answered that he could not do this, seeing that old Lizzie was a woman in good repute and fearing God as *Dom. Consul* might learn for himself; but that, nevertheless, he had had her summoned for the morrow, together with the other witnesses.

[xliv] These words are from Cicero, if I do not mistake.
[xlv] At this time it was believed that as a man bound himself to the devil by writing, so did the devil in like manner to the man.

Yea, in truth, an excellently devout and worthy woman! — for scarcely were we out of the village, when so fearful a storm of thunder, lightning, wind, and hail burst over our heads, that the corn all around us was beaten down as with a flail, and the horses before the coach were quite maddened; however, it did not last long. But my poor child had to bear all the blame again,[xlvi] inasmuch as *Dom. Consul* thought that it was not old Lizzie, which, nevertheless, was as clear as the sun at noonday! but my poor daughter who brewed the storm; — for, beloved reader, what could it have profited her, even if she had known the black art? This, however, did not strike *Dom. Consul*, and Satan, by the permission of the all-righteous God, was presently to use us still worse; for just as we got to the Master's Dam,[xlvii] he came flying over us in the shape of a stork, and dropped a frog so exactly over us that it fell into my daughter her lap: she gave a shrill scream, but I whispered her to sit still, and that I would secretly throw the frog away by one leg.

But the constable had seen it, and cried out, "Hey, sirs! hey, look at the cursed witch! what has the devil just thrown into her lap?" Whereupon the Sheriff and *Dom. Consul* looked round and saw the frog, which crawled in her lap, and the constable after he had blown upon it three times,[133] took it up and showed it to their lordships. Hereat *Dom. Consul* began to spew, and when he had done, he ordered the coachman to stop, got down from the coach, and said we might drive home, that he felt qualmish, and would go afoot and see if he got better. But first he privately whispered to the constable, which, howbeit, we heard right well, that when he got home he should lay my poor child in chains, but not so as to hurt her much; to which neither she nor I could answer save by tears and sobs. But the Sheriff had heard it too, and when his worship was out of sight he began to stroke my child her cheeks from behind her back, telling her to be easy, as he also had a word to say in the matter, and that the constable should not lay her in chains. But that she must leave off being so hard to him as she had been hitherto, and come and sit on the seat beside him, that he might privately give her some good advice as to what was to be done. To this she answered, with many tears, that she wished to sit only by her father, as she knew not how much longer she might sit by him at all; and she begged for nothing more save that his lordship would leave her in peace. But this he would not do, but pinched her back and sides with his knees; and as she bore with this, seeing that there was no help for it, he waxed bolder, taking it for a good sign. Meanwhile *Dom. Consul* called out close behind us (for being frightened he ran just after the coach), "Constable, constable, come here quick; here lies a hedgehog in the midst of the road!"[134] whereupon the constable jumped down from the coach.

This made the Sheriff still bolder; and at last my child rose up and said, "Father, let us also go afoot; I can no longer guard myself from him here behind!" But he

---

[xlvi] Such sudden storms were attributed to witches.
[xlvii] It is so called to the present day, and is distant a mile from Coserow.

pulled her down again by her clothes, and cried out angrily, "Wait, thou wicked witch, I will help thee to go afoot if thou art so wilful; thou shalt be chained to the block this very night." Whereupon she answered, "Do you do that which you cannot help doing; the righteous God, it is to be hoped, will one day do unto you what He cannot help doing."

Meanwhile we had reached the castle, and scarcely were we got out of the coach, when *Dom. Consul*, who had run till he was all of a sweat, came up together with the constable, and straightway gave over my child into his charge, so that I had scarce time to bid her farewell. I was left standing on the floor below, wringing my hands in the dark, and hearkened whither they were leading her, inasmuch as I had not the heart to follow, when *Dom. Consul*, who had stepped into a room with the Sheriff, looked out at the door again, and called after the constable to bring *Rea* once more before them. And when he had done so, and I went into the room with them, *Dom. Consul* held a letter in his hand, and, after spitting thrice, he began thus: "Wilt thou still deny, thou stubborn witch? Hear what the old knight, Hans von Nienkerken, writes to the court!" Whereupon he read out to us that his son was so disturbed by the tale the accursed witch had told of him that he had fallen sick from that very hour, and that he, the father, was not much better. That his son Rüdiger had indeed at times, when he went that way, been to see Pastor Schweidler, whom he had first known upon a journey; but that he swore that he wished he might turn black if he had ever used any folly or jesting with the cursed devil's whore his daughter; much less ever been with her by night on the Streckelberg, or embraced her there.

At this dreadful news we both (I mean my child and I) fell down in a swound together, seeing that we had rested our last hopes on the young lord; and I know not what further happened. For when I came to myself, my host, Conrad Seep, was standing over me, holding a funnel between my teeth, through which he ladled some warm beer down my throat, and I never felt more wretched in all my life; insomuch that Master Seep had to undress me like a little child, and to help me into bed.

CHAPTER XX

Of the malice of the Governor and of old Lizzie:
item, of the examination of witnesses.

The next morning my hairs, which till *datum* had been mingled with grey, were white as snow,[135] albeit the Lord otherwise blessed me wondrously. For near daybreak a nightingale flew into the elder-bush beneath my window, and sang so sweetly that straightway I thought it must be a good angel. For after I had hearkened a while to it, I was all at once able again to pray, which since last Sunday I could not do; and the spirit of our Lord Jesus Christ began to speak within me, "Abba, Father";[xlviii] and straightway I was of good cheer, trusting that God would once more be gracious unto me his wretched child; and when I had given him thanks for such great mercy, I fell into a refreshing slumber, and slept so long that the blessed sun stood high in the heavens when I awoke.

And seeing that my heart was still of good cheer, I sat up in my bed, and sang with a loud voice, "Be not dismayed, thou little flock": whereupon Master Seep came into the room, thinking I had called him. But he stood reverently waiting till I had done; and after marvelling at my snow-white hair, he told me it was already seven; *item*, that half my congregation, among others my ploughman, Claus Neels, were already assembled in his house to bear witness that day. When I heard this, I bade mine host forthwith send Claus to the castle, to ask when the court would open, and he brought word back that no one knew, seeing that *Dom. Consul* was already gone that morning to Mellenthin to see old Nienkerken, and was not yet come back. This message gave me good courage, and I asked the fellow whether he also had come to bear witness against my poor child? To which he answered, "Nay, I know nought save good of her, and I would give the fellows their due, only —"

These words surprised me, and I vehemently urged him to open his heart to me. But he began to weep, and at last said that he knew nothing. Alas! he knew but too much, and could then have saved my poor child if he had willed. But from fear of the torture he held his peace, as he since owned; and I will here relate what had befallen him that very morning.

He had set out betimes that morning, so as to be alone with his sweetheart, who was to go along with him (she is Steffen of Zempin his daughter, not farmer Steffen, but the lame gouty Steffen), and had got to Pudgla about five, where he found no one in the ale-house save old Lizzie Kolken, who straightway hobbled up to the castle; and when his sweetheart was gone home again, time hung heavy on his hands, and he climbed over the wall into the castle garden, where he threw himself on his face behind a hedge to sleep. But before long the Sheriff came with old Lizzie, and after they had looked all round and seen no one, they went into an arbour close by him, and conversed as follows: —

Ille. Now that they were alone together, what did she want of him?

Illa. She came to get the money for the witchcraft she had contrived in the village.

Ille. Of what use had all this witchcraft been to him? My child, so far from being frightened, defied him more and more; and he doubted whether he should ever have his will of her.

Illa. He should only have patience; when she was laid upon the rack she would soon learn to be fond.

[xlviii] Galations 4. 6.

Ille. That might be, but till then she (Lizzie) should get no money.

Illa. What! Must she then do his cattle a mischief?

Ille. Yes, if she felt chilly, and wanted a burning fagot to warm her *podex*,[136] she had better. Moreover, he thought that she had bewitched him, seeing that his desire for the parson's daughter was such as he had never felt before.

Illa. (Laughing.) He had said the same thing some thirty years ago, when he first came after her.

Ille. Ugh! thou old baggage, don't remind me of such things, but see to it that you get three witnesses, as I told you before, or else methinks they will rack your old joints for you after all.

Illa. She had the three witnesses ready, and would leave the rest to him. But that if she were racked she would reveal all she knew.

Ille. She should hold her ugly tongue, and go to the devil.

Illa. So she would, but first she must have her money.

Ille. She should have no money till he had had his will of my daughter.

Illa. He might at least pay her for her little pig which she herself had bewitched to death, in order that she might not get into evil repute.

Ille. She might choose one when his pigs were driven by, and say she had paid for it. Hereupon, said my Claus, the pigs were driven by, and one ran into the garden, the door being open, and as the swineherd followed it, they parted; but the witch muttered to herself, "Now help, devil, help, that I may —" but he heard no further.

The cowardly fellow, however, hid all this from me, as I have said above, and only said, with tears, that he knew nothing. I believed him, and sat down at the window to see when *Dom. Consul* should return; and when I saw him I rose and went to the castle, where the constable, who was already there with my child, met me before the judgment-chamber. Alas! she looked more joyful than I had seen her for a long time, and smiled at me with her sweet little mouth: but when she saw my snow-white hair, she gave a cry, which made *Dom. Consul* throw open the door of the judgment-chamber, and say, "Ha, ha! thou knowest well what news I have brought thee; come in, thou stubborn devil's brat!" Whereupon we stepped into the chamber to him, and he lift up his voice and spake to me, after he had sat down with the Sheriff, who was by.

He said that yester-even, after he had caused me to be carried like one dead to Master Seep his ale-house, and that my stubborn child had been brought to life again, he had once more adjured her, to the utmost of his power, no longer to lie before the face of the living God, but to confess the truth; whereupon she had borne herself very unruly, and had wrung her hands and wept and sobbed, and at last answered that the young *nobilis* never could have said such things, but that his father must have written them, who hated her, as she had plainly seen when the Swedish king was at Coserow. That he, *Dom. Consul*, had indeed doubted the truth of this at the time, but as a just judge had gone that morning right early with the *scriba* to Mellenthin, to question the young lord himself.

That I might now see myself what horrible malice was in my daughter. For that the old knight had led him to his son's bedside, who still lay sick from vexation, and that he had confirmed all his father had written, and had cursed the scandalous she-devil (as he called my daughter) for seeking to rob him of his knightly honour. "What sayest thou now?" he continued; "wilt thou still deny thy great wickedness? See here the *protocollum* which the young lord hath signed *manu propriâ!*"[137] But the wretched maid had meanwhile fallen on the ground again, and the constable had no sooner seen this than he ran into the kitchen, and came back with a burning brimstone match, which he was about to hold under her nose.

But I hindered him, and sprinkled her face with water, so that she opened her eyes, and raised herself up by a table. She then stood a while, without saying a word or regarding my sorrow. At last she smiled sadly, and spake thus: That she clearly saw how true was that spoken by the Holy Ghost, "Cursed be the man that trusteth in man";[xlix] and that the faithlessness of the young lord had surely broken her poor heart if the all-merciful God had not graciously prevented him, and sent her a dream that night, which she would tell, not hoping to persuade the judges, but to raise up the white head of her poor father.

"After I had sat and watched all the night," quoth she, "towards morning I heard a nightingale sing in the castle-garden so sweetly that my eyes closed, and I slept. Then methought I was a lamb, grazing quietly in my meadow at Coserow. Suddenly the Sheriff jumped over the hedge and turned into a wolf, who seized me in his jaws, and ran with me towards the Streckelberg, where he had his lair. I, poor little lamb, trembled and bleated in vain, and saw death before my eyes, when he laid me down before his lair, where lay the she-wolf and her young. But behold a hand, like the hand of a man, straightway came out of the bushes and touched the wolves, each one with one finger, and crushed them so that nought was left of them save a grey powder. Hereupon the hand took me up, and carried me back to my meadow."

Only think, beloved reader, how I felt when I heard all this, and about the dear nightingale too, which no one can doubt to have been the servant of God. I clasped my child with many tears, and told her what had happened to me, and we both won such courage and confidence as we had never yet felt, to the wonderment of *Dom. Consul*, as it seemed; but the Sheriff turned as pale as a sheet when she stepped towards their worships and said, "And now do with me as you will, the lamb fears not, for she is in the hands of the Good Shepherd!" Meanwhile *Dom. Camerarius* came in with the *scriba*, but was terrified as he chanced to touch my daughter's apron with the skirts of his coat; and stood and scraped at his coat as a woman scrapes a fish. At last, after he had spat out thrice,

---

[xlix] Jeremiah 17. 5.

he asked the court whether it would not begin to examine witnesses, seeing that all the people had been waiting some time both in the castle and at the alehouse. Hereunto they agreed, and the constable was ordered to guard my child in his room, until it should please the court to summon her. I therefore went with her, but, we had to endure much from the impudent rogue, seeing he was not ashamed to lay his arm round my child her shoulders and to ask for a kiss *in meâ presentiâ*. But, before I could get out a word, she tore herself from him, and said, "Ah, thou wicked knave, must I complain of thee to the court; hast thou forgotten what thou hast already done to me?" To which, he answered, laughing, "See, see! how coy"; and still sought to persuade her to be more willing, and not to forget her own interest; for that he meant as well by her as his master; she might believe it or not; with many other scandalous words besides which I have forgot; for I took my child upon my knees and laid my head on her neck, and we sat and wept.

CHAPTER XXI

De confrontatione testium.

When we were summoned before the court again, the whole court was full of people, and some shuddered when they saw us, but others wept; my child told the same tale as before. But when our old Ilse was called, who sat on a bench behind, so that we had not seen her, the strength wherewith the Lord had gifted her was again at an end, and she repeated the words of our Saviour, "He that eateth bread with me hath lift up his heel against me":[138] and she held fast by my chair. Old Ilse, too, could not walk straight for very grief, nor could she speak for tears, but she twisted and wound herself about before the court like a woman in travail. But when Dom. Consul threatened that the constable should presently help her to her words, she testified that my child had very often got up in the night and called aloud upon the foul fiend.

Q. Whether she had ever heard Satan answer her?

R. She never had heard him at all.

Q. Whether she had perceived that *Rea* had a familiar spirit, and in what shape? She should think upon her oath, and speak the truth.

R. She had never seen one.

Q. Whether she had ever heard her fly up the chimney?

R. Nay, she had always gone softly out at the door.

Q. Whether she never at mornings had missed her broom or pitch-fork?

R. Once the broom was gone, but she had found it again behind the stove, and may be left it there herself by mistake.

Q. Whether she had never heard *Rea* cast a spell or wish harm to this or that person?

R. No, never; she had always wished her neighbours nothing but good, and even in the time of bitter famine had taken the bread out of her own mouth to give it to others.

Q. Whether she did not know the salve which had been found in *Rea* her coffer?

R. Oh, yes! her young mistress had brought it back from Wolgast for her skin, and had once given her some when she had chapped hands, and it had done her a vast deal of good.

Q. Whether she had anything further to say?

R. No, nothing but good.

Hereupon my man Claus Neels was called up. He also came forward in tears, but answered every question with a "Nay," and at last testified that he had never seen nor heard anything bad of my child, and knew nought of her doings by night, seeing that he slept in the stable with the horses; and that he firmly believed that evil folks — and here he looked at old Lizzie — had brought this misfortune upon her, and that she was quite innocent.

When it came to the turn of this old limb of Satan, who was to be the chief witness, my child again declared that she would not accept old Lizzie's testimony against her, and called upon the court for justice, for that she had hated her from her youth up, and had been longer by habit and repute a witch than she herself.

But the old hag cried out, "God forgive thee thy sins; the whole village knows that I am a devout woman, and one serving the Lord in all things"; whereupon she called up old Zuter Witthahn and my church-warden Claus Bulk, who bore witness hereto. But old Paasch stood and shook his head; nevertheless when my child said, "Paasch, wherefore dost thou shake thy head?" he started, and answered, "Oh, nothing!"

Howbeit, *Dom. Consul* likewise perceived this, and asked him, whether he had any charge to bring against old Lizzie; if so, he should give glory to God, and state the same; *item*, it was competent to every one so to do; indeed the court required of him to speak out all he knew.

But from fear of the old dragon, all were still as mice, so that you might have heard the flies buzz about the inkstand. I then stood up, wretched as I was, and stretched out my arms over my amazed and faint-hearted people and spake, "Can ye thus crucify me together with my poor child? Have I deserved this at your hands? Speak, then; alas, will none speak?" I heard, indeed, how several wept aloud, but not one spake; and hereupon my poor child was forced to submit.

And the malice of the old hag was such that she not only accused my child of the most horrible witchcraft, but also reckoned to a day when she had given herself up to Satan to rob her of her maiden honour; and she said that Satan had, without doubt, then defiled her when she could no longer heal the cattle, and when they all died. Hereupon my child said nought, save that she cast down her eyes and blushed deep, for shame at such filthiness; and to the other blasphemous slander which the old hag uttered with many tears, namely, that my daughter had given up her (Lizzie's) husband, body and soul, to Satan, she answered as she had done before. But when the old hag came to her re-baptism in the sea, and gave out that while seeking for strawberries in the coppice she had recognised my child's voice, and stolen towards her, and perceived these devil's doings, my child fell in smiling, and answered, "Oh, thou evil woman! how couldst thou hear my voice speaking down by the sea, being thyself in the forest upon the mountain? surely thou liest, seeing that the murmur of the waves would make that impossible." This angered the old dragon, and seeking to get out of the blunder she fell still deeper into it, for she said, "I saw thee move thy lips, and from that I knew that thou didst call upon thy paramour the devil!" for my child straight-way replied, "Oh, thou ungodly woman! thou saidst thou wert in the forest when thou didst hear my voice; how then up in the forest couldst thou see whether I, who was below by the water, moved my lips or not?" —

Such contradictions amazed even *Dom. Consul*, and he began to threaten the old hag with the rack if she told such lies; whereupon she answered and said, "List, then, whether I lie! When she went naked into the water she had no mark on her body, but when she came out again I saw that she had between her breasts a mark the size of a silver penny, whence I perceived that the devil had given it her,[139] although I had not seen him about her, nor, indeed, had I seen any one, either spirit or child of man, for she seemed to be quite alone."

Hereupon the Sheriff jumped up from his seat, and cried, "Search must straightway be made for this mark"; whereupon *Dom. Consul* answered, "Yea, but not by us, but by two women of good repute," for he would not hearken to what my child said, that it was a mole, and that she had had it from her youth up, wherefore the constable his wife was sent for, and *Dom. Consul* muttered somewhat into her ear, and as prayers and tears were of no avail, my child was forced to go with her. Howbeit, she obtained this favour, that old Lizzie Kolken was not to follow her, as she would have done, but our old maid Ilse. I, too, went in my sorrow, seeing that I knew not what the women might do to her. She wept bitterly as they undressed her, and held her hands over her eyes for very shame.

Well-a-day, her body was just as white as my departed wife's; although in her childhood, as I remember, she was very yellow, and I saw with amazement the mole between her breasts, whereof I had never heard aught before. But she suddenly screamed violently and started back, seeing that the constable his wife, when nobody watched her, had run a needle into the mole, so deep that the red blood ran down over her breasts. I was sorely angered thereat, but the woman said that she had done it by order of the judge,[1] which, indeed, was true; for when

---

[1] It was believed that these marks were the infallible sign of a witch when they were insensible, and that they were given by the devil; and everyone suspected of witchcraft was invariably searched for them.

we came back into court, and the Sheriff asked how it was, she testified that there was a mark of the size of a silver penny, of a yellowish colour, but that it had feeling, seeing that *Rea* had screamed aloud when she had, unperceived, driven a needle therein. Meanwhile, however, *Dom. Camerarius* suddenly rose, and, stepping up to my child, drew her eyelids asunder, and cried out, beginning to tremble, "Behold the sign which never fails":[li] 140 whereupon the whole court started to their feet, and looked at the little spot under her right eyelid, which in truth had been left there by a stye, but this none would believe. *Dom. Consul* now said, "See, Satan hath marked thee on body and soul! and thou dost still continue to lie unto the Holy Ghost; but it shall not avail thee, and thy punishment will only be the heavier. Oh, thou shameless woman! thou hast refused to accept the testimony of old Lizzie; wilt thou also refuse that of these people, who have all heard thee on the mountain call upon the devil thy paramour, and seen him appear in the likeness of a hairy giant, and kiss and caress thee?"

Hereupon old Paasch, goodwife Witthahn, and Zuter came forward and bare witness, that they had seen this happen about midnight, and that on this declaration they would live and die; that old Lizzie had awakened them one Saturday night about eleven o'clock, had given them a can of beer, and persuaded them to follow the parson's daughter privately, and to see what she did upon the mountain. At first they refused but in order to get at the truth about the witchcraft in the village, they had at last, after a devout prayer, consented, and had followed her in God's name.

They had soon through the bushes seen the witch in the moonshine; she seemed to dig, and spake in some strange tongue the while, whereupon the grim arch-fiend suddenly appeared, and fell upon her neck. Hereupon they ran away in consternation, but, by the help of the Almighty God, on whom from the very first they had set their faith, they were preserved from the power of the Evil One. For, notwithstanding he had turned round on hearing a rustling in the bushes, he had had no power to harm them.

Finally, it was even charged to my child as a crime, that she had fainted on the road from Coserow to Pudgla, and none would believe that this had been caused by vexation at old Lizzie her singing, and not from a bad conscience, as stated by the judge.

When all the witnesses had been examined, *Dom. Consul* asked her whether she had brewed the storm, what was the meaning of the frog that dropped into her lap, *item*, the hedgehog which lay directly in his path? To all of which she answered, that she had caused the one as little as she knew of the other. Whereupon *Dom. Consul* shook his head, and asked her, last of all, whether she would have an advocate, or trust entirely in the good judgment of the court. To

---

[li] See, among other authorities, Delrio, *Disquisit. magicae*, lib. v. tit. xiv. No. 28.

this she gave answer that she would by all means have an advocate. Wherefore I sent my ploughman, Claus Neels, the next day to Wolgast to fetch the *Syndicus* Michelsen, who is a worthy man, and in whose house I have been many times when I went to the town, seeing that he courteously invited me.

I must also note here that at this time my old Ilse came back to live with me; for after the witnesses were gone she stayed behind in the chamber, and came boldly up to me, and besought me to suffer her once more to serve her old master and her dear young mistress; for that now she had saved her poor soul, and confessed all she knew. Wherefore she could no longer bear to see her old masters in such woeful plight, without so much as a mouthful of victuals, seeing that she had heard that old wife Seep, who had till *datum* prepared the food for me and my child, often let the porridge burn; *item*, oversalted the fish and the meat. Moreover, that I was so weakened by age and misery, that I needed help and support, which she would faithfully give me, and was ready to sleep in the stable, if needs must be; that she wanted no wages for it, I was only not to turn her away. Such kindness made my daughter to weep, and she said to me, "Behold, father, the good folks come back to us again; think you, then, that the good angels will forsake us for ever? I thank thee, old Ilse; thou shall indeed prepare my food for me, and always bring it as far as the prison-door, if thou mayest come no further; and mark, then, I pray thee, what the constable does therewith."

This the maid promised to do, and from this time forth took up her abode in the stable. May God repay her at the day of judgment for what she then did for me and for my poor child!

CHAPTER XXII

How the Syndicus Dom. Michelsen arrived and prepared his defence of my poor child.

The next day, at about three o'clock p.m., *Dom. Syndicus* came driving up, and got out of his coach at my inn. He had a huge bag full of books with him, but was not so friendly in his manner as was usual with him, but very grave and silent. And after he had saluted me in my own room, and had asked how it was possible for my child to have come to such misfortune, I related to him the whole affair, whereat, however, he only shook his head. On my asking him whether he would not see my child that same day, he answered, "Nay"; he would rather first study the *acta*.[141] And after he had eaten of some wild duck—which my old Ilse had roasted for him, he would tarry no longer, but straightway went up to the castle, whence he did not return till the following afternoon. His manner was not more friendly now than at his first coming, and I followed him with sighs when he asked me to lead him to my daughter. As we went in with the constable, and I, for the first time, saw my child in chains before me — she who in her whole life had never hurt a worm — I again felt as though I should die for very grief. But she smiled and cried out to *Dom. Syndicus*, "Are you indeed the good angel who will cause my chains to fall from my hands, as was done of yore to St. Peter?"[lii] To which he replied, with a sigh, "May the Almighty God grant it"; and as, save the chair whereon my child sat against the wall, there was none other in the dungeon (which was a filthy and stinking hole, wherein were more wood-lice than ever I saw in my life), *Dom. Syndicus* and I sat down on her bed, which had been left for her at my prayer; and he ordered the constable to go his ways until he should call him back. Hereupon he asked my child what she had to say in her justification; and she had not gone far in her defence when I perceived, from the shadow at the door, that some one must be standing without. I therefore went quickly to the door, which was half open, and found the impudent constable, who stood there to listen. This so angered *Dom. Syndicus* that he snatched up his staff in order to hasten his going, but the arch-rogue took to his heels as soon as he saw this. My child took this opportunity to tell her worshipful defensor what she had suffered from the impudence of this fellow, and to beg that some other constable might be set over her, seeing that this one had come to her last night again with evil designs, so that she at last had shrieked aloud and beaten him on the head with her chains; whereupon he had left her. This *Dom. Syndicus* promised to obtain for her; but with regard to the *defensio*, wherewith she now went on, he thought it would be better to make no further mention of the *impetus*[142] which the Sheriff had made on her chastity. "For," said he, "as the princely central court at Wolgast has to give sentence upon thee, this statement would do thee far more harm than good, seeing that the *praeses*[143] thereof is a cousin of the Sheriff, and ofttimes goes a-hunting with him. Besides, thou being charged with a capital crime hast no *fides*,[144] especially as thou canst bring no witnesses against him. Thou couldst, therefore, gain no belief even if thou didst confirm the charge on the rack, wherefrom, moreover, I am come hither to save thee by my *defensio*." These reasons seemed sufficient to us both, and we resolved to leave vengeance to Almighty God, who seeth in secret, and to complain of our wrongs to him, as we might not complain to men. But all my daughter said about old Lizzie — *item*, of the good report wherein she herself had, till now, stood with everybody — he said he would write down, and add thereunto as much and as well of his own as he was able, so as, by the help of Almighty God, to save her from the torture. That she was to make herself easy and commend herself to God; within two days he hoped to have his *defensio* ready and to read it to her. And now, when he called the constable back again, the fellow did not come, but sent his wife to lock the prison, and I took leave of my child with many tears: *Dom. Syndicus* told the woman the while what her impudent rogue of a husband had

---

[lii] The Acts of the Apostles 12. 7.

done, that she might let him hear more of it. Then he sent the woman away again and came back to my daughter, saying that he had forgotten to ascertain whether she really knew the Latin tongue, and that she was to say her *defensio* over again in Latin, if she was able. Hereupon she began and went on therewith for a quarter of an hour or more, in such wise that not only *Dom. Syndicus* but I myself also was amazed, seeing that she did not stop for a single word, save the word "hedgehog," which we both had forgotten at the moment when she asked us what it was. — *Summa. Dom. Syndicus* grew far more gracious when she had finished her oration, and took leave of her, promising that he would set to work forthwith.

After this I did not see him again till the morning of the third day at ten o'clock, seeing that he sat at work in a room at the castle, which the Sheriff had given him, and also ate there, as he sent me word by old Ilse when she carried him his breakfast next day.

At the above-named time he sent the new constable for me, who, meanwhile, had been fetched from Uzdom at his desire. For the Sheriff was exceeding wroth when he heard that the impudent fellow had attempted my child in the prison, and cried out in a rage, "S'death, and 'ouns, I'll mend thy coaxing!" Whereupon he gave him a sound thrashing with a dog-whip he held in his hand, to make sure that she should be at peace from him.

But, alas! the new constable was even worse than the old, as will be shown hereafter. His name was Master Köppner, and he was a tall fellow with a grim face, and a mouth so wide that at every word he said the spittle ran out at the corners, and stuck in his long beard like soap-suds, so that my child had an especial fear and loathing of him. Moreover, on all occasions he seemed to laugh in mockery and scorn, as he did when he opened the prison-door to us, and saw my poor child sitting in her grief and distress. But he straightway left us without waiting to be told, whereupon *Dom. Syndicus* drew his defence out of his pocket, and read it to us; we have remembered the main points thereof, and I will recount them here, but most of the *auctores*[145] we have forgotten.

1. He began by saying that my daughter had ever till now stood in good repute, as not only the whole village, but even my servants bore witness; *ergo*, she could not be a witch, inasmuch as the Saviour hath said, "A good tree cannot bring forth evil fruit, neither can a corrupt tree bring forth good fruit" (Matthew 7).

2. With regard to the witchcraft in the village, that belike was the contrivance of old Lizzie, seeing that she bore a great hatred towards *Rea*, and had long been in evil repute, for that the parishioners dared not to speak out, only from fear of the old witch; wherefore Zuter, her little girl, must be examined, who had heard old Lizzie her goodman tell her she had a familiar spirit, and that he would tell it to the parson; for that notwithstanding the above-named was but a child, still it was written in Psalm 8, "Out of the mouth of babes and sucklings hast thou ordained strength…."; and the Saviour himself appealed (Matthew 21) to the testimony of little children.

3. Furthermore, old Lizzie might have bewitched the crops, *item*, the fruit-trees, inasmuch as none could believe that *Rea*, who had ever shown herself a dutiful child, would have bewitched her own father's corn, or made caterpillars come on his trees; for no one, according to Scripture, can serve two masters.[146]

4. *Item*, she (old Lizzie) might very well have been the woodpecker that was seen by *Rea* and old Paasch on the Streckelberg, and herself have given over her goodman to the Evil One for fear of the parson, inasmuch as Spitzel *De Expugnatione Orci* asserts;[147] *item*, the *Malleus Maleficarum*[liii] proves beyond doubt that the wicked children of Satan ofttimes change themselves into all manner of beasts, as the foul fiend himself likewise seduced our first parents in the shape of a serpent (Genesis 3).

5. That old Lizzie had most likely made the wild weather when *Dom. Consul* was coming home with *Rea* from the Streckelberg, seeing it was impossible that *Rea* could have done it, as she was sitting in the coach, whereas witches when they raise storms always stand in the water, and throw it over their heads backwards; *item*, beat the stones soundly with a stick, as Hannold relates.[148] Wherefore she too, may be, knew best about the frog and the hedgehog.

6. That *Rea* was erroneously charged with that as a *crimen* which ought rather to serve as her justification, namely, her sudden riches. For the *Malleus Maleficarum* expressly says that a witch can never grow rich, seeing that Satan, to do dishonour to God, always buys them for a vile price, so that they should not betray themselves by their riches.[liv] [149] Wherefore that as *Rea* had grown rich, she could not have got her wealth from the foul fiend, but it must be true that she had found amber on the mountain; that the spells of old Lizzie might have been the cause why they could not find the vein of amber again, or that the sea might have washed away the cliff below, as often happens, whereupon the top had slipped down, so that only a *miraculum naturale* had taken place. The proof which he brought forward from Scripture we have quite forgotten, seeing it was but middling.

7. With regard to her re-baptism, the old hag had said herself that she had not seen the devil or any other spirit or man about *Rea*, wherefore she might in truth have been only naturally bathing, in order to greet the King of Sweden next day, seeing that the weather was hot, and that bathing was not of itself sufficient to impair the modesty of a maiden. For that she had as little thought any would see her as Bathsheba the daughter of Eliam, and wife of Uriah the Hittite, who in like manner did bathe herself, as is written (II Samuel 11. 2), without knowing that

---

[liii] The celebrated "Hammer for Witches" of Innocent VIII., which appeared in 1489, and gave directions for the whole course of proceeding to be observed at trials for witchcraft.
[liv] The original words of the "Hammer for Witches", tom. i. quest. 18, in answer to the question, *Cur maleficae non ditentur?* are, *Ut juxta complacentiam daemonis in contumeliam Creatoris, quantum possibile est, pro vilissimo pretio emantur, et secundo, ne in divitis notentur.*

David could see her. Neither could her mark be a mark given by Satan, inasmuch as there was feeling therein; *ergo*, it must be a natural mole, and it was a lie that she had it not before bathing. Moreover, that on this point the old harlot was nowise to be believed, seeing that she had fallen from one contradiction into another about it, as stated in the *acta*.

8. Neither was it just to accuse *Rea* of having bewitched Paasch his little daughter; for as old Lizzie was going in and out of the room, nay, even sat herself down on the little girl her belly when the pastor went to see her, it most likely was that wicked woman (who was known to have a great spite against *Rea*) that contrived the spell through the power of the foul fiend, and by permission of the all-just God; for that Satan was "a liar and the father of it," as our Lord Christ says (John 8).

9. With regard to the appearance of the foul fiend on the mountain in the shape of a hairy giant, that indeed was the heaviest *gravamen*,[150] inasmuch as not only old Lizzie, but likewise three trustworthy witnesses, had seen him. But who could tell whether it was not old Lizzie herself who had contrived this devilish apparition in order to ruin her enemy altogether; for that notwithstanding the apparition was not the young nobleman, as *Rea* had declared it to be, it still was very likely that she had not lied, but had mistaken Satan for the young lord, as he appeared in his shape; *exemplum*, for this was to be found even in Scripture: for that all *Theologi* of the whole Protestant Church were agreed that the vision which the witch of Endor showed to King Saul[151] was not Samuel himself, but the arch-fiend; nevertheless, Saul had taken it for Samuel. In like manner the old harlot might have conjured up the devil before *Rea*, who did not perceive that it was not the young lord, but Satan, who had put on that shape in order to seduce her; for as *Rea* was a fair woman, none could wonder that the devil gave himself more trouble for her than for an old withered hag, seeing he has ever sought after fair women to lie with them.[lv]

Lastly, he argued that *Rea* was in nowise marked as a witch, for that she neither had bleared and squinting eyes nor a hooked nose, whereas old Lizzie had both, which Theophrastus Paracelsus[152] declares to be an unfailing mark of a witch, saying, "Nature marketh none thus unless by abortion, for these are the chiefest signs whereby witches be known whom the spirit *Asiendens* hath subdued unto himself."

When *Dom. Syndicus* had read his *defensio*, my daughter was so rejoiced thereat that she would have kissed his hand, but he snatched it from her and breathed upon it thrice, whereby we could easily see that he himself was nowise in earnest with his *defensio*. Soon after he took leave in an ill-humour, after commending her to the care of the Most High, and begged that I would make my

---

[lv] Genesis 6. 2.

farewell as short as might be, seeing that he purposed to return home that very day, the which, alas! I very unwillingly did.

CHAPTER XXIII

How my poor child was sentenced to be put to the question.

After *acta* had been sent to the honourable the central court, about fourteen days passed over before any answer was received. My lord the Sheriff was especially gracious toward me the while, and allowed me to see my daughter as often as I would (seeing that the rest of the court were gone home), wherefore I was with her nearly all day. And when the constable grew impatient of keeping watch over me, I gave him a fee to lock me in together with my child. And the all-merciful God was gracious unto us, and caused us often and gladly to pray, for we had a steadfast hope, believing that the cross we had seen in the heavens would now soon pass away from us, and that the ravening wolf would receive his reward when the honourable high court had read through the *acta*, and should come to the excellent *defensio* which *Dom. Syndicus* had constructed for my child. Wherefore I began to be of good cheer again, especially when I saw my daughter her cheeks growing of a right lovely red. But on Thursday, 25th *mensis Augusti*, at noon, the worshipful court drove into the castle-yard again as I sat in the prison with my child, as I was wont; and old Ilse brought us our food, but could not tell us the news for weeping. But the tall constable peeped in at the door, grinning, and cried, "Oh, ho! they are come, they are come, they are come; now the tickling will begin": whereat my poor child shuddered, but less at the news than at sight of the fellow himself. Scarce was he gone than he came back again to take off her chains and to fetch her away. So I followed her into the judgment-chamber, where *Dom. Consul* read out the sentence of the honourable high court as follows: — That she should once more be questioned in kindness touching the articles contained in the indictment; and if she then continued stubborn she should be subjected to the *peine forte et dure*,[153] for that the *defensio* she had set up did not suffice, and that there were *indicia legitima praegnantia et sufficientia ad torturam ipsam*;[154] to wit —

1. *Mala fama.*
2. *Maleficium, publicè commissum.*
3. *Apparitio daemonis in monte.*[155]

Whereupon the most honourable central court cited about 20 *auctores*, whereof, howbeit, we remember but little. When *Dom. Consul* had read out this to my child, he once more lift up his voice and admonished her with many words to confess of her own free-will, for that the truth must now come to light.

Hereupon she steadfastly replied, that after the *defensio* of *Dom. Syndicus* she had indeed hoped for a better sentence; but that, as it was the will of God to try her yet more hardly, she resigned herself altogether into His gracious hands, and could not confess aught save what she had said before, namely, that she was innocent, and that evil men had brought this misery upon her. Hereupon *Dom. Consul* motioned the constable, who straightway opened the door of the next room, and admitted *Pastor Benzensis*[lvi] in his surplice, who had been sent for by the court to admonish her still better out of the word of God. He heaved a deep sigh, and said, "Mary, Mary, is it thus I must meet thee again?" Whereupon she began to weep bitterly, and to protest her innocence afresh. But he heeded not her distress, and as soon as he had heard her pray, "Our Father," "The eyes of all wait upon thee,"[156] and "God the Father dwell with us," he lift up his voice and declared to her the hatred of the living God to all witches and warlocks, seeing that not only is the punishment of fire awarded to them in the Old Testament, but that the Holy Ghost expressly saith in the New Testament (Galations 5), "That they which do such things shall not inherit the kingdom of God"; but "shall have their part in the lake which burneth with fire and brimstone, which is the second death" (Apocalypse 21).[157] Wherefore she must not be stubborn nor murmur against the court when she was tormented, seeing that it was all done out of Christian love, and to save her poor soul. That, for the sake of God and her salvation, she should no longer delay repentance, and thereby cause her body to be tormented, and give over her wretched soul to Satan, who certainly would not fulfil those promises in hell which he had made her here upon earth; seeing that "He was a murderer from the beginning — a liar and the father of it" (John 8). "Oh!" cried he, "Mary, my child, who so oft hast sat upon my knees, and for whom I now cry every morning and every night unto my God, if thou wilt have no pity upon thee and me, have pity at least upon thy worthy father, whom I cannot look upon without tears, seeing that his hairs have turned snow-white within a few days, and save thy soul, my child, and confess! Behold, thy Heavenly Father grieveth over thee no less than thy fleshly father, and the holy angels veil their faces for sorrow that thou, who wert once their darling sister, art now become the sister and bride of the devil. Return therefore, and repent! This day thy Saviour calleth thee, poor stray lamb, back into His flock, 'And ought not this woman, being a daughter of Abraham, whom Satan hath bound ... be loosed from this bond?' Such are His merciful words (Luke 13); *item*, 'Return, thou backsliding Israel, saith the Lord, and I will not cause mine anger to fall upon you, for I am merciful' (Jeremiah 3). Return then, thou back-sliding soul, unto the Lord thy God! He who heard the prayer of the idolatrous Manasseh when 'he besought the Lord his God and humbled himself' (II Chronicles 33); who, through Paul, accepted the repentance of the sorcerers at Ephesus (Acts 19), the same merciful God now crieth unto thee as unto the angel of the church of

---

[lvi] The minister at Bentz, a village situated at a short distance from Pudgla.

Ephesus, 'Remember, therefore, from whence thou art fallen, and repent' (Apocalypse 2). Oh, Mary, Mary, remember, my child, from whence thou art fallen, and repent!"

Hereupon he held his peace, and it was some time before she could say a word for tears and sobs; but at last she answered, "If lies are no less hateful to God than witchcraft, I may not lie, but must rather declare, to the glory of God, as I have ever declared, that I am innocent."

Hereupon *Dom. Consul* was exceeding wroth, and frowned and asked the tall constable if all was ready, *item*, whether the women were at hand to undress *Rea*; whereupon he answered with a grin, as he was wont, "Ho, ho, I have never been wanting in my duty, nor will I be wanting to-day; I will tickle her in such wise that she shall soon confess."

When he had said this, *Dom. Consul* turned to my daughter, and said, "Thou art a foolish thing, and knowest not the torment which awaits thee, and therefore is it that thou still art stubborn. Now, then, follow me to the torture-chamber, where the executioner shall show thee the *instrumenta*; and thou mayest yet think better of it when thou hast seen what the question is like."

Hereupon he went into another room, and the constable followed him with my child. And when I would have gone after them, *Pastor Benzensis* held me back, with many tears, and conjured me not to do so, but to tarry where I was. But I hearkened not unto him, and tore myself from him, and swore that so long as a single vein should beat in my wretched body I would never forsake my child. I therefore went into the next room, and from thence down into a vault, where was the torture-chamber, wherein were no windows, so that those without might not hear the cries of the tormented. Two torches were already burning there when I went in, and although *Dom. Consul* would at first have sent me away, after a while he had pity upon me, so that he suffered me to stay.

And now that hell-hound the constable stepped forward, and first showed my poor child the ladder, saying with savage glee, "See here! first of all thou wilt be laid on that, and thy hands and feet will be tied. Next, the thumb-screw here will be put upon thee, which straightway will make the blood to spirt out at the tips of thy fingers; thou mayest see that they are still red with the blood of old Gussy Biehlke, who was burnt last year, and who, like thee, would not confess at first. If thou still wilt not confess, I shall next put these Spanish boots on thee, and should they be too large, I shall just drive in a wedge, so that the calf, which is now at the back of thy leg, will be driven to the front, and the blood will shoot out of thy feet, as when thou squeezest blackberries in a bag.

"Again, if thou wilt not yet confess — holla!" shouted he, and kicked open a door behind him, so that the whole vault shook, and my poor child fell upon her knees for fright. Before long two women brought in a bubbling caldron, full of boiling pitch and brimstone. This caldron the hell-hound ordered them to set down on the ground, and drew forth, from under the red cloak he wore, a goose's wing, wherefrom he plucked five or six quills, which he dipped into the boiling brimstone. After he had held them a while in the caldron he threw them upon the earth, where they twisted about and spirted the brimstone on all sides. And then he called to my poor child again, "See! these quills I shall throw upon thy white loins, and the burning brimstone will presently eat into thy flesh down to the very bones, so that thou wilt thereby have a foretaste of the joys which await thee in hell."

When he had spoken thus far, amid sneers and laughter, I was so overcome with rage that I sprang forth out of the corner where I stood leaning my trembling joints against an old barrel, and cried, "O, thou hellish dog! sayest thou this of thyself, or have others bidden thee?" Whereupon, however, the fellow gave me such a blow upon the breast that I fell backwards against the wall, and *Dom. Consul* called out in great wrath, "You old fool, if you needs must stay here, at any rate leave the constable in peace, for if not I will have you thrust out of the chamber forthwith. The constable has said no more than is his duty; and it will thus happen to thy child if she confess not, and if it appear that the foul fiend have given her some charm against the torture."[lvii] [158] Hereupon this hell-hound went on to speak to my poor child, without heeding me, save that he laughed in my face: "Look here! when thou hast thus been well shorn, ho, ho, ho! I shall pull thee up by means of these two rings in the floor and the roof, stretch thy arms above thy head, and bind them fast to the ceiling; whereupon I shall take these two torches, and hold them under thy shoulders, till thy skin will presently become like the rind of a smoked ham. Then thy hellish paramour will help thee no longer, and thou wilt confess the truth. And now thou hast seen and heard all that I shall do to thee, in the name of God, and by order of the magistrates."

And now *Dom. Consul* once more came forward and admonished her to confess the truth. But she abode by what she had said from the first; whereupon he delivered her over to the two women who had brought in the caldron, to strip her naked as she was born, and to clothe her in the black torture-shift; after which they were once more to lead her barefooted up the steps before the worshipful court. But one of these women was the Sheriff his housekeeper (the other was the impudent constable his wife), and my daughter said that she would not suffer herself to be touched save by honest women, and assuredly not by the housekeeper, and begged *Dom. Consul* to send for her maid, who was sitting in her prison reading the Bible, if he knew of no other decent woman at hand. Hereupon the housekeeper began to pour forth a wondrous deal of railing and ill words, but *Dom. Consul* rebuked her, and answered my daughter that he would

---

[lvii] It was believed that when witches endured the torture with unusual patience, or even slept during the operation, which, strange to say, frequently occurred, the devil had gifted them with insensibility to pain by means of an amulet which they concealed in some secret part of their persons. — Zedler's Universal Lexicon, vol. xliv., art. "Torture".

let her have her wish in this matter too, and bade the impudent constable his wife call the maid hither from out of the prison. After he had said this, he took me by the arm, and prayed me so long to go up with him, for that no harm would happen to my daughter as yet, that I did as he would have me.

Before long she herself came up, led between the two women, barefooted, and in the black torture-shift, but so pale that I myself should scarce have known her. The hateful constable, who followed close behind, seized her by the hand, and led her before the worshipful court.

Hereupon the admonitions began all over again, and *Dom. Consul* bade her look upon the brown spots that were upon the black shift, for that they were the blood of old wife Bichlke, and to consider that within a few minutes it would in like manner be stained with her own blood. Hereupon she answered, "I have considered that right well, but I hope that my faithful Saviour, who hath laid this torment upon me, being innocent, will likewise help me to bear it, as he helped the holy martyrs of old; for if these, through God's help, overcame by faith the torments inflicted on them by blind heathens, I also can overcome the torture inflicted on me by blind heathens, who, indeed, call themselves Christians, but who are more cruel than those of yore; for the old heathens only caused the holy virgins to be torn of savage beasts, but ye which have received the new commandment, 'That ye love one another; as your Saviour hath loved you, that ye also love one another. By this shall all men know that ye are his disciples' (St. John xiii.); yourselves will act the part of savage beasts, and tear with your own hands the body of an innocent maiden, your sister, who has never done aught to harm you. Do, then, as ye list, but have a care how ye will answer it to the highest Judge of all. Again, I say, the lamb feareth nought, for it is in the hand of the good Shepherd."

When my matchless child had thus spoken, *Dom. Consul* rose, pulled off the black skull-cap which he ever wore, because the top of his head was already bald, bowed to the court, and said, "We hereby make known to the worshipful court that the question ordinary and extraordinary of the stubborn and blaspheming witch, Mary Schweidler, is about to begin, in the name of the Father, and of the Son, and of the Holy Ghost. Amen."

Hereupon all the court rose save the Sheriff, who had got up before, and was walking uneasily up and down in the room. But of all that now follows, and of what I myself did, I remember not one word, but will relate it all as I have received it from my daughter and other *testes*,[159] and they have told me as follows: —

That when *Dom. Consul* after these words had taken up the hour-glass which stood upon the table, and walked on before, I would go with him, whereupon *Pastor Benzensis* first prayed me with many words and tears to desist from my purpose, and when that was of no avail my child herself stroked my cheeks, saying, "Father, have you ever read that the Blessed Virgin stood by when her guileless Son was scourged? Depart, therefore, from me. You shall stand by the pile whereon I am burned, that I promise you; for in like manner did the Blessed Virgin stand at the foot of the cross. But, now, go; go, I pray you, for you will not be able to bear it, neither shall I."

And when this also failed, *Dom. Consul* bade the constable seize me, and by main force lock me into another room; whereupon, however, I tore myself away, and fell at his feet, conjuring him by the wounds of Christ not to tear me from my child; that I would never forget his kindness and mercy, but pray for him day and night; nay, that at the day of judgment I would be his intercessor with God and the holy angels if that he would but let me go with my child; that I would be quite quiet, and not speak one single word, but that I must go with my child, etc.

This so moved the worthy man that he burst into tears, and so trembled with pity for me that the hour-glass fell from his hands and rolled right before the feet of the Sheriff, as though God himself would signify to him that his glass was soon to run out; and, indeed, he understood it right well, for he grew white as any chalk when he picked it up and gave it back to *Dom. Consul*. The latter at last gave way, saying that this day would make him ten years older; but he bade the impudent constable (who also went with us) lead me away if I made any *rumor*[160] during the torture. And hereupon the whole court went below, save the Sheriff, who said his head ached, and that he believed his old *malum*, the gout, was coming upon him again, wherefore he went into another chamber; *item, Pastor Benzensis* likewise departed.

Down in the vault the constable first brought in tables and chairs, whereon the court sat, and *Dom. Consul* also pushed a chair toward me, but I sat not thereon, but threw myself upon my knees in a corner. When this was done they began again with their vile admonitions, and as my child, like her guileless Saviour before His unrighteous judges, answered not a word, *Dom. Consul* rose up and bade the tall constable lay her on the torture-bench.

She shook like an aspen leaf when he bound her hands and feet; and when he was about to bind over her sweet eyes a nasty old filthy clout wherein my maid had seen him carry fish but the day before, and which was still all over shining scales, I perceived it, and pulled off my silken neckerchief, begging him to use that instead, which he did. Hereupon the thumb-screw was put on her, and she was once more asked whether she would confess freely, but she only shook her poor blinded head and sighed with her dying Saviour, "Eli, Eli, lama sabachthani?" and then in Greek, "Θεέ μου, Θεέ μου, ἵνα τί με ἐγκατέλιπες;"[lviii] Whereat *Dom. Consul* started back, and made the sign of the cross (for inasmuch as he knew no Greek, he believed, as he afterwards said himself, that she was calling upon the devil to help her), and then called to the constable with a loud voice, "Screw!"

[lviii] "My God, My God, why hast Thou forsaken me?" — Matthew 27. 46.

But when I heard this I gave such a cry that the whole vault shook; and when my poor child, who was dying of terror and despair, had heard my voice she first struggled with her bound hands and feet like a lamb that lies dying in the slaughter-house, and then cried out, "Loose me, and I will confess whatsoe'er you will." Hereat *Dom. Consul* so greatly rejoiced, that while the constable unbound her, he fell on his knees, and thanked God for having spared him this anguish. But no sooner was my poor desperate child unbound, and had laid aside her crown of thorns (I mean my silken neckerchief), than she jumped off the ladder, and flung herself upon me, who lay for dead in a corner in a deep swound.

This greatly angered the worshipful court, and when the constable had borne me away, *Rea* was admonished to make her confession according to promise. But seeing she was too weak to stand upon her feet, *Dom. Consul* gave her a chair to sit upon, although *Dom. Camerarius* grumbled thereat, and these were the chief questions which were put to her by order of the most honourable high central court, as *Dom. Consul* said, and which were registered *ad protocollum*.

Q. Whether she could bewitch?

R. Yes, she could bewitch.

Q. Who taught her to do so?

R. Satan himself.

Q. How many devils had she?

R. One devil was enough for her.

Q. What was this devil called?

Illa (considering). His name was *Disidaemonia*.[lix]

Hereat *Dom. Consul* shuddered, and said that that must be a very terrible devil indeed, for that he had never heard such a name before, and that she must spell it, so that *Scriba* might make no *error*; which she did, and he then went on as follows: —

Q. In what shape had he appeared to her?

R. In the shape of the Sheriff, and sometimes as a goat with terrible horns.

Q. Whether Satan had re-baptized her, and where?

R. In the sea.

Q. What name had he given her?

R. —.[lx]

Q. Whether any of the neighbors had been by when she was re-baptized, and which of them?

R. Hereupon my matchless child cast up her eyes towards heaven, as though doubting whether she should file old Lizzie or not, but at last she said, "No."

Q. She must have had sponsors; who were they? and what gift had they given her as christening money?

[lix] Δεισιδαιμονία — Superstition. What an extraordinary woman!

[lx] It was impossible to decipher this name in the MS.

R. There were none there save spirits; wherefore old Lizzie could see no one when she came and looked on at her re-baptism.

Q. Whether she had ever lived with the devil?

R. She never had lived anywhere save in her father's house.

She did not choose to understand. He meant whether she had ever played the wanton with Satan, and known him carnally? Hereupon she blushed, and was so ashamed that she covered her face with her hands, and presently began to weep and to sob: and as, after many questions, she gave no answer, she was again admonished to speak the truth, or that the executioner should lift her up on the ladder again. At last she said, "No!" which, howbeit, the worshipful court would not believe, and bade the executioner seize her again, whereupon she answered, "Yes!"

Q. Whether she had found the devil hot or cold?[161]

R. She did not remember which.

Q. Whether she had ever conceived by Satan, and given birth to a changeling, and of what shape?

R. No, never.

Q. Whether the foul fiend had given her any sign or mark about her body, and in what part thereof?

R. That the mark had already been seen by the worshipful court.

She was next charged with all the witchcraft done in the village, and owned to it all, save that she still said that she knew nought of old Seden his death, *item*, of little Paasch her sickness, nor, lastly, would she confess that she had, by the help of the foul fiend, raked up my crop or conjured the caterpillars into my orchard. And albeit they again threatened her with the question, and even ordered the executioner to lay her on the bench and put on the thumb-screw to frighten her, she remained firm and said, "Why should you torture me, seeing that I have confessed far heavier crimes than these, which it will not save my life to deny?"

Hereupon the worshipful court at last were satisfied, and suffered her to be lifted off the torture-bench, especially as she confessed the *articulus principalis*;[162] to wit, that Satan had really appeared to her on the mountain in the shape of a hairy giant. Of the storm and the frog, *item*, of the hedgehog, nothing was said, inasmuch as the worshipful court had by this time seen the folly of supposing that she could have brewed a storm while she quietly sat in the coach. Lastly, she prayed that it might be granted to her to suffer death clothed in the garments which she had worn when she went to greet the King of Sweden; *item*, that they would suffer her wretched father to be driven with her to the stake, and to stand by while she was burned, seeing that she had promised him this in the presence of the worshipful court.

Hereupon she was once more given into the charge of the tall constable, who was ordered to put her into a stronger and severer prison. But he had not led her out of the chamber before the Sheriff his bastard, whom he had had by the housekeeper, came into the vault with a drum, and kept drumming and crying out, "Come to the roast goose! come to the roast goose!" whereat *Dom. Consul* was exceeding wroth, and ran after him, but he could not catch him, seeing that the young varlet knew all the ins and outs of the vault. Without doubt it was the Lord who sent me the swound, so that I should be spared this fresh grief; wherefore to Him alone be honour and glory. Amen.

CHAPTER XXIV

How in my presence the devil fetched old Lizzie Kolken.

When I recovered from my above-mentioned swound, I found my host, his wife, and my old maid standing over me, and pouring warm beer down my throat. The faithful old creature shrieked for joy when I opened my eyes again, and then told me that my daughter had not suffered herself to be racked, but had freely confessed her crimes and filed herself as a witch. This seemed pleasant news to me in my misery, inasmuch as I deemed the death by fire to be a less heavy punishment than the torture. Howbeit when I would have prayed I could not, whereat I again fell into heavy grief and despair, fearing that the Holy Ghost had altogether turned away His face from me, wretched man that I was. And albeit the old maid, when she had seen this, came and stood before my bed and began to pray aloud to me; it was all in vain, and I remained a hardened sinner. But the Lord had pity upon me, although I deserved it not, insomuch that I presently fell into a deep sleep, and did not awake until next morning when the prayer-bell rang; and then I was once more able to pray, whereat I greatly rejoiced, and still thanked God in my heart, when my ploughman Claus Neels came in and told me that he had come yesterday to tell me about my oats, seeing that he had gotten them all in; and that the constable came with him who had been to fetch old Lizzie Kolken, inasmuch as the honourable high court had ordered her to be brought up for trial. Hereat the whole village rejoiced, but *Rea* herself laughed, and shouted, and sang, and told him and the constable by the way (for the constable had let her get up behind for a short time), that this should bring great luck to the Sheriff. They need only bring her up before the court, and in good sooth she would not hold her tongue within her teeth, but that all men should marvel at her confession; that such a court as that was a laughing-stock to her, and that she spat, *salvâ veniâ*, upon the whole brotherhood, *et cet.*

Upon hearing this I once more felt a strong hope, and rose to go to old Lizzie. But I was not quite dressed before she sent the impudent constable to beg that I would go to her with all speed and give her the sacrament, seeing that she had become very weak during the night. I had my own thoughts on the matter, and followed the constable as fast as I could, though not to give her the sacrament, as indeed anybody may suppose. But in my haste, I, weak old man that I was, forgot to take my witnesses with me; for all the misery I had hitherto suffered had so clouded my senses that it never once came into my head. None followed me save the impudent constable; and it will soon appear how that this villain had given himself over body and soul to Satan to destroy my child, whereas he might have saved her. For when he had opened the prison (it was the same cell wherein my child had first been shut up), we found old Lizzie lying on the ground on a truss of straw, with a broom for a pillow (as though she were to fly to hell upon it, as she no longer could fly to Blockula[163]), so that I shuddered when I caught sight of her.

Scarce was I come in when she cried out fearfully, "I'm a witch, I'm a witch! Have pity upon me, and give me the sacrament quick, and I will confess everything to you!" And when I said to her, "Confess, then!" she owned that she, with the help of the Sheriff, had contrived all the witchcraft in the village, and that my child was as innocent thereof as the blessed sun in heaven. Howbeit that the Sheriff had the greatest guilt, inasmuch as he was a warlock and a witch's priest, and had a spirit far stronger than hers, called Dudaim,[lxi] [164] which spirit had given her such a blow on the head in the night as she should never recover. This same Dudaim it was that had raked up the crops, heaped sand over the amber, made the storm, and dropped the frog into my daughter her lap; *item*, carried off her old goodman through the air.

And when I asked her how that could be, seeing that her goodman had been a child of God until very near his end, and much given to prayer; albeit I had indeed marvelled why he had other thoughts in his last illness; she answered that one day he had seen her spirit, which she kept in a chest, in the shape of a black cat, and whose name was Kit, and had threatened that he would tell me of it; whereupon she, being frightened, had caused her spirit to make him so ill that he despaired of ever getting over it. Thereupon she had comforted him, saying that she would presently heal him if he would deny God, who, as he well saw, could not help him. This he promised to do; and when she had straight-way made him quite hearty again, they took the silver which I had scraped off the new sacrament cup, and went by night down to the seashore, where he had to throw it into the sea with these words: "When this silver returns again to the chalice, then shall my soul return to God." Whereupon the Sheriff, who was by, re-baptized him in the name of Satan, and called him Jack. He had had no sponsors save only herself, old Lizzie. Moreover, that on St. John's Eve, when he went with

---

[lxi] This remarkable word occurs in Genesis 30. 15 ff. as the name of a plant which produces fruitfulness in women; but the commentators are by no means agreed as to its nature and its properties. The LXX render it by *Mandragoras*, which has been understood by the most eminent ancient and modern theologians to mean the mandrake (Alraunwurzel) so famous in the history of witchcraft. In many instances the devils, strangely enough, receive Christian names; thus the familiar spirit of old Lizzie is afterwards called Kit, *i.e.*, Christopher.

them to Blockula for the first time (the Herrenberg[lxii] was their Blockula), they had talked of my daughter, and Satan himself had sworn to the Sheriff that he should have her. For that he would show the old one (wherewith the villain meant God) what he could do, and that he would make the carpenter's son sweat for vexation (fie upon thee, thou arch villain, that thou couldst thus speak of my blessed Saviour!). Whereupon her old goodman had grumbled, and as they had never rightly trusted him, the spirit Dudaim one day flew off with him through the air by the Sheriff's order, seeing that her own spirit, called Kit, was too weak to carry him. That the same Dudaim had also been the woodpecker who afterwards 'ticed my daughter and old Paasch to the spot with his cries, in order to ruin her. But that the giant who had appeared on the Streckelberg was not a devil, but the young lord of Mellenthin himself, as her spirit, Kit, had told her.

And this she said was nothing but the truth, whereby she would live and die; and she begged me, for the love of God, to take pity upon her, and, after her repentant confession, to speak forgiveness of her sins, and to give her the Lord's Supper; for that her spirit stood there behind the stove, grinning like a rogue, because he saw that it was all up with her now. But I answered, "I would sooner give the sacrament to an old sow than to thee, thou accursed witch, who not only didst give over thine own husband to Satan, but hast likewise tortured me and my poor child almost unto death with pains like those of hell." Before she could make any answer, a loathsome insect, about as long as my finger, and with a yellow tail, crawled in under the door of the prison. When she espied it she gave a yell, such as I never before heard, and never wish to hear again. For once, when I was in Silesia, in my youth, I saw one of the enemy's soldiers spear a child before its mother's face, and I thought that a fearful shriek which the mother gave; but her cry was child's play to the cry of old Lizzie. All my hair stood on end, and her own red hair grew so stiff that it was like the twigs of the broom whereon she lay; and then she howled, "That is the spirit Dudaim, whom the accursed Sheriff has sent to me — the sacrament, for the love of God, the sacrament! — I will confess a great deal more — I have been a witch these thirty years! — the sacrament, the sacrament!" While she thus bellowed and flung about her arms and legs, the loathsome insect rose into the air, and buzzed and whizzed about her where she lay, insomuch that it was fearful to see and to hear. And this she-devil called by turns on God, on her spirit Kit, and on me, to help her, till the insect all of a sudden darted into her open jaws, whereupon she straightway gave up the ghost, and turned all black and blue like a blackberry.

[lxii] A hill near Coserow. In almost all trials of witches hills of this kind in the neighbourhood of the accused are mentioned, where the devil, on Walpurgis Night and St. John's Eve, feasts, dances, and wantons with them, and where warlock priests administer Satanic sacraments, which are mere mockeries of those of Divine institution.

I heard nothing more save that the window rattled, not very loud, but as though one had thrown a pea against it, whereby I straightway perceived that Satan had just flown through it with her soul. May the all-merciful God keep every mother's child from such an end, for the sake of Jesus Christ our blessed Lord and Saviour! Amen.

As soon as I was somewhat recovered, which, however, was not for a long time, inasmuch as my blood had turned to ice, and my feet were as stiff as a stake; I began to call out after the impudent constable, but he was no longer in the prison. Thereat I greatly marvelled, seeing that I had seen him there but just before the vermin crawled in, and straightway I suspected no good, as, indeed, it turned out; for when at last he came upon my calling him, and I told him to let this carrion be carted out which had just died in the name of the devil, he did as though he was amazed; and when I desired him that he would bear witness to the innocence of my daughter, which the old hag had confessed on her death-bed, he pretended to be yet more amazed, and said that he had heard nothing. This went through my heart like a sword, and I leaned against a pillar without, where I stood for a long time: but as soon as I was come to myself I went to *Dom. Consul*, who was about to go to Usedom and already sat in his coach. At my humble prayer he went back into the judgment-chamber with the *Camerarius* and the *Scriba*, whereupon I told all that had taken place, and how the wicked constable denied that he had heard the same. But they say that I talked a great deal of nonsense beside; among other things, that all the little fishes had swam into the vault to release my daughter. Nevertheless, *Dom. Consul*, who often shook his head, sent for the impudent constable, and asked him for his testimony. But the fellow pretended that as soon as he saw that old Lizzie wished to confess, he had gone away, so as not to get any more hard words, wherefore he had heard nothing. Hereupon I, as *Dom. Consul* afterwards told the pastor of Benz, clenched my fists and answered, "What, thou arch-rogue, didst thou not crawl about the room in the shape of a reptile?" whereupon he would hearken to me no longer, thinking me distraught, nor would he make the constable take an oath, but left me standing in the midst of the room, and got into his coach again.

Neither do I know how I got out of the room; but next morning when the sun rose, and I found myself lying in bed at Master Seep his ale-house, the whole *casus* seemed to me like a dream; neither was I able to rise, but lay a-bed all the blessed Saturday and Sunday, talking all manner of *allotria*.[165] It was not till towards evening on Sunday, when I began to vomit and threw up green bile (no wonder!), that I got somewhat better. About this time *Pastor Benzensis* came to my bedside, and told me how distractedly I had borne myself, but so comforted me from the word of God, that I was once more able to pray from my heart. May the merciful God reward my dear gossip,[166] therefore, at the day of judgment! For prayer is almost as brave a comforter as the Holy Ghost himself, from whom it comes; and I shall ever consider that so long as a man can still pray, his misfortunes are not unbearable, even though in all else "his flesh and his heart faileth" (Psalm 73).

CHAPTER XXV

*How Satan sifted me like wheat, whereas my
daughter withstood him right bravely.*

On Monday I left my bed betimes, and as I felt in passable good case, I went up to the castle to see whether I might peradventure get to my daughter, but I could not find either constable, albeit I had brought a few groats with me to give them as beer-money; neither would the folks that I met tell me where they were; *item*, the impudent constable his wife, who was in the kitchen making brimstone matches.[167] And when I asked her when her husband would come back, she said not before to-morrow morning early; *item*, that the other constable would not be here any sooner. Hereupon I begged her to lead me to my daughter herself, at the same time showing her the two groats; but she answered that she had not the keys, and knew not how to get at them: moreover, she said she did not know where my child was now shut up, seeing that I would have spoken to her through the door; *item*, the cook, the huntsman, and whomsoever else I met in my sorrow, said they knew not in what hole the witch might lie.

Hereupon I went all round about the castle, and laid my ear against every little window that looked as though it might be her window, and cried, "Mary, my child, where art thou?" *Item*, at every grating I found I kneeled down, bowed my head, and called in like manner into the vault below. But all in vain; I got no answer anywhere. The Sheriff at length saw what I was about, and came down out of the castle to me with a very gracious air, and, taking me by the hand, he asked me what I sought? But when I answered him that I had not seen my only child since last Thursday, and prayed him to show pity upon me, and let me be led to her, he said that could not be, but that I was to come up into his chamber, and talk further of the matter. By the way he said, "Well, so the old witch told you fine things about me, but you see how Almighty God has sent his righteous judgment upon her. She has long been ripe for the fire; but my great long-suffering, wherein a good magistrate should ever strive to be like unto the Lord, has made me overlook it till *datum*, and in return for my goodness she raises this outcry against me." And when I replied, "How does your Lordship know that the witch raised such an outcry against you?" he first began to stammer, and then said, "Why, you yourself charged me thereon before the judge. But I bear you no anger therefor, and God knows that I pity you, who are a poor, weak old man, and would gladly help you if I were able." Meanwhile he led me up four or five flights of stairs, so that I, old man that I am, could follow him no further, and stood still gasping for breath. But he took me by the hand and said, "Come, I must first show you how matters really stand, or I fear you will not accept my help, but will plunge yourself into destruction." Hereupon we stepped out upon a terrace at the top of the castle, which looked toward the water; and the villain went on to say, "Reverend Abraham, can you see well afar off?" and when I answered that I once could see very well, but that the many tears I had shed had now peradventure dimmed my eyes, he pointed to the Streckelberg, and said, "Do you, then, see nothing there?" *Ego*. "Nought save a black speck, which I cannot make out." *Ille*. "Know, then, that that is the pile whereon your daughter is to burn at ten o'clock to-morrow morning, and which the constables are now raising." When this hell-hound had thus spoken, I gave a loud cry and swounded. Oh, blessed Lord! I know not how I lived through such distress; thou alone didst strengthen me beyond nature, in order, "after so much weeping and wailing, to heap joys and blessings upon me; without thee I never could have lived through such misery: therefore to thy name ever be all honour and glory, O thou God of Israel!"[lxiii]

When I came again to myself I lay on a bed in a fine room, and perceived a taste in my mouth like wine. But as I saw none near me save the Sheriff, who held a pitcher in his hand, I shuddered and closed mine eyes, considering what I should say or do. This he presently observed, and said, "Do not shudder thus; I mean well by you, and only wish to put a question to you, which you must answer me on your conscience as a priest. Say, reverend Abraham, which is the greater sin, to commit whoredom, or to take the lives of two persons?" and when I answered him, "To take the lives of two persons," he went on, "Well, then, is not that what your stubborn child is about to do? Rather than give herself up to me, who have ever desired to save her, and who can even yet save her, albeit her pile is now being raised, she will take away her own life and that of her wretched father, for I scarcely think that you, poor man, will outlive this sorrow. Wherefore do you, for God his sake, persuade her to think better of it while I am yet able to save her. For know that about ten miles from hence I have a small house in the midst of the forest, where no human being ever goes; thither will I send her this very night, and you may dwell there with her all the days of your life, if so it please you. You shall live as well as you can possibly desire, and to-morrow morning I will spread a report betimes that the witch and her father have run away together during the night, and that nobody knows whither they are gone." Thus spake the serpent to me, as whilom to our mother Eve; and, wretched sinner that I am, the tree of death which he showed me seemed to me also to be a tree of life, so pleasant was it to the eye. Nevertheless I answered, "My child will never save her miserable life by doing aught to peril the salvation of her soul." But now, too, the serpent was more cunning than all the beasts of the field (especially such an old fool as I), and spake thus: "Why, who would have her peril the salvation of her soul? Reverend Abraham, must I teach you Scripture? Did not our Lord Christ pardon Mary Magdalene, who lived in open whoredom? and did he not speak forgiveness to the poor adulteress who had committed a still greater *crimen*?

[lxiii] Tobit 3. 22–23, Luther's Version.

nay, more, doth not St. Paul expressly say that the harlot Rahab was saved, Hebrews 11? *item*, St. James 2 says the same. But where have ye read that any one was saved who had wantonly taken her own life and that of her father? Wherefore, for the love of God, persuade your child not to give herself up, body and soul, to the devil, by her stubbornness, but to suffer herself to be saved while it is yet time. You can abide with her, and pray away all the sins she may commit, and likewise aid me with your prayers, who freely own that I am a miserable sinner, and have done you much evil, though not so much evil by far, reverend Abraham, as David did to Uriah, and he was saved, notwithstanding he put the man to a shameful death, and afterwards lay with his wife.[168] Wherefore I, poor man, likewise hope to be saved, seeing that my desire for your daughter is still greater than that which this David felt for Bathsheba; and I will gladly make it all up to you twofold as soon as we are in my cottage."

When the tempter had thus spoken, methought his words were sweeter than honey, and I answered, "Alas, my lord, I am ashamed to appear before her face with such a proposal." Whereupon he straightway said, "Then do you write it to her; come, here is pen, ink, and paper."

And now, like Eve, I took the fruit and ate, and gave it to my child that she might eat also; that is to say, that I recapitulated on paper all that Satan had prompted, but in the Latin tongue, for I was ashamed to write it in mine own; and lastly I conjured her not to take away her own life and mine, but to submit to the wondrous will of God. Neither were mine eyes opened when I had eaten (that is, written), nor did I perceive that the ink was gall instead of honey, and I translated my letter to the Sheriff (seeing that he understood no Latin), smiling like a drunken man the while; whereupon he clapped me on the shoulder, and after I had made fast the letter with his signet, he called his huntsman, and gave it to him to carry to my daughter; *item*, he sent her pen, ink, and paper, together with his signet, in order that she might answer it forthwith.

Meanwhile he talked with me right graciously, praising my child and me, and made me drink to him many times from his great pitcher, wherein was most goodly wine; moreover, he went to a cupboard and brought out cakes for me to eat, saying that I should now have such every day. But when the huntsman came back in about half an hour with her answer, and I had read the same, then, first, were mine eyes opened, and I knew good and evil; had I had a fig-leaf, I should have covered them therewith for shame; but as it was, I held my hand over them and wept so bitterly that the Sheriff waxed very wroth, and cursing bade me tell him what she had written. Thereupon I interpreted the letter to him, the which I likewise place here, in order that all may see my folly, and the wisdom of my child. It was as follows:[lxiv] —

[lxiv] It is evidently written by a female hand, and probably the original letter; there are, however, no traces of sealing-wax or wax upon it, whence I infer that it was sent open, which, from its

"IESVS!

Pater infelix!

Ego cras non magis pallebo rogum aspectura, et rogus non magis erubescet, me suscipiens, quam pallui et iterum erubescui, literas tuas legens. Quid? et te, pium patrem, pium servum Domini, ita Satanas sollicitavit, ut communionem facias cum inimicis meis, et non intelligas: in tali vitâ esse mortem, et in tali morte vitam? Scilicet si clementissimus Deus Mariae Magdalenae aliisque ignovit, ignovit, quia resipiscerent ob carnis debilitatem, et non iterum peccarent. Et ego peccarem cum quavis detestatione carnis, et non semel, sed iterum atque iterum sine reversione usque ad mortem? Quomodo clementissimus Deus haec sceleratissima ignoscere posset? infelix pater! recordare quid mihi dixisti de sanctis martyribus et virginibus Domini, qua omnes mallent vitam quam pudicitiam perdere. His et ego sequar, et sponsus meus, Jesus Christus, et mihi miserae, ut spero, coronam aeternam dabit, quamvis eum non minus offendi ob debilitatem carnis ut Maria, et me sontem declaravi, cum insons sum. Fac igitur, ut valeas et ora pro me apud Deum et non apud Satanam, ut et ego mox coram Deo pro te orare possim.

MARIA S., captiva."

---

being written in a foreign language, would have been perfectly safe. I have purposely left the few grammatical errors it contains, as the smallest alteration of this gem would appear to me in the light of a treason against the character of this incomparable woman.

Translation.

Jesus!

Unhappy Father!

I shall not to-morrow grow more pale at sight of the pile, nor will the pile grow more red on receiving me, than I grew pale and then red while reading thy letter. How? and hath Satan so tempted three, pious father, pious servant of the Lord, that thou hast made common cause with mine enemies, and that thou understandest not that in such life is death, and in such death is life? For if the all-merciful God forgave Mary Magdalene and other sinners, He forgave them because they repented of the weakness of their flesh, and sinned not again. And shall I sin with so great abhorrence of the flesh, and that not once but again and again without return even until death? How could the all-merciful God forgive this to the vilest of women? Unhappy father! remember what thou hast told me of the holy martyrs, and of the virgins of the Lord, who all lost their lives rather than lose their chastity. These will I follow, hoping that my spouse Jesus Christ will also give to wretched me a crown of eternal glory, although, indeed, I have not less offended through the weakness of the flesh than Mary, declaring myself to be guilty, whereas I am innocent. Be strong, therefore, and pray for me unto God, and not unto the devil, so that I may soon pray for thee before the face of God.

Mary S., a Prisoner.

When the Sheriff heard this, he flung the pitcher which he held in his hand to the ground, so that it flew in pieces, and cried, "The cursed devil's whore! the constable shall make her squeak for this a good hour longer"; with many more such things beside, which he said in his malice, and which I have now forgotten; but he soon became quite gracious again, and said, "She is foolish; do you go to her and see whether you cannot persuade her to her own good as well as yours; the huntsman shall let you in, and should the fellow listen, give him a good box on the ears in my name; do you hear, reverend Abraham? Go now forthwith and bring me back an answer as quickly as possible!" I therefore followed the huntsman, who led me into a vault where was no light save what fell through a hole no bigger than a crown-piece; and here my daughter sat upon her bed and wept. Any one may guess that I straightway began to weep too, and was no better able to speak than she. We thus lay mute in each other's arms for a long time, until I at last begged her to forgive me for my letter, but of the Sheriff his message I said nought, although I had purposed so to do. But before long we heard the Sheriff himself call down into the vault from above, "What (and here he gave me a heavy curse) are you doing there so long? Come up this moment, reverend Johannes!" Thus I had scarce time to give her one kiss before the huntsman came back with the keys and forced us to part; albeit we had as yet scarcely spoken, save that I had told her in a few words what had happened with old Lizzie. It would be hard to believe into what grievous anger the Sheriff fell when I told him that my daughter remained firm and would not hearken unto him; he struck me on the breast, and said, "Go to the devil then, thou infamous parson!" and when I turned myself away and would have gone, he pulled me back, and said, "If thou breathest but one word of all that has passed, I will have thee burnt too, thou grey-headed old father of a witch; so look to it!" Hereupon I plucked up a heart, and answered that that would be the greatest joy to me, especially if I could be burnt to-morrow with my child. Hereunto he made no answer, but clapped to the door behind me. Well, clap the door as thou wilt, I greatly fear that the just God will one day clap the doors of heaven in thy face!

CHAPTER XXVI

How I received the Holy Sacrament with my daughter and the old maidservant, and how she was then led for the last time before the court, with the drawn sword and the outcry, to receive sentence.

Now any one would think that during that heavy Tuesday night I should not have been able to close mine eyes; but know, dear reader, that the Lord can do more than we can ask or understand, and that his mercy is new every morning. For toward daybreak I fell asleep as quietly as though I had had no care upon my heart; and when I awoke I was able to pray more heartily than I had done for a long time; so that, in the midst of my tribulation, I wept for joy at such great mercy from the Lord. But I prayed for nought save that he would endow my child with strength and courage to suffer the martyrdom he had laid upon her with Christian patience, and to send his angel to me, woeful man, so to pierce my heart with grief when I should see my child burn that it might straightway cease to beat, and I might presently follow her. And thus I still prayed when the maid came in all dressed in black, and with the silken raiment of my sweet lamb hanging over her arm; and she told me, with many tears, that the dead-bell had already tolled from the castle tower, for the first time, and that my child had sent for her to dress her, seeing that the court was already come from Usedom, and that in about two hours she was to set out on her last journey. Moreover, she had sent her word that she was to take her some blue and yellow flowers for a garland; wherefore she asked me what flowers she should take; and seeing that a jar filled with fire lilies and forget-me-nots stood in my window, which she had placed there yesterday, I said, "Thou canst gather no better flowers for her than these, wherefore do thou carry them to her, and tell her that I will follow thee in about half an hour, in order to receive the sacrament with her." Hereupon the faithful old creature prayed me to suffer her to go to the sacrament with us, the which I promised her. And scarce had I dressed myself and put on my surplice when *Pastor Benzensis* came in at the door and fell upon my neck, weeping, and as mute as a fish. As soon as he came to his speech again he told me of the great *miraculum* (*daemonis* I mean)[169] which had befallen at the burial of old Lizzie. For that, just as the bearers were about to lower the coffin into the grave, a noise was heard therein, as though of a carpenter boring through a deal board; wherefore they thought the old hag must be come to life again, and opened the coffin. But there she lay as before, all black and blue in the face, and as cold as ice; but her eyes had started wide open, so that all were horror-stricken, and expected some devilish apparition; and, indeed, a live rat presently jumped out of the coffin and ran into a skull which lay beside the grave. Thereupon they all ran away, seeing that old Lizzie had ever been in evil repute as a witch. Howbeit at last he himself went near the grave again, whereupon the rat disappeared, and all the others took courage and followed him. This the man told me, and any one may guess that this was in fact Satan, who had flown down the hag her throat as an insect, whereas his proper shape was that of a rat: albeit I wonder what he could so long have been about in the carrion; unless indeed it were that the evil spirits are as fond of all that is loathsome as the angels of God are of all that is fair and lovely. Be that as it may; *Summa*: I was not a little shocked at what he told me, and asked him what he now thought of the Sheriff? whereupon he shrugged his shoulders, and said that he had indeed been a wicked fellow as long as he could remember him, and that it was full ten years since he had given him any first-fruits; but that he did not believe that he was a warlock, as old Lizzie had said. For although he had indeed never been to the table of the Lord in his church, he had heard that he often went at Stettin, with his Princely Highness the Duke, and that the pastor at the castle church had shown him the entry in his communion-book.[170] Wherefore he likewise could not believe that he had brought this misery upon my daughter, if she were innocent, as the hag had said; besides, that my daughter had freely confessed herself a witch. Hereupon I answered, that she had done that for fear of the torture; but that she was not afraid of death; whereupon I told him, with many sighs, how the sheriff had yesterday tempted me, miserable and unfaithful servant, to evil, insomuch that I had been willing to sell my only child to him and to Satan, and was not worthy to receive the sacrament to-day. Likewise how much more steadfast a faith my daughter had than I, as he might see from her letter, which I still carried in my pocket; herewith I gave it into his hand, and when he had read it, he sighed as though he had been himself a father, and said, "Were this true, I should sink into the earth for sorrow; but come, brother, come, that I may prove her faith myself."

Hereupon we went up to the castle, and on our way we found the greensward before the hunting-lodge, *item*, the whole space in front of the castle, already crowded with people, who, nevertheless, were quite quiet as we went by: we gave our names again to the huntsman. (I have never been able to remember his name, seeing that he was a Polak; he was not, however, the same fellow who wooed my child, and whom the Sheriff had therefore turned off.) The man presently ushered us into a fine large room, whither my child had been led when taken out of her prison. The maid had already dressed her, and she looked lovely as an angel. She wore the chain of gold with the effigy round her neck again, *item*, the garland in her hair, and she smiled as we entered, saying, "I am ready!" Whereat the reverend Martinus was sorely angered and shocked, saying, "Ah, thou ungodly woman, let no one tell me further of thine innocence! Thou art about to go to the holy sacrament, and from thence to death, and thou flauntest as a child of this world about to go to the dancing-room." Whereupon she answered and said, "Be not wroth with me, dear godfather, because that I would go into the presence of my good King of Heaven in the same garments wherein I appeared some time since before the good King of Sweden. For it strengthens my weak and trembling flesh, seeing I hope that my righteous Saviour will in like manner take me to his heart, and will also hand his effigy upon my neck when I stretch out my hands to him in all humility, and recite my *carmen*, saying, 'O Lamb of God, innocently slain upon the cross, give my thy peace, O Jesu!'" These words softened my dear gossip, and he spoke, saying, "Ah, child, child, I thought to have reproached thee, but thou hast constrained me to weep with thee: art thou, then, indeed innocent?" "Verily," said she, "to you, my honoured godfather, I may now own that I am innocent, as truly as I trust that God will aid me in my last hour through Jesus Christ. Amen."

When the maid heard this, she made such outcries that I repented that I had suffered her to be present, and we all had enough to do to comfort her from the word of God till she became somewhat more tranquil; and when this was done, my dear gossip thus spake to my child: "If, indeed, thou dost so steadfastly maintain thine innocence, it is my duty, according to my conscience as a priest, to inform the worshipful court thereof"; and he was about to leave the room. But she withheld him, and fell upon the ground and clasped his knees, saying, "I beseech you, by the wounds of Jesus, to be silent. They would stretch me on the rack again, and uncover my nakedness, and I, wretched weak woman, would in such torture confess all that they would have me, especially if my father again be there, whereby both my soul and my body are tortured at once: wherefore stay, I pray you, stay; is it, then, a misfortune to die innocent, and is it not better to die innocent than guilty?"

My good gossip at last gave way, and after standing awhile and praying to himself, he wiped away his tears, and then spake the exhortation to confession, in the words of Isaiah 43. 1–2, "But now thus saith the Lord that created thee, O Jacob, and he that formed thee, O Israel, Fear not; for I have redeemed thee, I have called thee by thy name; thou art mine. When thou passest through the waters, I will be with thee; and through the rivers, they shall not overflow thee: when thou walkest through the fire, thou shalt not be burned, neither shall the flame kindle upon thee. For I am the Lord thy God, the Holy One of Israel, thy Saviour."

And when he had ended this comfortable address, and asked her whether she would willingly bear until her last hour that cross which the most merciful God according to his unsearchable will had laid upon her, she spake such beautiful words that my gossip afterwards said he should not forget them so long as he should live, seeing that he had never witnessed a bearing at once so full of faith and joy, and withal so deeply sorrowful. She spake after this manner: "Oh, holy cross, which my Jesus hath sanctified by his innocent suffering; oh, dear cross, which is laid upon me by the hand of a merciful Father; oh, blessed cross, whereby I am made like unto my Lord Jesus, and am called unto eternal glory and blessedness: how! shall I not willingly bear thee, thou sweet cross of my bridegroom, of my brother?" The reverend Johannes had scarce given us absolution, and after this, with many tears, the holy sacrament, when we heard a loud trampling upon the floor, and presently the impudent constable looked into the room and asked whether we were ready, seeing that the worshipful court was now waiting for us; and when he had been told that we were ready, my child would have first taken leave of me, but I forbade her, saying, "Not so; thou knowest that which thou hast promised me; … 'and whither thou goest I will go, and where thou lodgest I will lodge: … where thou diest will I die …'[lxv] if that the Lord, as I hope, will hear the ardent sighs of my poor soul." Hereupon she let me

---

[lxv] Ruth 1. 16.

go, and embraced only the old maid-servant, thanking her for all the kindness she had shown her from her youth up, and begging her not to go with her to make her death yet more bitter by her cries. The faithful old creature was unable for a long time to say a word for tears. Howbeit at last she begged forgiveness of my child for that she unwittingly accused her, and said, that out of her wages she had bought five pounds' weight of flax to hasten her death; that the shepherd of Pudgla had that very morning taken it with him to Coserow, and that she should wind it closely round her body; for that she had seen how old wife Schurne, who was burnt in Liepe, had suffered great torments before she came to her death, by reason of the damp wood.

But ere my child could thank her for this, the dreadful outcry of blood began in the judgment-chamber; for a voice cried as loudly as might be, "Woe upon the accursed witch, Mary Schweidler, because that she hath fallen off from the living God!"[171] Then all the folk without cried, "Woe upon the accursed witch!" When I heard this I fell back against the wall, but my sweet child stroked my cheeks with her darling hands, and said, "Father, father, do but remember that the people likewise cried out against the innocent Jesus, 'Crucify him, crucify him!' Shall not we then drink of the cup which our Heavenly Father hath prepared for us?"[172]

Hereupon the door opened, and the constable walked in, amid a great tumult among the people, holding a drawn sword in his hand, which he bowed thrice before my child, and cried, "Woe upon the accursed witch, Mary Schweidler, because that she hath fallen off from the living God!" and all the folks in the hall and without the castle cried as loud as they could, "Woe upon the accursed witch!"

Hereupon he said, "Mary Schweidler, come before the high and worshipful court to hear sentence of death passed upon thee!" Whereupon she followed him with us two miserable men (for *Pastor Benzensis* was no less cast down than myself). As for the old maid-servant, she lay on the ground for dead.

After we had with great pains pushed our way through all the people, the constable stood still before the open judgment-chamber, and once more bowed his sword before my child and cried for the third time, "Woe upon the accursed witch, Mary Schweidler, because that she hath fallen off from the living God!" And all the people, as well as the cruel judges themselves, cried as loud as they could, "Woe upon the accursed witch!"

When we had entered the room, *Dom. Consul* first asked my worthy gossip whether the witch had abode by her free avowal in confession; whereupon, after considering a short time, he answered, that he had best ask herself, for there she stood. According, taking up a paper which lay before him on the table, he spake as follows: — "Mary Schweidler, now that thou hast confessed, and received the holy and most honourable sacrament of the Lord's Supper, answer me once again these following questions: —

"1. Is it true that thou hast fallen off from the living God and given thyself up to Satan?

"2. Is it true that thou hadst a spirit called *Disidaemonia*, who re-baptized thee and carnally knew thee?

"3. Is it true that thou hast done all manner of mischief to the cattle?

"4. Is it true that Satan appeared to thee on the Streckelberg in the likeness of a hairy giant?"

When she had with many sighs said "Yes" to all these questions, he rose, took a wand in one hand and a second paper in the other, put his spectacles on his nose, and said, "Now, then, hear thy sentence." (This sentence I since copied: he would not let me see the other *Acta*, but pretended that they were at Wolgast. The sentence, however, was word for word as follows.)

"We, the Sheriff and the Justices appointed to serve the high and worshipful criminal court. Inasmuch as Mary Schweidler, the daughter of Abraham Schweidlerus, the pastor of Coserow, hath, after the appointed inquisition, repeatedly made free confession that she hath a devil named *Disidaemonia*, the which did re-baptize her in the sea, and did also know her carnally; *item*, that she by his help did mischief to the cattle; that he also appeared to her on the Streckelberg in the likeness of a hairy giant. We do therefore by these presents make known and direct that *Rea* be first duly torn four times on each breast with red-hot iron pincers, and after that be burned to death by fire, as a rightful punishment to herself and a warning to others. Nevertheless we, in pity for her youth, are pleased of our mercy to spare her the tearing with red-hot pincers, so that she shall only suffer death by the simple punishment of fire. Wherefore she is hereby condemned and judged accordingly on the part of the criminal court.

"*Publicatum* at the castle of Pudgla, the 30th day *mensis Augusti, anno Salutis* 1630."[lxvi]

As he spake the last word he brake his wand in two and threw the pieces before the feet of my innocent lamb,[173] saying to the constable, "Now, do your duty!" But so many folks, both men and women, threw themselves on the ground to seize the pieces of the wand (seeing they are said to be good for the gout in the joints, *item*, for cattle when troubled with lice), that the constable fell to the earth over a woman who was on her knees before him, and his approaching death was

---

[lxvi] Readers who are unacquainted with the atrocious administration of justice in those days, will be surprised at this rapid and arbitrary mode of proceeding. But I have seen authentic witch-trials wherein a mere notary condemned the accused to the torture and to death without the smallest hesitation; and it may be considered as a mark of humanity whenever the acts on which judgement was given were sent to an university, or to some other tribunal. For the sentence of death appears to have been almost invariably passed by the inferior courts, and no appeal seems to have been possible; indeed in these affairs their worships, as in this case, usually made incredible haste, which, it must be admitted, is perhaps the only good quality which the modern courts of justice might borrow from the old ones.

thus foreshadowed to him by the righteous God. Something of the same sort likewise befell the Sheriff now for the second time; for when the worshipful court rose, throwing down tables, stools, and benches, a table, under which two boys were fighting for the pieces of the wand, fell right upon his foot, whereupon he flew into a violent rage, and threatened the people with his fist, saying that they should have fifty right good lashes a-piece, both men and women, if they were not quiet forthwith, and did not depart peaceably out of the room. This frighted them, and after the people were gone out into the street, the constable took a rope out of his pocket, wherewith he bound my lamb her hands so tightly behind her back that she cried aloud; but when she saw how this wrung my heart, she straightway constrained herself and said, "Oh, father, remember that it fared no better with the blessed Saviour!" Howbeit, when my dear gossip, who stood behind her, saw that her little hands, and more especially her nails, had turned black and blue, he spoke for her to the worshipful court, whereupon the abominable Sheriff only said, "Oh, let her be; let her feel what it is to fall off from the living God." But *Dom. Consul* was more merciful, inasmuch as, after feeling the cords, he bade the constable bind her hands less cruelly and slacken the rope a little, which accordingly he was forced to do. But my dear gossip was not content herewith, and begged that she might sit in the cart without being bound, so that she should be able to hold her hymn-book, for he had summoned the school to sing a hymn by the way for her comfort, and he was ready to answer for it with his own head that she should not escape out of the cart. Moreover; it is the custom for fellows with pitchforks always to go with the carts wherein condemned criminals, and more especially witches, are carried to execution. But this the cruel Sheriff would not suffer, and the rope was left upon her hands, and the impudent constable seized her by the arm and led her from the judgment-chamber. But in the hall we saw a great *scandalum*,[174] which again pierced my very heart. For the housekeeper and the impudent constable his wife were fighting for my child her bed, and her linen, and wearing apparel, which the housekeeper had taken for herself, and which the other woman wanted to have. The latter now called to her husband to help her, whereupon he straightway let go my daughter and struck the housekeeper on her mouth with his fist, so that the blood ran out therefrom, and she shrieked and wailed fearfully to the Sheriff, who followed us with the court. He threatened them both in vain, and said that when he came back he would inquire into the matter and give to each her due share. But they would not hearken to this, until my daughter asked *Dom. Consul* whether every dying person, even a condemned criminal, had power to leave his goods and chattels to whomsoever he would? and when he answered, "Yes, all but the clothes, which belong of right to the executioner," she said, "Well, then, the constable may take my clothes, but none shall have my bed save my faithful old maid-servant Ilse!" Hereupon the housekeeper began to curse and revile my child loudly, who heeded her not, but stepped out at the door toward the cart, where there stood so many people that nought could be seen save head against head. The folks crowded about us so tumultuously that the Sheriff, who, meanwhile, had mounted his grey horse, constantly smote them right and left across their eyes with his riding-whip, but they nevertheless would scarce fall back. Howbeit, at length he cleared the way, and when about ten fellows with long pitchforks, who for the most part also had rapiers at their sides, had placed themselves round about our cart, the constable lifted my daughter up into it, and bound her fast to the rail. Old Paasch, who stood by, lifted me up, and my dear gossip was likewise forced to be lifted in, so weak had he become from all the distress. He motioned his sexton, Master Krekow, to walk before the cart with the school, and bade him from time to time lead a verse of the goodly hymn, "On God alone I rest my fate,"[75] which he promised to do. And here I will also note, that I myself sat down upon the straw by my daughter, and that our dear confessor the reverend Martinus sat backwards. The constable was perched up behind with his drawn sword. When all this was done, *item*, the court mounted up into another carriage, the Sheriff gave the order to set out.

CHAPTER XXVII

Of that which befell us by the way: Item, of the fearful death of the sheriff at the mill.

We met with many wonders by the way, and with great sorrow; for hard by the bridge, over the brook which runs into the Schmolle,[lxvii] stood the housekeeper her hateful boy, who beat a drum and cried aloud, "Come to the roast goose! come to the roast goose!" whereupon the crowd set up a loud laugh, and called out after him, "Yes, indeed, to the roast goose! to the roast goose!" Howbeit, when Master Krekow led the second verse the folks became somewhat quieter again, and most of them joined in singing it from their books, which they had brought with them. But when he ceased singing awhile the noise began again as bad as before. Some cried out, "The devil hath given her these clothes, and hath adorned her after that fashion"; and seeing the Sheriff had ridden on before, they came close round the cart, and felt her garments, more especially the women and young maidens. Others, again, called loudly, as the young varlet had done, "Come to the roast goose! come to the roast goose!" whereupon one fellow answered, "She will not let herself be roasted yet; mind ye that: she will quench the fire!" This, and much filthiness beside, which I may not for very shame write down, we were forced to hear, and it especially cut me to the heart to hear a fellow swear that he would have some of her ashes, seeing he had not been able to get any of the wand,

---

[lxvii] A lake near Pudgla.

and that nought was better for the fever and the gout than the ashes of a witch. I motioned the *Custos* to begin singing again, whereupon the folks were once more quiet for a while — *i.e.*, for so long as the verse lasted; but afterwards they rioted worse than before. But we were now come among the meadows, and when my child saw the beauteous flowers which grew along the sides of the ditches, she fell into deep thought, and began again to recite aloud the sweet song of St. Augustinus as follows: —[176]

> Flos perpetuus rosarum ver agit perpetuum,
> Candent lilia, rubescit crocus, sudat balsamum,
> Virent prata, vernant sata, rivi mellis influunt,
> Pigmentorum spirat odor liquor et aromatum,
> Pendent poma floridorum non lapsura nemorum,
> Non alternat luna vices, sol vel cursus syderum,
> Agnus est faelicis urbis lumen inocciduum.[lxviii]

By this *Casus*[177] we gained that all the folk ran cursing away from the cart, and followed us at the distance of a good musket-shot, thinking that my child was calling on Satan to help her. Only one lad, of about five-and-twenty, whom, however, I did not know, tarried a few paces behind the cart, until his father came, and seeing he would not go away willingly, pushed him into the ditch, so that he sank up to his loins in the water. Thereat even my poor child smiled, and asked me whether I did not know any more Latin hymns wherewith to keep the stupid and foul-mouthed people still further from us. But, dear reader, how could I then have been able to recite Latin hymns, even had I known any? But my *confrater*, the reverend Martinus, knew such an one; albeit it is indeed heretical; nevertheless, seeing that it above measure pleased my child, and that she made him repeat to her sundry verses thereof three and four times, until she could say them after him, I said nought; otherwise I have ever been very severe against aught that is heretical. Howbeit I comforted myself therewith that our Lord God would forgive her in consideration of her ignorance. And the first line ran as follows: — *Dies irae, dies illa.*[lxix] [178] But these two verses pleased her more than all the rest, and she recited them many times with great edification, wherefore I will insert them here.

[lxviii] Around them, bright with endless Spring, perpetual roses bloom,
  Warm balsams gratefully exude luxurious perfume;
  Red crocuses, and lilies white, shine dazzling in the sun;
  Green meadows yield them harvests green, and streams with honey run;
  Unbroken droop the laden boughs, with heavy fruitage bent,
  Of incense and of odours strange the air is redolent:
  And neither sun, nor moon, nor stars dispense their changeful light,
  But the Lamb's eternal glory makes the happy city bright!

[lxix] Day of wrath, that dreadful day; one of the most beautiful of the Catholic hymns.

Judex ergo cum sedebit
Quidquid latet apparebit,
Nil inultum remanebit:
Item,
Rex tremendae majestatis!
Qui salvandos salvas gratis,
Salva me, fons pietatis![lxx] 179

When the men with the pitchforks, who were round about the cart, heard this, and at the same time saw a heavy storm coming up from the Achterwater,[lxxi] they straightway thought no other but that my child had made it; and, moreover, the folk behind cried out, "The witch hath done this; the damned witch hath done this!" and all the ten, save one, who stayed behind, jumped over the ditch, and ran away. But *Dom. Consul*, who, together with the worshipful court, drove behind us, no sooner saw this than he called to the constable, "What is the meaning of all this?" Whereupon the constable cried aloud to the Sheriff, who was a little way on before us, but who straightway turned him about, and when he had heard the cause, called after the fellows that he would hang them all up on the first tree, and feed his falcons with their flesh, if they did not return forthwith. This threat had its effect; and when they came back he gave each of them about half a dozen strokes with his riding-whip, whereupon they tarried in their places, but as far off from the cart as they could for the ditch.

Meanwhile, however, the storm came up from the southward, with thunder, lightning, hail, and such a wind, as though the all-righteous God would manifest his wrath against these ruthless murderers; and the tops of the lofty beeches around us were beaten together like besoms, so that our cart was covered with leaves as with hail, and no one could hear his own voice for the noise. This happened just as we were entering the forest from the convent dam, and the Sheriff now rode close behind us, beside the coach wherein was *Dom. Consul*. Moreover, just as we were crossing the bridge over the mill-race, we were seized by the blast, which swept up a hollow from the Achterwater with such force that we conceived it must drive our cart down the abyss, which was at least forty feet deep or more; and seeing that, at the same time, the horses did as though they were upon ice, and could not stand, the driver halted to let the storm pass over, the which the Sheriff no sooner perceived than he galloped up and bade him go

---

[lxx] The judge ascends his awful throne,
   He makes each secret sin be known,
   And all with shame confess their own.

   Thou mighty formidable king!
   Thou mercy's unexhausted spring,
   Some comfortable pity bring. — *Old Version*.

[lxxi] A wash formed by the river Peene.

on forthwith. Whereupon the man flogged on the horses, but they slipped about after so strange a fashion that our guards with the pitchforks fell back, and my child cried aloud for fear; and when we were come to the place where the great waterwheel turned just below us, the driver fell with his horse, which broke one of its legs. Then the constable jumped down from the cart, but straightway fell too on the slippery ground; *item*, the driver, after getting on his legs again, fell a second time. Hereupon the Sheriff, with a curse, spurred on his grey charger, which likewise began to slip as our horses had also done. Nevertheless, he came sliding towards us, without, however, falling down; and when he saw that the horse with the broken leg still tried to get up, but always straightway fell again on the slippery ground, he hallooed and beckoned the fellows with pitchforks to come and unharness the mare; *item*, to push the cart over the bridge, lest it should be carried down the precipice. Presently a long flash of lightning shot into the water below us, followed by a clap of thunder so sudden and so awful that the whole bridge shook, and the Sheriff his horse (our horses stood quite still) started back a few paces, lost its footing, and, together with its rider, shot headlong down upon the great mill-wheel below, whereupon a fearful cry arose from all those that stood behind us on the bridge. For a while nought could be seen for the white foam, until the Sheriff his legs and body were borne up into the air by the wheel, his head being stuck fast between the fellies; and thus, fearful to behold, he went round and round upon the wheel. Naught ailed the grey charger, which swam about in the mill-pond below. When I saw this I seized the hand of my innocent lamb, and cried, "Behold, Mary, our Lord God yet liveth! 'and he rode upon a cherub, and did fly; yea, he did fly upon the wings of the wind. Then did he beat them small as the dust before the wind; he did cast them out as the dirt in the streets.'[lxxii] Look down, and see what the Almighty God hath done." While she hereupon raised her eyes towards heaven with a sigh, we heard *Dom. Consul* calling out behind us as loudly as he could: and seeing that none could understand his words for the fearful storm and the tumult of the waters, he jumped down from the coach, and would have crossed the bridge on foot, but straightway he fell upon his nose, so that it bled, and he crept back again on his hands and feet, and held a long talk with *Dom. Camerarius*, who, howbeit, did not stir out of the coach. Meanwhile the driver and the constable had unyoked the maimed horse, bound it, and dragged it off the bridge, and now they came back to the cart and bade us get down therefrom and cross the bridge on foot, the which we did after the constable had unbound my child with many curses and ill words, threatening that, in return for her malice, he would keep her roasting till late in the evening. (I could not blame him much therefore; for truly this was a strange thing!) But albeit my child herself got safe across, we two — I mean reverend Martinus and

---

[lxxii] Psalm 18. 10, 42.

myself — like all the others, fell two or three times to the ground. At length we all, by God his grace, got safe and sound to the miller's house, where the constable delivered my child into the miller his hands, to guard her on forfeit of his life, while he ran down to the mill-pond to save the Sheriff his grey charger. The driver was bidden the while to get the cart and the other horses off the bewitched bridge. We had, however, stood but a short time with the miller, under the great oak before his door, when *Dom. Consul*, with the worshipful court, and all the folks, came over the little bridge, which is but a couple of musket-shots off from the first one, and he could scarce prevent the crowd from falling upon my child and tearing her in pieces, seeing that they all, as well as *Dom. Consul* himself, imagined that none other but she had brewed the storm and bewitched the bridge (especially as she herself had not fallen thereon), and had likewise caused the Sheriff his death; all of which, nevertheless, were foul lies, as ye shall hereafter hear. He, therefore, railed at her for a cursed she-devil, who, even after having confessed and received the holy Sacrament, had not yet renounced Satan; but that nought should save her, and she should, nevertheless, receive her reward. And, seeing that she kept silence, I hereupon answered, "Did he not see that the all-righteous God had so ordered it, that the Sheriff, who would have robbed my innocent child of her honour and her life, had here forfeited his own life as a fearful example to others?" But *Dom. Consul* would not see this, and said that a child might perceive that our Lord God had not made this storm, or did I peradventure believe that our Lord God had likewise bewitched the bridge? I had better cease to justify my wicked child, and rather begin to exhort her to repent, seeing that this was the second time that she had brewed a storm, and that no man with a grain of sense could believe what I said, etc.

Meanwhile the miller had already stopped the mill, *item*, turned off the water, and some four or five fellows had gone with the constable down to the great water-wheel to take the Sheriff out of the fellies, wherein he had till *datum* still been carried round and round. This they could not do until they had first sawn out one of the fellies; and when at last they brought him to the bank, his neck was found to be broken, and he was as blue as a corn-flower. Moreover, his throat was frightfully torn, and the blood ran out of his nose and mouth. If the people had not reviled my child before, they reviled her doubly now, and would have thrown dirt and stones at her, had not the worshipful court interfered with might and main, saying that she would presently receive her well-deserved punishment.

Also, my dear gossip, the Reverend Martinus, climbed up into the cart again, and admonished the people not to forestall the law; and seeing that the storm had somewhat abated, he could now be heard. And when they had become somewhat more quiet, *Dom. Consul* left the corpse of the Sheriff in charge with the miller, until such time as, by God's help, he should return. *Item*, he caused the grey charger to be tied up to the oak-tree till the same time, seeing that the miller swore that he had no room in the mill, inasmuch as his stable was filled with straw; but that he would give the grey horse some hay, and keep good watch over him. And now were we wretched creatures forced to get into the cart again, after that the unsearchable will of God had once more dashed all our hopes. The constable gnashed his teeth with rage, while he took the cords out of his pocket to bind my poor child to the rail withal. As I saw right well what he was about to do, I pulled a few groats out of my pocket, and whispered into his ear, "Be merciful, for she cannot possibly run away, and do you hereafter help her to die quickly, and you shall get ten groats more from me!" This worked well, and albeit he pretended before the people to pull the ropes tight, seeing they all cried out with might and main, "Haul hard, haul hard!" in truth he bound her hands more gently than before, and even without making her fast to the rail; but he sat up behind us again with the naked sword, and after that *Dom. Consul* had prayed aloud, "God the Father, dwell with us," likewise the *Custos* had led another hymn (I know not what he sang, neither does my child), we went on our way, according to the unfathomable will of God, after this fashion: the worshipful court went before, whereas all the folks, to our great joy, fell back, and the fellows with the pitchforks lingered a good way behind us, now that the Sheriff was dead.

CHAPTER XXVIII

How my daughter was at length saved by the help of the all-merciful, yea, of the all-merciful God.

Meanwhile, by reason of my unbelief, wherewith Satan again tempted me, I had become so weak that I was forced to lean my back against the constable his knees, and expected not to live till even we should come to the mountain; for the last hope I had cherished was now gone, and I saw that my innocent lamb was in the same plight. Moreover, the reverend Martinus began to upbraid her, saying that he, too, now saw that all her oaths were lies, and that she really could brew storms. Hereupon, she answered with a smile, although, indeed, she was as white as a sheet, "Alas, reverend godfather, do you then really believe that the weather and the storms no longer obey our Lord God? Are storms, then, so rare at this season of the year, that none save the foul fiend can cause them? Nay, I have never broken the baptismal vow you once made in my name, nor will I ever break it, as I hope that God will be merciful to me in my last hour, which is now at hand." But the reverend Martinus shook his head doubtingly, and said, "The Evil One must have promised thee much, seeing thou remainest so stubborn even unto thy life's end, and blasphemest the Lord thy God; but wait, and thou wilt soon learn with horror that the devil 'is a liar, and the father of it'" (St. John 8). Whilst he yet spake this, and more of a like kind, we came to Uekeritze, where all the people, both great and small, rushed out of their doors, also Jacob Schwarten his wife, who, as we afterwards heard, had only been brought to bed the night before, and her goodman came running after her to fetch her back, in vain. She told him he was a fool, and had been one for many a weary day, and that if she had to crawl up the mountain on her bare knees, she would go to see the parson's witch burned; that she had reckoned upon it for so long, and if he did not let her go, she would give him a thump on the chaps, etc.

Thus did the coarse and foul-mouthed people riot around the cart wherein we sat, and as they knew not what had befallen, they ran so near us that the wheel went over the foot of a boy. Nevertheless, they all crowded up again, more especially the lasses, and felt my daughter her clothes, and would even see her shoes and stockings, and asked her how she felt. *Item*, one fellow asked whether she would drink somewhat, with many more fooleries besides, till at last, when several came and asked her for her garland and her golden chain, she turned towards me and smiled, saying, "Father, I must begin to speak some Latin again, otherwise the folks will leave me no peace." But it was not wanted this time; for our guards, with the pitchforks, had now reached the hindmost, and, doubtless, told them what had happened, as we presently heard a great shouting behind us, for the love of God to turn back before the witch did them a mischief; and as Jacob Schwarten his wife heeded it not, but still plagued my child to give her her apron to make a christening coat for her baby, for that it was pity to let it be burnt, her goodman gave her such a thump on her back with a knotted stick which he had pulled out of the hedge that she fell down with loud shrieks; and when he went to help her up she pulled him down by his hair, and, as reverend Martinus said, now executed what she had threatened; inasmuch as she struck him on the nose with her fist with might and main, until the other people came running up to them, and held her back. Meanwhile, however, the storm had almost passed over, and sank down toward the sea.

And when we had gone through the little wood, we suddenly saw the Streckelberg before us, covered with people, and the pile and stake upon the top, upon the which the tall constable jumped up when he saw us coming, and beckoned with his cap with all his might. Thereat my senses left me, and my sweet lamb was not much better; for she bent to and fro like a reed, and stretching her bound hands towards heaven, she once more cried out:

> Rex tremendae majestatis!
> Qui salvandos salvas gratis,
> Salva me, fons pietatis![lxxiii]

And, behold, scarce had she spoken these words, when the sun came out and formed a rainbow right over the mountain most pleasant to behold; and it is clear

---

[lxxiii] Thou mighty formidable king!
    Thou mercy's unexhausted spring,
    Some comfortable pity bring.

that this was a sign from the merciful God, such as he often gives us, but which we blind and unbelieving men do not rightly mark. Neither did my child heed it; for albeit she thought upon that first rainbow which shadowed forth our troubles, yet it seemed to her impossible that she could now be saved, wherefore she grew so faint, that she no longer heeded the blessed sign of mercy, and her head fell forward (for she could no longer lean it upon me, seeing that I lay my length at the bottom of the cart), till her garland almost touched my worthy gossip his knees. Thereupon he bade the driver stop for a moment, and pulled out a small flask filled with wine, which he always carries in his pocket when witches are to be burnt,[lxxiv] in order to comfort them therewith in their terror. (Henceforth, I myself will ever do the like, for this fashion of my dear gossip pleases me well.) He first poured some of this wine down my throat, and afterwards down my child's; and we had scarce come to ourselves again, when a fearful noise and tumult arose among the people behind us, and they not only cried out in deadly fear, "The Sheriff is come back! the Sheriff is come again!" but as they could neither run away forwards or backwards (being afraid of the ghost behind and of my child before them), they ran on either side, some rushing into the coppice, and others wading into the Achterwater up to their necks. *Item*, as soon as *Dom. Camerarius* saw the ghost come out of the coppice with a grey hat and a grey feather, such as the Sheriff wore, riding on the grey charger, he crept under a bundle of straw in the cart: and *Dom. Consul* cursed my child again, and bade the coachman drive on as madly as they could, even should all the horses die of it, when the impudent constable behind us called to him, "It is not the Sheriff, but the young lord of Nienkerken, who will surely seek to save the witch: shall I, then, cut her throat with my sword?" At these fearful words my child and I came to ourselves again, and the fellow had already lift up his naked sword to smite her, seeing *Dom. Consul* had made him a sign with his hand, when my dear gossip, who saw it, pulled my child with all his strength back into his lap. (May God reward him on the day of judgment, for I never can.) The villain would have stabbed her as she lay in his lap; but the young lord was already there, and seeing what he was about to do, thrust the boarspear, which he held in his hand, in between the constable's shoulders, so that he fell headlong on the earth, and his own sword, by the guidance of the most righteous God, went into his ribs on one side, and out again at the other. He lay there and bellowed, but the young lord heeded him not, but said to my child, "Sweet maid, God be praised that you are safe!" When, however, he saw her bound hands, he gnashed his teeth, and, cursing her judges, he jumped off his horse, and cut the rope with his sword, which he held in his right hand, took her hand in his, and said, "Alas, sweet maid, how

---

[lxxiv] Which so often happened at that time, that in many parishes of Pomerania six or seven of these unhappy women were brought to the stake every year.

have I sorrowed for you! but I could not save you, as I myself also lay in chains, which you may see from my looks."

But my child could answer him never a word, and fell into a swound again for joy; howbeit, she soon came to herself again, seeing my dear gossip still had a little wine by him. Meanwhile the dear young lord did me some injustice, which, however, I freely forgive him; for he railed at me and called me an old woman, who could do nought save weep and wail. Why had I not journeyed after the Swedish king, or why had I not gone to Mellenthin myself to fetch his testimony, as I knew right well what he thought about witchcraft? (But, blessed God, how could I do otherwise than believe the judge, who had been there? Others, besides old women, would have done the same; and I never once thought of the Swedish king; and say, dear reader, how could I have journeyed after him, and left my own child? But young folks do not think of these things seeing they know not what a father feels.)

Meanwhile, however, *Dom. Camerarius*, having heard that it was the young lord, had again crept out from beneath the straw, *item, Dom. Consul* had jumped down from the coach and ran towards us, railing at him loudly, and asking him by what power and authority he acted thus, seeing that he himself had heretofore denounced the ungodly witch? But the young lord pointed with his sword to his people, who now came riding out of the coppice, about eighteen strong, armed with sabres, pikes, and muskets, and said, "There is my authority, and I would let you feel it on your back if I did not know that you were but a stupid ass. When did you hear any testimony from me against this virtuous maiden? You lie in your throat if you say you did." And as *Dom. Consul* stood and straightway forswore himself, the young lord, to the astonishment of all, related as follows: — That as soon as he heard of the misfortune which had befallen me and my child, he ordered his horse to be saddled forthwith, in order to ride to Pudgla to bear witness to our innocence: this, however, his old father would nowise suffer, thinking that his nobility would receive a stain if it came to be known that his son had conversed with a reputed witch by night on the Streckelberg. He had caused him therefore, as prayers and threats were of no avail, to be bound hand and foot, and confined in the donjon-keep, where till *datum* an old servant had watched him, who refused to let him escape, notwithstanding he offered him any sum of money; whereupon he fell into the greatest anguish and despair at the thought that innocent blood would be shed on his account; but that the all-righteous God had graciously spared him this sorrow; for his father had fallen sick from vexation, and lay a-bed all this time, and it so happened that this very morning about prayer-time the huntsman, in shooting at a wild duck in the moat, had by chance sorely wounded his father's favourite dog, called Packan, which had crept howling to his father's bedside, and had died there; whereupon the old man, who was weak, was so angered that he was presently seized with a fit and gave up the ghost too. Hereupon his people released him, and after he had closed his father's eyes and prayed an "Our Father" over him, he straightway set out with all the people he could find in the castle in order to save the innocent maiden. For he testified here himself before all, on the word and honour of a knight, nay, more, by his hopes of salvation, that he himself was that devil which had appeared to the maiden on the mountain in the shape of a hairy giant; for having heard by common report that she ofttimes went thither, he greatly desired to know what she did there, and that from fear of his hard father he disguised himself in a wolf's skin, so that none might know him, and he had already spent two nights there, when on the third the maiden came, and he then saw her dig for amber on the mountain, and that she did not call upon Satan, but recited a Latin *carmen* aloud to herself. This he would have testified at Pudgla, but, from the cause aforesaid, he had not been able: moreover, his father had laid his cousin, Claus von Nienkerken, who was there on a visit, in his bed, and made him bear false witness; for as *Dom. Consul* had not seen him (I mean the young lord) for many a long year, seeing he had studied in foreign parts, his father thought that he might easily be deceived, which accordingly happened.

When the worthy young lord had stated this before *Dom. Consul* and all the people, which flocked together on hearing that the young lord was no ghost, I felt as though a millstone had been taken off my heart; and seeing that the people (who had already pulled the constable from under the cart, and crowded round him, like a swarm of bees) cried to me that he was dying, but desired first to confess somewhat to me, I jumped from the cart as lightly as a young bachelor, and called to *Dom. Consul* and the young lord to go with me, seeing that I could easily guess what he had on his mind. He sat upon a stone, and the blood gushed from his side like a fountain (now that they had drawn out the sword); he whimpered on seeing me, and said that he had in truth hearkened behind the door to all that old Lizzie had confessed to me, namely, that she herself, together with the Sheriff, had worked all the witchcraft on man and beast, to frighten my poor child, and force her to play the wanton. That he had hidden this, seeing that the Sheriff had promised him a great reward for so doing; but that he would now confess it freely, since God had brought my child her innocence to light. Wherefore he besought my child and myself to forgive him. And when *Dom. Consul* shook his head, and asked whether he would live and die on the truth of this confession, he answered, "Yes!" and straightway fell on his side to the earth and gave up the ghost.

Meanwhile time hung heavy with the people on the mountain, who had come from Coserow, from Zitze, from Gnitze, etc., to see my child burnt, and they all came running down the hill in long rows like geese, one after the other, to see what had happened. And among them was my ploughman, Claus Neels. When the worthy fellow saw and heard what had befallen us, he began to weep aloud for joy; and straightway he too told what he had heard the Sheriff say to old Lizzie in the garden, and how he had promised a pig in the room of her own little pig, which she had herself bewitched to death in order to bring my child into evil repute. *Summa*: all that I have noted above, and which till *datum* he had kept to himself for fear of the question. Hereat all the people marvelled, and gently bewailed her misfortunes; and many came, among them old Paasch, and would have kissed my daughter her hands and feet, as also mine own, and praised us now as much as they had before reviled us. But thus it ever is with the people. Wherefore my departed father used to say:

> The people's hate is death,
> Their love a passing breath!

My dear gossip ceased not from fondling my child, holding her in his lap, and weeping over her like a father (for I could not have wept more myself than he wept). Howbeit she herself wept not, but begged the young lord to send one of his horsemen to her faithful old maid-servant at Pudgla, to tell her what had befallen us, which he straightway did to please her. But the worshipful court (for *Dom. Gamerarius* and the *scriba* had now plucked up a heart, and had come down from the coach) was not yet satisfied, and *Dom. Consul* began to tell the young lord about the bewitched bridge, which none other save my daughter could have bewitched. Hereto the young lord gave answer that this was indeed a strange thing, inasmuch as his own horse had also broken a leg thereon, whereupon he had taken the Sheriff his horse, which he saw tied up at the mill; but he did not think that this could be laid to the charge of the maiden, but that it came about by natural means, as he had half discovered already, although he had not had time to search the matter thoroughly. Wherefore he besought the worshipful court and all the people, together with my child herself, to return back thither, where, with God's help, he would clear her from this suspicion also, and prove her perfect innocence before them all.

Thereunto the worshipful court agreed; and the young lord, having given the Sheriff his grey charger to my ploughman to carry the corpse, which had been laid across the horse's neck, to Coserow, the young lord got into the cart by us, but did not seat himself beside my child, but backward by my dear gossip: moreover, he bade one of his own people drive us instead of the old coachman, and thus we turned back in God his name. *Custos Benzensis*, who, with the children, had run in among the vetches by the wayside (my defunct *Custos* would not have done so, he had more courage), went on before again with the young folks, and by command of his reverence the pastor led the Ambrosian *Te Deum*, which deeply moved us all, more especially my child, insomuch that her book was wetted with her tears, and she at length laid it down and said, at the same time giving her hand to the young lord, "How can I thank God and you for that which you have done for me this day?" Whereupon the young lord answered, saying, "I have greater cause to thank God than yourself, sweet maid, seeing that you have suffered in your dungeon unjustly, but I justly, inasmuch as by my thoughtlessness I brought this misery upon you. Believe me that this morning when, in my donjon-keep, I first heard the sound of the dead-bell, I thought to have died; and when it tolled for the third time, I should have gone distraught in my grief, had not the Almighty God at that moment taken the life of my strange father, so that your innocent life should be saved by me. Wherefore I have vowed a new tower, and whatsoe'er beside may be needful, to the blessed house of God; for nought more bitter could have befallen me on earth than your death, sweet maid, and nought more sweet than your life!"

But at these words my child only wept and sighed; and when he looked on her, she cast down her eyes and trembled, so that I straightway perceived that my sorrows were not yet come to an end, but that another barrel of tears was just tapped for me, and so indeed it was. Moreover, the ass of a *Custos*, having finished the *Te Deum* before we were come to the bridge, straightway struck up the next following hymn, which was a funeral one, beginning, "The body let us now inter."[180] (God be praised that no harm has come of it till *datum*.) My beloved gossip rated him not a little, and threatened him that for his stupidity he should not get the money for the shoes which he had promised him out of the Church-dues. But my child comforted him, and promised him a pair of shoes at her own charges, seeing that peradventure a funeral hymn was better for her than a song of gladness.

And when this vexed the young lord, and he said, "How now, sweet maid, you know not how enough to thank God and me for your rescue, and yet you speak thus?" She answered, smiling sadly, that she had only spoken thus to comfort the poor *Custos*. But I straightway saw that she was in earnest, for that she felt that although she had escaped one fire, she already burned in another.

Meanwhile we were come to the bridge again, and all the folks stood still, and gazed open-mouthed, when the young lord jumped down from the cart, and after stabbing his horse, which still lay kicking on the bridge, went on his knees, and felt here and there with his hand. At length he called to the worshipful court to draw near, for that he had found out the witchcraft. But none save *Dom. Consul* and a few fellows out of the crowd, among whom was old Paasch, would follow him; *item*, my dear gossip and myself, and the young lord, showed us a lump of tallow about the size of a large walnut, which lay on the ground, and wherewith the whole bridge had been smeared, so that it looked quite white, but, which all the folks in their fright had taken for flour out of the mill; *item*, with some other *materia*, which stunk like fitchock's[181] dung, but what it was we could not find out. Soon after a fellow found another bit of tallow, and showed it to the people; whereupon I cried, "Aha! none hath done this but that ungodly miller's man, in revenge for the stripes which the Sheriff gave him for reviling my child." Whereupon I told what he had done, and *Dom. Consul*, who also had heard thereof, straightway sent for the miller.

He, however, did as though he knew nought of the matter, and only said that his man had left his service about an hour ago. But a young lass, the miller's maid-servant, said that that very morning, before daybreak, when she had got up to let out the cattle, she had seen the man scouring the bridge. But that she had given it no further heed, and had gone to sleep for another hour; and she pretended to know no more than the miller whither the rascal was gone. When the young lord had heard this news, he got up into the cart, and began to address the people, seeking to persuade them no longer to believe in witchcraft, now that they had seen what it really was. When I heard this, I was horror-stricken (as was but right) in my conscience, as a priest, and I got upon the cartwheel, and whispered into his ear, for God his sake, to leave this *materia*, seeing that if the people no longer feared the devil, neither would they fear our Lord God.[lxxv]

The dear young lord forthwith did as I would have him, and only asked the people whether they now held my child to be perfectly innocent? and when they had answered, "Yes!" he begged them to go quietly home, and to thank God that he had saved innocent blood. That he, too, would now return home, and that he hoped that none would molest me and my child if he let us return to Coserow alone. Hereupon he turned hastily towards her, took her hand and said: "Farewell, sweet maid, I trust that I shall soon clear your honour before the world, but do you thank God therefor, not me." He then did the like to me and to my dear gossip, whereupon he jumped down from the cart, and went and sat beside *Dom. Consul* in his coach. The latter also spake a few words to the people, and likewise begged my child and me to forgive him (and I must say it to his honour, that the tears ran down his cheeks the while), but he was so hurried by the young lord that he brake short his discourse, and they drove off over the little bridge, without so much as looking back. Only *Dom. Consul* looked round once, and called out to me, that in his hurry he had forgotten to tell the executioner that no one was to be burned to-day: I was therefore to send the churchwarden of Uekeritze up the mountain, to say so in his name; the which I did. And the bloodhound was still on the mountain, albeit he had long since heard what had befallen; and when the bailiff gave him the orders of the worshipful court, he began to curse so fearfully that it might have awakened the dead; moreover, he plucked off his cap, and trampled it under foot, so that any one might have guessed what he felt.

But to return to ourselves, my child sat as still and as white as a pillar of salt, after the young lord had left her so suddenly and so unawares, but she was somewhat comforted when the old maid-servant came running with her coats tucked up to her knees, and carrying her shoes and stockings in her hands. We heard her afar off, as the mill had stopped, blubbering for joy, and she fell at least three times on the bridge, but at last she got over safe, and kissed now mine and

---

[lxxv] Maybe a profound truth.

now my child her hands and feet; begging us only not to turn her away, but to keep her until her life's end; the which we promised to do. She had to climb up behind where the impudent constable had sat, seeing that my dear gossip would not leave me until I should be back in mine own manse. And as the young lord his servant had got up behind the coach, old Paasch drove us home, and all the folks who had waited till *datum* ran beside the cart, praising and pitying as much as they had before scorned and reviled us. Scarce, however, had we passed through Uekeritze, when we again heard cries of "Here comes the young lord, here comes the young lord!" so that my child started up for joy, and became as red as a rose; but some of the folks ran into the buckwheat, by the road, again, thinking it was another ghost. It was, however, in truth, the young lord who galloped up on a black horse, calling out as he drew near us, "Notwithstanding the haste I am in, sweet maid, I must return and give you safe-conduct home, seeing that I have just heard that the filthy people reviled you by the way, and I know not whether you are yet safe." Hereupon he urged old Paasch to mend his pace, and as his kicking and trampling did not even make the horses trot, the young lord struck the saddle-horse from time to time with the flat of his sword, so that we soon reached the village and the manse. Howbeit, when I prayed him to dismount a while, he would not, but excused himself, saying that he must still ride through Usedom to Anclam, but charged old Paasch, who was our bailiff, to watch over my child as the apple of his eye, and should anything unusual happen he was straightway to inform the town-clerk at Pudgla, or *Dom. Consul* at Usedom, thereof, and when Paasch had promised to do this, he waved his hand to us, and galloped off as fast as he could.

But before he got round the corner by Pagel his house, he turned back for the third time: and when we wondered thereat, he said we must forgive him, seeing his thoughts wandered to-day.

That I had formerly told him that I still had my patent of nobility,[182] the which he begged me to lend him for a time. Hereupon I answered that I must first seek for it, and that he had best dismount the while. But he would not, and again excused himself, saying he had no time. He therefore stayed without the door, until I brought him the patent, whereupon he thanked me and said, "Do not wonder hereat, you will soon see what my purpose is." Whereupon he struck his spurs into his horse's sides and did not come back again.

CHAPTER XXIX

Of our next great sorrow, and final joy.

And now might we have been at rest, and have thanked God on our knees by day and night. For, besides mercifully saving us out of such great tribulation, he turned the hearts of my beloved flock, so that they knew not how to do enough for us. Every day they brought us fish, meat, eggs, sausages, and whatsoe'er besides they could give me, and which I have since forgotten. Moreover they, every one of them, came to church the next Sunday, great and small (except goodwife Kliene of Zempin, who had just got a boy, and still kept her bed), and I preached a thanks-giving sermon on Job 5, 17th, 18th, and 19th verses, "Behold, happy is the man whom God correcteth; therefore despise not thou the chastening of the Almighty: for he maketh sore, and bindeth up; and his hands make whole. He shall deliver thee in six troubles, yea, in seven there shall no evil touch thee." And during my sermon I was ofttimes forced to stop by reason of all the weeping, and to let them blow their noses. And I might truly have compared myself to Job, after that the Lord had mercifully released him from his troubles, had it not been for my child, who prepared much fresh grief for me.

She had wept when the young lord would not dismount, and now that he came not again, she grew more uneasy from day to day. She sat and read first the Bible, then the hymn-book, *item*, the history of Dido in *Virgilius*,[183] or she climbed up the mountain to fetch flowers (likewise sought after the vein of amber there, but found it not, which shows the cunning and malice of Satan). I saw this for a while with many sighs, but spake not a word (for, dear reader, what could I say?) until it grew worse and worse; and as she now recited her *carmina* more than ever both at home and abroad, I feared lest the people should again repute her a witch, and one day I followed her up the mountain. Well-a-day, she sat on the pile, which still stood there, but with her face turned towards the sea, reciting the *versus* where Dido mounts the funeral pile in order to stab herself for love of Aeneas: —

> At trepida et coeptis immanibus effera Dido
> Sanguineam volvens aciem, maculisque trementes
> Interfusa genas, et pallida morte future
> Interiora domus irrumpit limina et altos
> Conscendit furibunda rogos....[lxxvi] [184]

When I saw this, and heard how things really stood with her, I was affrighted beyond measure, and cried, "Mary, my child, what art thou doing?" She started when she heard my voice, but sat still on the pile, and answered, as she covered her face with her apron, "Father, I am burning my heart." I drew near to her and pulled the apron from her face, saying, "Wilt thou, then, again kill me with grief?"

[lxxvi] But furious Dido, with dark thoughts involv'd,
Shook at the mightly mischief she resolv'd.
With livid spots distinguish'd was her face,
Red were her rolling eyes, and discompos'd her face:
Ghastly she gazed, with pain she drew her breath,
And nature shiver'd at approaching death.
Then swiftly to the fatal place she pass'd,
And mounts the funeral pile with furious haste.
                                                    Dryden's *Virgil*.

whereupon she covered her face with her hands, and moaned, "Alas, father, wherefore was I not burned here? My torment would then have endured but for a moment, but now it will last as long as I live!" I still did as though I had seen nought, and said, "Wherefore, dear child, dost thou suffer such torment?" whereupon she answered, "I have long been ashamed to tell you; for the young lord, the young lord, my father, do I suffer this torment! He no longer thinks of me; and albeit he saved my life he scorns me, or he would surely have dismounted and come in a while; but we are of far too low degree for him!" Hereupon I indeed began to comfort her and to persuade her to think no more of the young lord; but the more I comforted her, the worse she grew. Nevertheless I saw that she did yet in secret cherish a strong hope by reason of the patent of nobility which he had made me give him. I would not take this hope from her, seeing that I felt the same myself, and to comfort her I flattered her hopes, whereupon she was more quiet for some days, and did not go up the mountain, the which I had forbidden her. Moreover, she began again to teach little Paasch her god-daughter, out of whom, by the help of the all-righteous God, Satan was now altogether departed. But she still pined, and was as white as a sheet; and when soon after a report came that none in the castle at Mellenthin knew what was become of the young lord, and that they thought he had been killed, her grief became so great that I had to send my ploughman on horseback to Mellenthin to gain tidings of him. And she looked at least twenty times out of the door and over the paling to watch for his return; and when she saw him coming she ran out to meet him as far as the corner by Pagels. But, blessed God! he brought us even worse news than we had heard before, saying, that the people at the castle had told him that their young master had ridden away the self-same day whereon he had rescued the maiden. That he had, indeed, returned after three days to his father's funeral, but had straightway ridden off again, and that for five weeks they had heard nothing further of him, and knew not whither he was gone, but supposed that some wicked ruffians had killed him.

And now my grief was greater than ever it had been before; so patient and resigned to the will of God as my child had shown herself heretofore, and no martyr could have met her last hour stronger in God and Christ, so impatient and despairing was she now. She gave up all hope, and took it into her head that in these heavy times of war the young lord had been killed by robbers. Nought availed with her, not even prayer, for when I called upon God with her, on my knees, she straightway began so grievously to bewail that the Lord had cast her off, and that she was condemned to nought save misfortunes in this world; that it pierced through my heart like a knife, and my thoughts forsook me at her words. She lay also at night, and "like a crane or a swallow so did she chatter; she did mourn like a dove; her eyes did fail with looking upward,"[lxxvii] because no

---

[lxxvii] Isaaiah 38. 14.

sleep came upon her eyelids. I called to her from my bed, "Dear child, wilt thou, then, never cease? sleep, I pray thee!" and she answered and said, "Do you sleep, dearest father; I cannot sleep until I sleep the sleep of death. Alas, my father; that I was not burned!" But how could I sleep when she could not? I indeed said, each morning, that I had slept a while, in order to content her; but it was not so; but, like David, "all the night made I my bed to swim; I watered my couch with my tears."[lxxviii] Moreover I again fell into heavy unbelief, so that I neither could nor would pray. Nevertheless the Lord "did not deal with me after my sins, nor reward me according to mine iniquities. For as the heaven is high above the earth, so great was his mercy toward" me, miserable sinner![lxxix]

For mark what happened on the very next Saturday! Behold, our old maid-servant came running in at the door, quite out of breath, saying that a horseman was coming over the Master's Mount, with a tall plume waving on his hat, and that she believed it was the young lord. When my child, who sat upon the bench combing her hair, heard this, she gave a shriek of joy, which would have moved a stone under the earth, and straightway ran out of the room to look over the paling. She presently came running in again, fell upon my neck, and cried without ceasing, "The young lord! the young lord!" whereupon she would have run out to meet him, but I forbade her, saying she had better first bind up her hair, which she then remembered, and laughing, weeping, and praying, all at once, she bound up her long hair. And now the young lord came galloping round the corner, attired in a green velvet doublet with red silk sleeves, and a grey hat with a heron's feather therein; *summa*, gaily dressed as beseems a wooer. And when we now ran out at the door, he called aloud to my child in the Latin, from afar off, "*Quomodo stat dulcissima virgo?*"[185] Whereupon she gave answer, saying, "*Bene te aspecto.*"[186] He then sprang smiling off his horse, and gave it into the charge of my ploughman, who meanwhile had come up together with the maid; but he was affrighted when he saw my child so pale, and taking her hand spake in the vulgar tongue, "My God! what is it ails you, sweet maid? you look more pale than when about to go to the stake." Whereupon she answered, "I have been at the stake daily since you left us, good my lord, without coming into our house, or so much as sending us tidings of whither you were gone."

This pleased him well, and he said, "Let us first of all go into the chamber, and you shall hear all." And when he had wiped the sweat from his brow, and sat down on the bench beside my child, he spake as follows: — That he had straightway promised her that he would clear her honour before the whole world, and the self-same day whereon he left us he made the worshipful court draw up an authentic record of all that had taken place, more especially the confession of the impudent constable, *item*, that of my ploughboy, Claus Neels; wherewith he

---

[lxxviii] Psalm 6. 6.
[lxxix] Psalm 103. 10–11.

rode throughout the same night, as he had promised, to Anclam, and next day to Stettin, to our gracious sovereign Duke Bogislaw: who marvelled greatly when he heard of the wickedness of his Sheriff, and of that which he had done to my child: moreover, he asked whether she were the pastor's daughter who once upon a time had found the signet-ring of his Princely Highness Philippus Julius of most Christian memory in the castle garden at Wolgast? and as he did not know thereof, the Duke asked, whether she knew Latin? And he, the young lord, answered yes, that she knew the Latin better than he did himself. His Princely Highness said, "Then, indeed, it must be the same," and straightway he put on his spectacles, and read the *acta* himself. Hereupon, and after his Princely Highness had read the record of the worshipful court, shaking his head the while, the young lord humbly besought his Princely Highness to give him an *amende honorable*[187] for my child, *item, literas commendatitias*[188] for himself to our most gracious Emperor at Vienna,[189] to beg for a renewal of my patent of nobility, seeing that he was determined to marry none other maiden than my daughter so long as he lived.

When my child heard this, she gave a cry of joy, and fell back in a swound with her head against the wall. But the young lord caught her in his arms, and gave her three kisses (which I could not then deny him, seeing, as I did with joy, how matters went), and when she came to herself again, he asked her, whether she would not have him, seeing that she had given a cry at his words? Whereupon she said, "Whether I will not have you, my lord! Alas! I love you as dearly as my God and my Saviour! You first saved my life, and now you have snatched my heart from the stake, whereon, without you, it would have burned all the days of my life!" Hereupon I wept for joy, when he drew her into his lap, and she clasped his neck with her little hands.

They thus sat and toyed a while, till the young lord again perceived me, and said, "What say you thereto; I trust it is also your will, reverend Abraham?" Now, dear reader, what could I say, save my hearty good-will? seeing that I wept for very joy, as did my child, and I answered, how should it not be my will, seeing that it was the will of God? But whether the worthy, good young lord had likewise considered that he would stain his noble name if he took to wife my child, who had been habit and repute a witch, and had been well-nigh bound to the stake?

Hereupon he said, By no means; for that he had long since prevented this, and he proceeded to tell us how he had done it, namely, his Princely Highness had promised him to make ready all the *scripta* which he required, within four days, when he hoped to be back from his father's burial. He therefore rode straightway back to Mellenthin, and after paying the last honour to my lord his father, he presently set forth on his way again, and found that his Princely Highness had kept his word meanwhile. With these *scripta* he rode to Vienna, and albeit he met with many pains, troubles, and dangers by the way (which he would relate to us at some other time), he nevertheless reached the city safely. There he by chance met with a Jesuit with whom he had once upon a time had his *locamentum* for a few days at Prague, while he was yet a *studiosus*, and this man, having heard his business, bade him be of good cheer, seeing that his Imperial Majesty stood sorely in need of money in these hard times of war, and that he, the Jesuit, would manage it all for him. This he really did, and his Imperial Majesty not only renewed my patent of nobility, but likewise confirmed the *amende honorable* to my child granted by his Princely Highness the Duke, so that he might now maintain the honour of his betrothed bride against all the world, as also hereafter that of his wife.

Hereupon he drew forth the *acta* from his bosom, and put them into my hand, saying, "And now, reverend Abraham, you must also do me a pleasure, to wit, to-morrow morning, when I hope to go with my betrothed bride to the Lord's table, you must publish the banns between me and your daughter,[190] and on the day after you must marry us. Do not say nay thereto, for my pastor, the reverend Philippus, says that this is no uncommon custom among the nobles in Pomerania, and I have already given notice of the wedding for Monday at mine own castle, whither we will then go, and where I purpose to bed my bride." I should have found much to say against this request, more especially that in honour of the Holy Trinity he should suffer himself to be called three times in church according to custom, and that he should delay a while the espousals; but when I perceived that my child would gladly have the marriage held right soon, for she sighed and grew red as scarlet, I had not the heart to refuse them, but promised all they asked. Whereupon I exhorted them both to prayer, and when I had laid my hands upon their heads, I thanked the Lord more deeply than I had ever yet thanked him, so that at last I could no longer speak for tears, seeing that they drowned my voice.

Meanwhile the young lord his coach had driven up to the door, filled with chests and coffers: and he said, "Now, sweet maid, you shall see what I have brought you," and he bade them bring all the things into the room. Dear reader, what fine things were there, such as I had never seen in all my life! All that women can use was there, especially of clothes, to wit, bodices, plaited gowns, long robes, some of them bordered with fur, veils, aprons, *item*, the bridal shift with gold fringes, whereon the merry lord had laid some six or seven bunches of myrtle to make herself a wreath withal.[191] *Item*, there was no end to the rings, neck-chains, eardrops, etc., the which I have in part forgotten. Neither did the young lord leave me without a gift, seeing he had brought me a new surplice (the enemy had robbed me of my old one), also doublets, hosen, and shoes, *summa*, whatsoever appertains to a man's attire; wherefore I secretly besought the Lord not to punish us again in his sore displeasure for such pomps and vanities. When my child beheld all these things she was grieved that she could bestow upon him nought save her heart alone, and the chain of the Swedish king, the which she hung round his neck, and begged him, weeping the while, to take it as a bridal gift. This he at length promised to do, and likewise to carry it with him into the grave: but that my child must first wear it at her wedding, as well as the blue silken gown, for that this and no other should be her bridal dress, and this he made her promise to do.

And now a merry chance befell with the old maid, the which I will here note. For when the faithful old soul had heard what had taken place, she was beside herself for joy, danced and clapped her hands, and at last said to my child, "Now to be sure you will not weep when the young lord is to lie in your bed," whereat my child blushed scarlet for shame, and ran out of the room; and when the young lord would know what she meant therewith, she told him that he had already once slept in my child her bed when he came from Gutzkow with me, whereupon he bantered her all the evening after that she was come back again. Moreover, he promised the maid that as she had once made my child her bed for him, she should make it again, and that on the day after to-morrow she and the ploughman too should go with us to Mellenthin, so that masters and servants should all rejoice together after such great distress.

And seeing that the dear young lord would stop the night under my roof, I made him lie in the small closet together with me (for I could not know what might happen). He soon slept like a top, but no sleep came into my eyes, for very joy, and I prayed the livelong blessed night, or thought over my sermon. Only near morning I dozed a little; and when I rose the young lord already sat in the next room with my child, who wore the black silken gown which he had brought her, and, strange to say, she looked fresher than even when the Swedish king came, so that I never in all my life saw her look fresher or fairer. *Item*, the young lord wore his black doublet, and picked out for her the best bits of myrtle for the wreath she was twisting. But when she saw me, she straightway laid the wreath beside her on the bench, folded her little hands, and said the morning prayer, as she was ever wont to do, which humility pleased the young lord right well, and he begged her that in future she would ever do the like with him, the which she promised.

Soon after we went to the blessed church to confession, and all the folk stood gaping open-mouthed because the young lord led my child on his arm. But they wondered far more when, after the sermon, I first read to them in the vulgar tongue the *amende honorable* to my child from his Princely Highness, together with the confirmation of the same by his Imperial Majesty, and after that my patent of nobility; and, lastly, began to publish the banns between my child and the young lord. Dear reader, there arose a murmur throughout the church like the buzzing of a swarm of bees. (N.B. These *scripta* were burnt in the fire which broke out in the castle a year ago, as I shall hereafter relate, wherefore I cannot insert them here *in origne*.)

Hereupon my dear children went together with much people to the Lord's table, and after church nearly all the folks crowded round them and wished them joy. *Item*, old Paasch came to our house again that afternoon, and once more besought my daughter's forgiveness because that he had unwittingly offended her; that he would gladly give her a marriage-gift, but that he now had nothing at all; howbeit that his wife should set one of her hens in the spring, and he would take the chickens to her at Mellenthin himself. This made us all to laugh, more especially the young lord, who at last said: "As thou wilt bring me a marriage-gift, thou must also be asked to the wedding, wherefore thou mayest come to-morrow with the rest."

Whereupon my child said: "And your little Mary, my god-child, shall come too, and be my bridemaiden, if my lord allows it." Whereupon she began to tell the young lord all that that had befallen the child by the malice of Satan, and how they laid it to her charge until such time as the all-righteous God brought her innocence to light; and she begged that since her dear lord had commanded her to wear the same garments at her wedding which she had worn to salute the Swedish king, and afterwards to go to the stake, he would likewise suffer her to take for her bridemaiden her little god-child, as *indicium secundum*[192] of her sorrows.

And when he had promised her this, she told old Paasch to send hither his child to her, that she might fit a new gown upon her which she had cut out for her a week ago, and which the maid would finish sewing this very day. This so went to the heart of the good old fellow that he began to weep aloud, and at last said, she should not do all this for nothing, for instead of the one hen his wife should set three for her in the spring.

When he was gone, and the young lord did nought save talk with his betrothed bride, both in the vulgar and in the Latin tongue, I did better — namely, went up the mountain to pray, wherein, moreover, I followed my child's example, and clomb up upon the pile, there in loneliness to offer up my whole heart to the Lord as an offering of thanksgiving, seeing that with this sacrifice he is well pleased, as in Psalm 51. 19,[193] "The sacrifice of God is a troubled spirit; a broken and contrite heart, O God, shalt thou not despise."

That night the young lord again lay in my room, but next morning, when the sun had scarce risen —

* * * * *

Here end these interesting communications, which I do not intend to dilute with any additions of my own. My readers, more especially those of the fair sex, can picture to themselves at pleasure the future happiness of this excellent pair.

All further historical traces of their existence, as well as that of the pastor, have disappeared, and nothing remains but a tablet fixed in the wall of the church at Mellenthin, on which the incomparable lord, and his yet more incomparable wife, are represented.[194] On his faithful breast still hangs "the golden chain, with the effigy of the Swedish King." They both seem to have died within a short time of each other, and to have been buried in the same coffin. For in the vault under the church there is still a large double coffin, in which, according to tradition, lies a chain of gold of incalculable value. Some twenty years ago, the owner of Mellenthin, whose unequalled extravagance had reduced him to the verge of beggary, attempted to open the coffin in order to take out this precious relic, but he was not able. It appeared as if some powerful spell held it firmly together; and it has remained unopened down to the present time. May it remain so until the last awful day, and may the impious hand of avarice or curiosity never desecrate these holy ashes of holy beings!

THE END.

NOTES TO THE TEXT

∼

1. Coserow is one of the oldest settlements on the German Baltic island of Usedom, first mentioned in records in 1347. For centuries the village's economy was based on fishing and agriculture. In 1815 it became part of the Prussian province of Pomerania.
2. The thirteenth-century church, originally constructed from field stones, was expanded in the fifteenth century, and contains a number of treasures including a carved medieval winged altar. Meinhold served as minister there from 1821 to 1827, and includes in his novel names and events connected with the church around 1630.
3. Balthasar Bekker (1634–1698), a Dutch Protestant theologian, published *De Betoverde Weereld* in 1691. A disciple of Descartes, he was an important figure in the early Enlightenment debates about witchcraft, who opposed superstition and questioned belief in sorcery and demonic possession.
4. The German pastor Georg Conrad Horst (1779–1832) published his six-volume history of magical texts and early occult practices entitled *Zauber-Bibliothek* between 1821 and 1826.
5. The style and content of Meinhold's novel are clearly influenced by the accounts of witch trials published in the *Pommersche Provinzial-Blätter für Stadt und Land*, for example vol. 5 (1824), pp. 86–118 and 249–56.
6. The concept of animal magnetism was popularised by the German physician Franz Anton Mesmer (1734–1815) who postulated that there was a natural transference of energy between animate and inanimate objects which could be directed for healing or other purposes. The theory was investigated seriously by scientists from around 1780 to 1850, and was commonly referred to as 'mesmerism'.
7. An assembly of bishops convened to discuss matters of doctrine and governance. Ancyra (today Ankara, capital of Turkey) was the seat of administration for the Roman province of Galatia.
8. The *Malleus maleficarum* was the infamous medieval witch-hunting manual written by the German Catholic clergyman and inquisitor Heinrich Kramer (*c.* 1430–1505) to assist prosecutors in the detection, interrogation and conviction of witches. It was published in 1487, two years earlier than Meinhold claims. The inclusion of a papal bull by Innocent VIII at the beginning of the book gave the distorted impression that the Pope had commissioned or endorsed this particular work. Kramer was reportedly denounced by the Catholic Church in 1490, but the contents of his treatise

continued to be influential in the witchcraft trials of the sixteenth and seventeenth centuries.
9. Friedrich von Spee (1591–1635) was a German Jesuit whose most noted work, *Cautio criminalis* (1631), was the first publication expressing arguments against the use of torture in witch trials and calling for legal reform.
10. Christian Thomasius (1655–1728) was a jurist who became Chancellor of the University of Halle. He was one of the foremost opponents of witch-hunting and torture in Germany.
11. A work of fiction depicting unusual or stirring events.
12. An indirect jibe at the liberal theologian David F. Strauss (1808–1874), whose historical investigation of the Gospel narratives in *The Life of Christ, Critically Examined* (1835) had so angered Meinhold that he conceived this work as a response (see Introduction, pp. 3–5).
13. Johannes Micraelius (1597–1658) was a German philosopher and historian whose six-volume history of Pomerania was first published by Georg Rhete in Stettin between 1639 and 1640. The fifth volume, to which Meinhold refers here, covers the years 1627 to 1637. Meinhold uses the Kunckel edition of 1723.
14. The Thirty Years' War (1618–1648) had a devastating effect on the population of Germany which suffered famine and disease as a result of the actions of marauding armies. The war reached Usedom in 1628.
15. A starched and wired female headdress, popular between the twelfth and fifteenth centuries, and retained as a distinctive item of clothing for nuns.
16. Moreover, in addition: throughout the text this word features frequently in lists of information.
17. Liturgical vessels, usually made of precious metal.
18. The former convent at Pudagla was extended in 1574 by Ernst Ludwig, Duke of Pomerania, into a residence for his widowed mother Maria of Saxony.
19. Philipp Julius (1584–1625) was the last Duke of Pomerania-Wolgast.
20. Dues, perquisites.
21. A reference to the Reformation, in particular the aim to rid the Church of its perceived corruption and exploitation of the poor.
22. Coastal village near Coserow, on the isthmus of Usedom.
23. Meinhold draws on the widespread early modern European stereotype regarding the physical appearance of witches. Cf. the description by the English Puritan cleric John Gaule, who opposed aspects of witch-hunting: 'every old woman with a wrinkled face, a furr'd brow, a hairy lip, a gobber tooth, a squint eye, a squeaking voice, or a scolding tongue, having a ragged coate on her back, a skullcap on her head, a spindle in her hand, and a Dog or Cat by her side; is not only suspected, but pronounced for a witch.' (*Select Cases of Conscience Touching Witches and Witchcraft* (London: Clutterbuck, 1646), pp. 4–5.)

24. The text contains a number of references to wolves. The threat to livestock and humans was taken very seriously in Germany, and wolves were hunted to extinction by the late nineteenth century. As each region was cleansed of these predators, a 'wolf stone' was erected in the place where the last one was killed. The fear of wolves is emblematised in many German fairy tales.
25. 'Summa' is used regularly in the text to introduce a summary of essential points.
26. The 56-meter-high Streckelberg is a hill on the island of Usedom, the north-east side of which consists of cliffs with numerous caves. Legends abound in this area of the caves being used as hiding places for pirates, in particular the privateer Klaus Störtebeker (c. 1360–1401). The Streckelberg is the site of key events in the novel.
27. Church bells were an important means of public communication, and were used not only to call people to worship and to tell the time, but to summon workers to the fields at particular intervals of the agricultural year, to announce celebrations such as weddings or fairs, and to intimate warnings, curfews and funerals. Different ringing sounds and styles were used to convey a range of messages, with regional variations.
28. Damerow was an outlying estate of the village of Coserow, situated on the narrowest part of the isthmus, with the Baltic on one side and the lagoon known as the Achterwater on the other.
29. The allusion is to the manna and quail provided by God for the Israelites while they travelled in the desert. See Exodus 16.
30. Horsehair was employed in the construction of small snares for birds, with rowan berries or elderberries used as bait. The birds were strangled by the snares. Thrushes were mainly trapped by this method (the translator uses 'fieldfares', a type of thrush). The birds' German name (Drosseln) is sometimes said to be derived from the verb 'erdrosseln', meaning 'to throttle'.
31. 'Gott, der Vater, wohn' uns bei' is a hymn of unknown authorship, adapted by Luther for publication in Johann Walter's *Eyn geystlich Gesangk Buchleyn* (Wittenberg, 1524). It was translated into English in 1854 by Richard Massie (1800–1887) as 'God the Father, be our stay'.
32. Alas, the enemy is here!
33. Come back out, these are friends!
34. These are the communion vessels referred to earlier. The chalice is a cup for wine, the paten a small round dish for bread.
35. See I Kings 17. 6.
36. The text draws on motifs from the Exodus narrative, in particular here the role of Moses as leader of a flawed community which incurs God's anger.
37. The work of the ancient Roman poet Virgil, probably the famous epic poem the *Aeneid* to which reference is made later.

38. Parallel passage, i.e. text from another part of the Bible on the same subject. The verses referred to here are Luke 12. 24 and Matthew 6. 26.
39. By introducing the idea of an error corrected by an editor, Meinhold reinforces the ruse of authenticity. The quoted lines are indeed attributed to the Benedictine monk and cardinal Peter Damian (c. 1007–1072), taken from his hymn 'de gloria paradisi' on the heavenly Jerusalem, which was adapted from a meditation by Augustine.
40. Village in the north of Usedom.
41. Lieper Winkel is a peninsula of the island of Usedom, consisting of eight small villages. This area suffered greatly during the Thirty Years' War as a result of plague and repeated raids. A census taken at the end of the war showed that the population had been reduced to thirty-three families.
42. Micraelius mentions instances of both cannibalism and suicide among the rural population in 1630 when food was extremely scarce (see vol. 5, p. 174). Micraelius uses the alternative name 'Dandemin' for the village in this anecdote.
43. Grace: a prayer of thanks for food, or to invoke a blessing on it.
44. Teacher. It was the duty of pastors to establish a school in each village and to employ a teacher, providing them with free board and lodging and a modest salary.
45. Reference to the miracle at the wedding in Cana, where Jesus turns water into wine. See John 2. 1–11.
46. 'Believe, and thou hast eaten already' is the formula used by Augustine to explain the figurative meaning of Christ's sermon in John 6. 25–58 on eating the Bread of Life.
47. The hymn by the Lutheran theologian Paul Eber (1511–1569) 'Wenn wir in höchsten Nöten sein' was translated into English by Catherine Winkworth (1827–78) as 'When in the hour of utmost need' for the 1858 hymn collection *Lyra Germanica*.
48. For the record, report.
49. This alludes to a Biblical motif indicating that those who defy God will suffer punishment. See, for example, Psalm 2. 9: 'Thou shalt dash them in pieces like a potter's vessel'; Isaiah 30. 14: 'and he shall break it as the breaking of the potters' vessel that is broken in pieces'; and Jeremiah 19. 11: 'Even so will I break this people and this city, as one breaketh a potter's vessel.'
50. The parable of the beggar Lazarus is related in Luke 16. 19–31. The Book of Job addresses the theme of undeserved human suffering.
51. See Matthew 7. 9.
52. Towns in Western Pomerania. Anklam, the larger of the two, was the head of navigation on the Peene river, and belonged to the Hanseatic League. Lassan originated as a fishing village.
53. Village on the peninsula known as Lieper Winkel.

54. Hagar, the mother of Abraham's son Ishmael, was banished with her child to the desert, where she was saved by an angel sent by God. See Genesis 21. 14–21.
55. Peter's denial of Christ was prompted by the questions of a servant girl in the courtyard of the High Priest's palace where Jesus was under arrest. See Matthew 26. 69–75, Mark 14. 66–72, Luke 22. 54–62 and John 18. 15–27.
56. King of Judah during the Assyrian siege of Jerusalem in 701 BC. His reign is documented in II Kings 18–20, Isaiah 36–39 and II Chronicles 29–32.
57. The Baltic region is home to the world's largest known deposits of amber, a fossilised tree resin which is highly valued as a gemstone.
58. Town situated on the mainland, adjacent to the island of Usedom.
59. Fir cones were used as kindling, but were a poor source of fuel as they burned up quickly.
60. Chronograms (from the Greek 'time writing') are sentences in which particular letters such as L, I, V, M etc. can be rearranged and interpreted as Roman numerals indicating a date. In the first example, the uppercase numerals VVVDMIICIII add up to 1620. The first part of this line is based on Psalm 79. 5, and the translation is: 'How long will you be angry, Lord?; be a father to us.' In the second example, the uppercase numerals IVVDXMVCII add up to 1628. The translation is: 'And in your right hand bring aid, gracious Christ.' When written in dactylic hexameter ('metrum heroicum' = epic metre), these are referred to as chronosticha. Contrary to the narrator's assertion, however, the examples cited are not written in hexameter.
61. An example of the use of the footnotes to reinforce the literary hoax. Here a modern editor highlights the narrator's ignorance. The reference to skin turning black may be linked with starvation or with typhoid fever. Germany suffered huge losses through hunger and disease during the Thirty Years' War, as well as from military causes, and historians estimate that it took around a century for the population to return to the level of 1618.
62. Possibly a Latinisation of the German word 'Losament', derived from the French 'logement'. The term was used from the sixteenth to eighteenth centuries to refer to a temporary military dwelling made of canvas, wood or wickerwork.
63. Bogislaw X (1454–1523), Duke of Pomerania, made a pilgrimage to Jerusalem in 1496-98. A tragicomedy on the subject of this visit was published by Johann von Kitzscher in 1501.
64. A further example of editorial game-playing. This information is indeed included in Micraelius's account, though he uses the spelling 'Kikepost' (p. 170).
65. Bogislaw XIII (1560–1637) was the last Duke of Pomerania. On the death of his cousin Philipp Julius, the last Duke of Wolgast, he became ruler of all West Pomerania in 1625.

66. Gracious princes, which of you has lost this ring?
67. I am the daughter of the pastor of Coserow.
68. Sweet girl, it is I who have lost it.
69. But who are you, and where do you come from?
70. The reference to Anna Maria van Schurman is problematic in that the spreading of her reputation across Europe postdates the action of the novel. Born in 1607, she would have been only three years older than the protagonist Mary. As historical records indicate that Schurman did not begin learning Latin until the age of eleven, it cannot be the case that Pastor Schweidler taught his daughter Latin from a very young age in response to this role-model. This is an example of the anachronisms contained in the novel, resulting from the fact that Meinhold took much of his information from later sources. The lengthy editorial note relies heavily on an entry on Schurman in volume 35 of Zedler's *Universal-Lexicon* (columns 1677–81). In later life Schurman joined the contemplative religious community founded by the French Pietist Jean de Labadie (1610–1674) and became one of the movement's most famous apologists through her work *Eukleria seu melioris partis electio* (*On Choosing the Better Part*), published in 1673. The 'Muckers' was a derogatory nickname (meaning hypocrites or bigots) for a Pietist-based sect formed in Königsberg by Johannes Ebel (1784–1861).
71. Natural ability.
72. Duff Gordon intervenes on several occasions to clarify variations between the Lutheran and the King James Bible. Here the verse from Psalm 33 is slightly different in the two versions. (See also note 93.)
73. Stipend, allowance.
74. Endowment certificate.
75. Allusion to the Gospel miracle of the feeding of the five thousand, in which Christ used five small loaves and two fish to feed a large crowd of followers near the town of Bethsaida on the north coast of the Sea of Galilee. See Matthew 14. 13–21, Mark 6. 31–44, Luke 9. 10–17, and John 6. 5–15.
76. Law of retaliation laid down in Exodus 21. 24 and Leviticus 34. 19–20.
77. Spitting three times on the ground, especially near a place where danger was perceived to exist, was used in folkloric tradition as a means of defence against evil. The text is ambivalent here, however, as in witchcraft spitting was also a powerful form of cursing.
78. Form of public execution in which the condemned were tied to a large wooden cartwheel and beaten until their bones were broken.
79. The important figure of Rüdiger von Nienkerken is loosely based on a noble family associated with this region. The Pomeranian historian Thomas Kantzow refers to the family as 'Newenkirchen' (vol. 1, p. 422), while Micraelius names them as 'Neukirchen' (vol. 6, pp. 322, 362). Meinhold took inspiration from a local fourteenth-century legend of a young lord von

Nienkerken who was buried with his wife at the church in Mellenthin. By including a medieval lithograph depicting this couple in the first edition of his novel, however, he unwittingly undermined the claim that the work was an authentic historical document (see note 194).
80. Without stopping.
81. A sign or prediction.
82. The Rose noble was an English gold coin introduced in 1464, during the reign of King Edward IV. Its design featured a rose, it weighed about 116 grains (7.8g) and was worth ten shillings. The coin was discontinued after 1470.
83. Married woman's bonnet; it was considered unseemly for a married woman to show her hair.
84. Against me.
85. Word-for-word.
86. Treasury.
87. The disciple who betrayed Christ, prompting the events which led to his death.
88. In Book 2 of Virgil's *Aeneid*, Aeneas tells the story of the Trojan horse and the fall of Troy.
89. At this point in the text it becomes clear that the pastor's daughter is older than his references to her as a 'child' might suggest.
90. Pregnant.
91. Supernatural creatures such as imps, thought to be the servants of witches, were sought in witch-hunts as evidence of sorcery.
92. Instigator, source.
93. 'Honour thy father and thy mother' is the fourth commandment in the Lutheran tradition.
94. The works of St Augustine of Hippo (354–430).
95. Nobleman.
96. The Dutch physician and occultist Johann Weyer (or Wier) (1515–1588) was one of the earliest opponents of witch-hunting. In his most famous work, *De praestigiis daemonum et incantationibus ac veneficiis*, (*On the Illusions of the Demons and on Spells and Poisons*, 1563), he argued that women accused of witchcraft were in fact suffering from mental disturbance or melancholia. He did, however, defend the notion of the existence and power of the devil and of demons of various ranks, but believed that it was magicians rather than witches who could invoke these powers. Johannes Bodinus is the latinized name of Jean Bodin (1530–1596), a French jurist and writer on demonology. His major work on witchcraft, *De la démonomanie des sorciers* (*On the Demon-Mania of Witches*), was published in 1580.
97. It was a common folk-belief that witches could transform themselves or others into animals.

98. The Augsburg confession, which consisted of the 28 articles of Christian faith held by Lutherans and as such was one of the most important documents of the Reformation, was presented to the Holy Roman Emperor Charles V at the Diet of Augsburg on 25 June 1530.
99. The Swedish king Gustavus Adolphus visited Usedom during the Thirty Years' War, landing with his army in the village of Peenemünde on 26 June 1630. The visit is recorded by Micraelius in vol. 5, p. 180.
100. The *Theatrum Europeum* was a history of the German-speaking lands, noted for its depiction of the Thirty Years' War. Begun by Matthäus Merian (1593–1650), it was published in 21 volumes between 1633 and 1738. Meinhold refers here to vol. 2 (1629–33).
101. Celebratory poem.
102. Alternative name for Greifswald.
103. Dialogue.
104. Poetic inspiration.
105. The 'Te Deum', also known as the Ambrosian hymn because of its association with St Ambrose, takes its title from the opening words in Latin, 'Te Deum laudamus' (We praise thee, O God).
106. Poem in elegiac metre, in which couplets are composed of a dactylic hexameter followed by a dactylic pentameter.
107. Sweetest and loveliest girl, who appears to me like an angel of the Lord in the colours of the sky, if only you were always with me, no harm would ever befall me.
108. Accept this modest wreath, and this.
109. This verse is an adaptation of the concluding lines of the neo-Latin poem 'Consolatio' by the German humanist Helius Eobanus Hessus (1488–1540). The original (*c.* 1523) was composed for William of Brunswick, and Meinhold re-writes it to fit the context of Gustavus Adolphus. See Harry Vredeveld, 'Pia fraus: Anachronisms, Fake Latin, and Stolen Colors in Wilhelm Meinhold's *Maria Schweidler, die Bernsteinhexe*', *Monatshefte*, 106 (2014), 200–12 (pp. 205–08).
110. Come closer, patriotic maid, that I may kiss you.
111. This is for your beauty. And if by God's favour I return victorious, I will expect the promised poem and two kisses besides.
112. Goodbye.
113. The superstitious practice of spitting is intended to ward off evil.
114. The German original makes direct reference here to the 'peinliche Gerichtsordnung', formally the Constitutio Criminalis Carolina, which was the first criminal code in Germany, introduced in 1530 under Holy Roman Emperor Charles V. This legislation defined witchcraft as a serious crime, punishable by execution with fire, and its introduction laid the basis for a surge of witch trials across the country.

115. The archetypal image of Satan as a 'roaring lion, seeking whom he may devour' comes from I Peter 5. 8.
116. The temptation of Christ in the wilderness is documented in Matthew 4. 1–11, Mark 1. 12–13, and Luke 4. 1–13.
117. See note 31. On the previous occasion Duff Gordon translates this as 'God the Father, be with us.'
118. Warning.
119. The words of Christ's response when tempted by the devil are also used to rebuke Peter in Matthew 16. 23 and Mark 8. 33.
120. Senior mayor, top-ranking official of the municipality.
121. Chamberlain.
122. Court clerk.
123. Mayor.
124. The accused.
125. The story of Susannah is one of the additions to the book of Daniel excluded from Protestant Bibles as apocryphal.
126. Evidence.
127. Alternative name for the Brocken, the highest mountain in the Harz range, celebrated in folklore as a witches' gathering place.
128. The megalithic grave site on Usedom gave rise to legends of giants who formerly inhabited the island. This mythology is perhaps alluded to here.
129. 'If you will pardon my language'. The use of this phrase makes little sense here as Duff Gordon has chosen in her translation to obviate the vulgarity of the German original in which the man is described as defecating in the street in front of the coach.
130. The last words of Christ on the cross; see Matthew 27. 46.
131. The original quotation, slightly different from what is cited here, comes from Cicero's *Orator* 65. 219, and the words are attributed to Crassus. Cicero's text is: 'Nam ubi libido dominatur, innocentiae leve praesidium est.' (For where lust predominates, light-armed is the protection of innocence.) The words 'Innocentia, quid est innocentia?' (Innocence, what is innocence?) are not Ciceronian.
132. Te Deum, see note 105.
133. Ritual act of exorcistic significance, performed to ward off evil.
134. Hedgehogs were associated with witches and considered a bad omen.
135. Historians and novelists utilized this popular myth to dramatize their accounts, but the reference here undermines Meinhold's literary hoax for modern readers, enabling them to identify the story as fictional.
136. Bottom, backside.
137. Report signed in his own hand.
138. Christ here predicts his betrayal; see John 13. 18.
139. The witch's mark was believed to be a physical indication of a pact with the

devil, and in early accounts of witch trials women's bodies were searched for such a mark.

140. Martin Delrio (1551–1608) was a Jesuit theologian of Spanish descent. His highly popular work *Magical Investigations* (*Disquisitiones magicae*), which was published in three volumes in Leuven in 1599 and 1600, reproduced many of the ideas contained in the Malleus Maleficarum.
141. Files, records.
142. Attack.
143. Judge.
144. Credibility.
145. Informants, sources.
146. See Matthew 6. 24 and Luke 16. 13.
147. The Augsburg clergyman Gottlieb Spitzel (1639-91) used the name Theophilus Spizelius as author of *De expugnatione Orci. Die gebrochene Macht der Finsternis oder zerstörte teufflische Bunds- und Buhlfreundschafft mit den Menschen*, published in 1687. This reference is an anachronism, as Spitzel was not yet born in 1630, the year of Maria's trial.
148. The Jesuit theologian Christoph Haunold (1610-1689) uncritically incorporates conventional thinking about witchcraft in his work *Controversiae de iustitia et iure privatorum universo*, 6 vols (Ingolstadt, 1671–74). Again this is an anachronism, as Haunold's work postdates the action of the novel.
149. Why can witches not grow rich? In order that, in accordance with the devil's desire to insult the creator, they may be bought for the lowest possible price, and may not become conspicuous because of their riches.
150. Complaint or charge against the accused.
151. See I Samuel 28. 3–25.
152. Theophrastus Paracelsus (1493–1541) was an unorthodox scientist and physician with a strong interest in sorcery and the occult.
153. French legal term, referring to the method of torture by which increasingly heavy stones were placed on a defendant's chest. While this method was used in the Salem witch trials in America of the 1690s, the French phrase is not the best translation here as it does not fit the cultural context of German witch trials.
154. Weighty, sufficient reasons for torture in terms of the law.
155. 1. Malicious rumour; 2. Sorcery performed in public; 3. The appearance of the devil on the mountain.
156. Prayer taken from Psalm 145. 15.
157. Revelation 21. 8.
158. Johann Heinrich Zedler (1706–1751) created the most significant German-language encyclopaedia of the eighteenth century, the *Großes vollständiges Universal-Lexicon aller Wissenschaften und Künste*. It contains a long section on torture (vol. 44, columns 1451–1554).

159. Witnesses.
160. Sound.
161. The German original is altered substantially here by the translator, perhaps for reasons of propriety for a Victorian readership. In the original a dash is placed after the letter Q., and a footnote reference is inserted which states: 'I can only express this disgusting question in Latin: 'num semen Daemonis calidum fuerit aut frigidum' (whether the devil's semen had been warm or cold), to which she answered that she could no longer remember. This question, by the way, features in *all* witch trials and is inexplicably *always* answered with the word 'frigidum' (cold)'. The words in Latin are not translated in the original, as if to render them in German would be indelicate.
162. Primary charge.
163. In Swedish folklore, a gathering place for witches, reached only by magical flight. This meadow associated with witches' Sabbaths is frequently mentioned in witch-hunts. The name originates from Blåkulla, a Swedish island in the Baltic.
164. Dudaim is a Hebrew word for the mandrake plant. In the author's footnote 'the LXX' refers to the Septuagint, the Koine Greek translation of the Hebrew Bible, which takes its name from the 70 Jewish scholars who first translated the five books of Moses into Greek.
165. Nonsense.
166. Brother, friend.
167. Thin pieces of wood, both ends of which were sharpened and dipped in sulphur; used for lighting candles and lamps.
168. The story of David and Bathsheba is related in II Samuel 11.
169. Demonic miracle.
170. This refers to the practice in some churches of keeping an attendance record of communicants, as a means both of encouraging religious observance and of checking on the payment of dues.
171. The second part of the curse draws on Hebrews 3. 12.
172. See Matthew 20. 22 and Mark 10. 38, where 'drinking of the cup' refers to sharing in Christ's suffering.
173. The staff of office represents the official's power, and he breaks it after pronouncing the death penalty to symbolize the finality of this judgement. In modern times this was replaced by the tradition of the judge breaking the nib of his pen.
174. Disgraceful action.
175. The German hymn for the dying 'Ich hab' mein' Sach' Gott heimgestellt' was written by the Lutheran pastor Johann Leon (*c.* 1530–1597) and later adapted as a chorale prelude by Johann Sebastian Bach. 'On God alone I rest my fate' seems to be Duff Gordon's own rendering of the opening line. The

hymn was in fact translated into English by Johann Christian Jacobi (1670–1750) as 'My life I now to God resign'.
176. See note 39. On the first occasion on which this is sung, Meinhold intervenes as 'editor' to point out that the eleventh-century versification is by Peter Damian.
177. Unexpected event, development.
178. Medieval Latin hymn in 19 stanzas depicting the day of judgement, often attributed to the Franciscan friar Thomas of Celano (1190–1260). The sixth and eighth stanzas are quoted here.
179. The translation cited by Duff Gordon in the footnote as the 'Old Version' is by the poet Wentworth Dillon, fourth Earl of Roscommon (c. 1633–85).
180. The German burial hymn 'Nun laßt uns den Leib begraben' was composed by Michael Weisse (1488–1534). The English translation by Catherine Winkworth (1827–78), 'Now lay we calmly in the grave', was not published until 1858.
181. Polecat.
182. Formally executed document recording the granting of an aristocratic title to an individual.
183. The love-story of Aeneas and Dido, Queen of Carthage, is related in the fourth book of Virgil's *Aeneid*. Dido commits suicide in despair when Aeneas abandons her. She mounts a ceremonial funeral pyre before killing herself with her sword.
184. For the English version of this passage from Vergil's *Aeneid*, Duff Gordon cites the translation by the English poet and critic John Dryden (1631–1700). In Meinhold's text the German translation used in the footnote is by Friedrich Schiller.
185. How are you, sweet maiden?
186. Well, now that I see you.
187. Formal apology, reparation.
188. Letter of recommendation, testimonial.
189. Ferdinand II (1578–1637).
190. The public announcement in church of an impending marriage, intended to enable anyone aware of an impediment (e.g. a pre-existing marriage or lack of consent) to make this known.
191. Myrtle was sacred in Greek mythology to Aphrodite, the goddess of love, and has been used since ancient times in bridal bouquets.
192. Secondary witness.
193. Psalm 51. 19 in the Lutheran Bible; Psalm 51. 17 in the King James Bible. Here Duff Gordon does not point out the discrepancy as she does on other occasions.
194. The first edition of the novel included an illustration of this tablet on the church wall. The fact that the couple portrayed are wearing medieval

costume rather than dress appropriate to the seventeenth century betrayed the story's lack of authenticity as an historical account. An unsigned article in the Augsburg *Allgemeine Zeitung* of 17 December 1843 drew attention to this discrepancy. The author was the prominent author and journalist Lewin Schücking, who liked the novel in spite of the question surrounding its status as fact or fiction and encouraged Annette von Droste-Hülshoff to read it (see letter of 23 January 1844 in Annette von Droste-Hülshoff, *Werke, Briefwechsel*, ed. by Winfried Woesler, 14 vols (Tübingen: Niemeyer, 1978–2000), XII.1: *Briefe an die Droste 1841–1848. Text*, ed. by Stefan Thürmer (1995), p. 122).

BIBLIOGRAPHY

AUSTIN, SARAH, trans., *Characteristics of Goethe from the German of Falk, Von Müller, Etc.* (London: Wilson, 1833)
——, trans., *Fragments from German Prose Writers* (London: Murray, 1841)
'The Author of *The Amber Witch*', *The Eclectic Magazine of Foreign Literature, Science and Art*, 21 (1850), ed. by John Holmes Agnew and Walter Hilliard Bidwell (New York: Leavitt, Trow and Co.), p. 419
B[LACKIE], J[OHN] S[TUART], 'The Importance of the German Language, and Reasons for its More General Cultivation in this Country', *The Edinburgh Literary Journal; Or, Weekly Register of Criticism and Belles Lettres*, 2 vols (Edinburgh: Constable, 1829), II, 163–66
BEKKER, BALTHASAR, *De Betoverde Weereld* (Amsterdam: Daniel van den Dalen, 1691)
BETHKE, WALTHER, ed., *Wilhelm Meinholds Briefe* (Greifswald: Universitätsverlag, 1935)
BLEILER, E. F., 'Introduction to the Dover Edition', in *Five Victorian Ghost Novels*, ed. by E. F. Bleiler (New York: Dover, 1971), pp. v–xiv
BLIND, MATHILDE, *George Eliot* (London: Allen, 1883)
BODIN, JEAN, *De la démonomanie des sorciers* (Paris: Jacques du Puys, 1580)
BRIDGWATER, PATRICK, *Anglo-German Interactions in the Literature of the 1890s* (Oxford: Legenda, 1999)
——, 'Who's Afraid of Sidonia von Bork?', in *The Novel in Anglo-German Context: Cultural Cross-Currents and Affinities*, ed. by Susanne Stark (Amsterdam: Rodopi, 2000), pp. 213–28
BURNS, BARBARA, 'Truth, Fiction and Deception in Meinhold's *Maria Schweidler, die Bernsteinhexe*', *Neophilologus*, 95 (2011), 627–38
CARLYLE, THOMAS, *Critical and Miscellaneous Essays*, 4 vols (Boston: Munroe, 1839)
DAVIS, JOHN R., *The Victorians and Germany* (Oxford: Lang, 2007)
DELRIO, MARTIN, *Disquisitiones magicae*, 3 vols (Leuven, 1599–1600)
DUFF GORDON, Lucie, Lady, *Letters from Egypt, 1863–1865*, ed. by Sarah Austin (London: Macmillan, 1865)
——, *Last Letters From Egypt*, ed. by Janet Ross (London: Macmillan, 1875)
DROSTE-HÜLSHOFF, ANNETTE VON, *Werke, Briefwechsel*, ed. by Winfried Woesler, 14 vols (Tübingen: Niemeyer, 1978–2000), XII.1: *Briefe an die Droste 1841–1848. Text*, ed. by Stefan Thürmer (1995)
ELTON, OLIVER, *A Survey of English Literature, 1830–1880*, 2 vols (London: Arnold, 1920)
FRANK, KATHERINE, *Lucie Duff Gordon: A Passage to Egypt* (London: Penguin, 1995)
GAULE, JOHN, *Select Cases of Conscience Touching Witches and Witchcraft* (London: Clutterbuck, 1646)

GEORGE, MARION, 'Vom historischen Fakt zur Sinnfigur der Moderne. Zur Gestalt der Hexe in Tiecks Novelle *Hexensabbat* (1832)', in *Hexen: Historische Faktizität und fiktive Bildlichkeit / Sorcières: Faits historiques, imagerie et fiction*, ed. by Marion George and Andrea Rudolph (Dettelbach: Röll, 2004), pp. 253–70

GOETHE, JOHANN WOLFGANG VON, *Sämtliche Werke*, ed. by Hendrik Birus et al., 40 vols (Frankfurt a.M.: Deutscher Klassiker Verlag, 1986–2000), XXII: *Ästhetische Schriften 1824–1832*, ed. by Anne Bohnenkamp (1999)

GOSSE, EDMUND, *Leaves and Fruit* (London: Heinemann, 1927)

HAUNOLD, CHRISTOPH, *Controversiae de iustitia et iure privatorum universo*, 6 vols (Ingolstadt, 1671–74)

'Heine and Lady Duff Gordon', *Otago Witness*, 5 July 1894, p. 41

HAKEN, JOHANN CHRISTIAN LUDWIG, ed., *Pommersche Provinzial-Blätter für Stadt und Land*, 6 vols (Stettin: Effenbarts, 1820–25)

HELLER, CARL, *Chronik der Stadt Wolgast* (Greifswald: Kunike, 1829)

HORST, GEORG CONRAD, *Zauber-Bibliothek: Oder, Von Zauberei, Theurgie und Mantik, Zauberern, Hexen, und Hexenprocessen, Dämonen, Gespenstern, und Geistererscheinungen*, 6 vols (Mainz: Kupferberg, 1821–26)

HUFTON, OLWEN, *The Prospect Before Her: A History of Women in Western Europe, Vol. I: 1500–1800* (London: HarperCollins, 1995)

KANTZOW, THOMAS, *Pomerania, Oder Ursprunck, Altheit und Geschichte der Völcker und Lande Pomern, Caßuben, Wenden, Stettin, Rhügen. In vierzehn Büchern*, ed. by Johann Gottfried Ludwig Kosegarten, 2 vols (Greifswald: Mauritius, 1816–17)

KIPPEL, MARKUS, *Die Stimme der Vernunft über einer Welt des Wahns. Studien zur literarischen Rezeption der Hexenprozesse (19.–20. Jahrhundert)* (Berlin: Lit, 2001)

KRAMER, HEINRICH, *Malleus maleficarum* (Speyer, 1487)

LEPPLA, RUPPRECHT, *Wilhelm Meinhold und die chronikalische Erzählung* (Berlin: Ebering, 1928)

MAIERHOFER, WALTRAUD, *Hexen — Huren — Heldenweiber: Bilder des Weiblichen in Erzähltexten über den Dreißigjährigen Krieg* (Cologne: Böhlau, 2005)

MATURIN, CHARLES, *Fatal Revenge; Or, The Family of Montorio* (London: Longman, Hurst, Rees, and Orme, 1807)

MATUSZAK-LOOSE, BERNADETTA, 'Infame Handlung wird bestraft — Zu Wilhelm Meinholds Roman *Maria Schweidler, die Bernsteinhexe*', in *Die Kunst der Infamie. Vom Sängerkrieg zum Medienkrieg*, ed. by Hubertus Fischer (Frankfurt: Lang, 2003), pp. 201–25

MEINHOLD, WILHELM, *Maria Schweidler, die Bernsteinhexe. Der interessanteste aller bisher bekannten Hexenprocesse; nach einer defecten Handschrift ihres Vaters, des Pfarrers Abraham Schweidler in Coserow auf Usedom, herausgegeben von W. Meinhold, Doctor der Theologie und Pfarrer* (Berlin: Duncker und Humblot, 1843)

——, 'Die Bernsteinhexe von Wilhelm Meinhold. In ihrer ursprünglichen, neuhochdeutschen Gestalt vom Jahre 1826', *Novellen-Zeitung*, 3 July 1844, pp. 2–8

——, *Gesammelte Schriften*, 7 vols (Leipzig: Weber, 1846–48), VII: *Sidonia von Bork die Klosterhexe, angebliche Vertilgerin des gesammten herzoglich-pommerschen Regentenhauses* (1848)

——, *The Amber Witch*, trans. by Lady Duff Gordon (London: Murray, 1846)

——, *Sidonia the Sorceress: The Supposed Destroyer of the Whole Reigning Ducal House of Pomerania*, trans. by Jane Elgee (London: Simms and McIntyre (The Parlour Library), 1849)

——, *The Amber Witch*, intro. by Joseph Jacobs (London: Nutt, 1895)

——, *The Amber Witch*, intro. by J. W. Mackail (London: Oxford University Press (World's Classics), 1928)

——, *Die Hexe von Coserow*, with an Afterword by Winfried Freund (Rostock: Hinstorff, 2000)

MEYER, RICHARD M., *Die deutsche Literatur des neunzehnten Jahrhunderts*, 4th edn, 2 vols (Berlin: Bondi, 1910)

MICRAELIUS, JOHANNES, *Antiquitates Pomeraniae, oder Sechs Bücher vom alten Pommerlande*, 6 vols (Stettin: Kunckel, 1723)

NORTON, CAROLINE, 'Lady Duff Gordon and Her Works', *Macmillan's Magazine*, September 1869, pp. 457–62

'An Old and Famous Story', *New York Times*, 17 March 1895, p. 31

OTTO, CHRISTIAN and FÖRSTER, ERNST, ed., *Wahrheit aus Jean Paul's Leben*, 8 vols (Breslau: Max und Komp., 1826–33)

OXENFORD, JOHN, trans., *The Autobiography of Goethe: Truth and Poetry, From My Own Life*, (London: Bohn, 1848)

PALGRAVE, FRANCIS, 'Goethe's *Life of Himself*', *Edinburgh Review*, 26 (1816), 304–37

PATER, WALTER, *Appreciations* (London: Macmillan, 1889)

PETERSON, WILLIAM S., *A Bibliography of the Kelmscott Press* (Oxford: Clarendon, 1984)

PÜCKLER-MUSKAU, Hermann Fürst von, *Tour in England, Ireland, and France, in the Years 1826, 1827, 1828, and 1829: With Remarks on the Manners and Customs of the Inhabitants, and Anecdotes of Distinguished Public Characters*, trans. by Sarah Austin (London: Wilson, 1832)

ROSS, JANET, *Three Generations of English Women: Memoirs and Correspondence of Mrs John Taylor, Mrs Sarah Austin and Lady Duff Gordon* (London: Murray, 1888)

RUDOLPH, ANDREA, 'Provinzen als Sinnräume einer ethischen Moderne. Wilhelm Meinhold's Chroniknovelle *Die Bernsteinhexe* (1843)', in *Kulturraumformung. Sprachpolitische, kulturpolitische, ästhetische Dimensionen*, ed. by Maria Katarzyna Lasatowicz (Berlin: trafo, 2004), pp. 149–77

RYSAN, JOSEF, *Wilhelm Meinhold's 'Bernsteinhexe': A Study in Witchcraft and Cultural History* (Chicago: University of Chicago, 1948)

SCHURMAN, ANNA MARIA VAN, *Eukleria seu melioris partis electio* (Altona: Cornelius van der Meulen, 1673)

SCOTT, WALTER, *Briefe über Dämonologie und Hexerei*, trans. by Georg Nikolaus Bärmann (Zwickau: Schumann, 1833)

——, *Waverley Novels*, 25 vols (London: Dryburgh, 1929)

SKRINE, PETER, 'Historical Realism', in *Perspectives on German Realist Writing. Eight Essays*, ed. by Mark G. Ward (Lewiston, NY: Mellen, 1995), pp. 113–24

SPEE, FRIEDRICH VON, *Cautio criminalis* (Rinteln, 1631)

SPIZELIUS, THEOPHILUS (GOTTLIEB SPITZEL), *De expugnatione Orci. Die gebrochene Macht der Finsternis oder zerstörte teufflische Bunds- und Buhlfreundschafft mit den Menschen* (Augsburg, 1687)

STRAUSS, DAVID FRIEDRICH, *Das Leben Jesu, kritisch bearbetiet*, 2 vols (Tübingen: Osiander, 1835–36)

——, *The Life of Jesus, Critically Examined*, trans. by George Eliot, 3 vols (London: Chapman, 1846)

VARNHAGEN VON ENSE, KARL AUGUST, *Tagebücher*, 14 vols (Leipzig: Brockhaus, 1861–70)

VREDEVELD, HARRY, 'Pia fraus: Anachronisms, Fake Latin, and Stolen Colors in Wilhelm Meinhold's *Maria Schweidler, die Bernsteinhexe*', *Monatshefte*, 106 (2014), 200–12

WALTER, JOHANN, *Eyn geystlich Gesangk Buchleyn* (Wittenberg, 1524)

WEYER, JOHANN, *De praestigiis daemonum et incantationibus ac venificiis* (Basel: Oporinus, 1563)

WILDE, OSCAR, *Complete Shorter Fiction*, ed. by Isobel Murray (Oxford: Oxford University Press, 1980)

WINKWORTH, CATHERINE, *Lyra Germanica: Second Series: The Christian Life* (London: Longman, Brown, Green, Longmans and Roberts; New York: Randolph, 1858)

ZEDLER, JOHANN HEINRICH and others, ed., *Grosses vollständiges Universal-Lexicon aller Wissenschaften und Künste*, 68 vols (Halle: Zedler, 1731–54)

MHRA European Translations

The guiding principle of this series is to make available translations that had a significant impact on the receiving culture at the time of their publication, but that are now either completely or relatively inaccessible. Aimed at an academic market, titles in this series will also reflect current areas of scholarly debate and/or topics studied on undergraduate and postgraduate courses.

Each volume will include a substantial introduction, and textual and explanatory notes. The introduction will describe the ways in which this particular translation (or these translations) shaped literary and/or intellectual currents in the receiving culture, and will provide a coherently argued account of the omissions and distortions of the translation/s.

Titles will be selected by members of the Editorial Board and edited by leading academics.

Alison Finch
General Editor

Editorial Board

Professor Malcolm Cook (French)
Professor Alison Finch (French)
Professor Ritchie Robertson (Germanic)
Dr Mark Davie (Italian)
Professor David Treece (Portuguese)
Professor David Gillespie (Slavonic)
Dr Duncan Wheeler (Spanish)
Dr Jonathan Thacker (Spanish)

Published titles

1. *Böece de Confort remanié. Edition critique*
   (Glynnis M. Cropp, 2011)
2. *Luise Gottsched, Der Lockenraub/
   Alexander Pope, The Rape of the Lock*
   (Hilary Brown, 2014)
3. *Pedro Calderón de la Barca, 'La devoción de la cruz'/
   August Wilhelm Schlegel, 'Die Andacht zum Kreuze'*
   (Carol Tully, 2012)

For details of how to order please visit our website at:
www.translations.mhra.org.uk

www.ingramcontent.com/pod-product-compliance
Lightning Source LLC
LaVergne TN
LVHW021810070125
800741LV00002B/182